Toward Improved
Urban Education

Toward Improved Urban Education

edited by **Frank W. Lutz**
Pennsylvania State University

Charles A. Jones Publishing Company
Worthington, Ohio

Foreword

Urban schools are in trouble. Vast numbers of teachers and administrators have felt ill-equipped by traditional training to cope with the tough demands of today's schools. But colleges and universities have made dramatic moves toward remedying this problem. Interestingly, the original land grant colleges have provided a model for those institutions looking to become involved in the direct solution of urban problems. The land grant colleges were committed to the concept of direct service. Agricultural research was designed to directly aid farmers produce better crop yields. Students were expertly trained to return to the fields as agronomists. Field agents from the universities visited farmers in the field and disseminated information and research data.

On the other hand, emphasis on pure research, scholarly publications, inquiry after truth for its own sake, and other desirable and necessary pursuits that have made our universities so great at one time resulted in a de-emphasis of the concept of direct service and deep immersion in current practical problems. Our great universities have reversed this trend. Direct service and problem solving have begun to reassume their rightful place in value structure of the modern university. Cooperative relationships between researchers, practitioners, and social agencies are common, fruitful, and profitable. University personnel are devoting their time, energy, and expertise to running programs that attempt to use the latest research for greatest impact on specific problems. Universities now run public school programs, share their research capability, donate top-grade professors, engage in community projects, send student teachers into the inner city, run Teacher Corps and Job Corps centers.

The authors of this book are in the forefront of this reimmersion of the university in the events rampaging outside of the ivied walls. Virtually all of the contributors have had very recent firing-line experience as teachers or urban administrators. Some engage in periodic and extended involvement in the day-to-day problems of schools. One author, for example, has recently traded places with a secondary school principal for a period of time. All of the contributors are adept at experiencing problems first hand, retreating to evaluate and theorize, presenting solutions to practitioners, and then returning to the scene to test solutions.

This kind of involvement is imperative. Without it the university scholar cannot expect to grow or provide relevant and workable solutions. Development of theory and research is crucial. But it is of limited value unless applied to the explosive problems in schools. It is not enough that the university professor have prior experience in the field. If he is to keep his theory abreast of changing times and to maintain credibility with those urban administrators and teachers who come to him for the theoretical groundwork against which to measure their daily activities, then the university professor must experience practical problems as a matter of daily routine.

A potential vehicle for accomplishing this might be for universities to conduct teacher and administrator training in urban schools. Currently operative public schools could be transformed into laboratories. Professors, graduate and undergraduate students, and research people would form the staff of the school. Teachers would be trained by teaching part-time under supervision and studying theory right there in the school. Students seeking to become administrators would help administer the school. Professors would teach public school students as well as prospective teachers and administrators. They would also administer the laboratory, thus sharpening their own practical skills, and use the school as a laboratory to develop theory and test solutions. In that way public schools would profit from the applications of research as well as receive better trained teachers and administrators. Universities would profit from direct participation in urban problems. The union of scholar and practitioner would be complete.

The contributors to this book represent a fine example of the potential of such a new breed of university scholar-practitioner. They have stood in the midst of the urban maelstrom and tested their values as well as their theory. They have produced a book worthy of serious attention.

Mark R. Shedd
Superintendent of Schools
Philadelphia, Pennsylvania

Preface

This book was made possible through the efforts of many people and results from the concern about urban education expressed by the National Conference of Professors of Educational Administration. Fifteen chapters covering many of the major problems of urban education are herewith presented, along with introductory and concluding statements by the Editor. The Editor benefited from the wisdom of the authors as he prepared the introductory remarks and hopes they express the ideas of the writers. The ideas in the introductory and concluding statements are drawn largely from the chapters; however, the Editor assumes complete responsibility for statements in these sections.

One of the qualities all of the authors have in common is their dedication to the study of school administration and the fact that all have worked and lived in urban cities most of their lives. This has united them in an interest in the National Conference of Professors of Educational Administration, which is dedicated to improving the teaching of school administration. Each author has donated his efforts so that the royalties from this book may benefit the aims of the organization.

The Editor is therefore grateful for the cooperation of the many scholars who contributed their time and effort to this work. Each chapter was written expressly for this book, and the time expended by the authors was great. The Editor can only hope that his efforts to bring the chapters into a meaningful text can somehow compensate the authors for their contributions.

Frank W. Lutz

Contributors

Harry J. Hartley, *New York University*

W. Deane Wiley, *Southern Illinois University at Edwardsville*

Robert W. Heller, *State University of New York at Buffalo*

Stanley Lisser, *Center for Urban Education, New York*

Anthony N. Baratta, *Fordham University*

Raphael O. Nystrand and Luvern L. Cunningham, *Ohio State University*

Frank W. Lutz, *Pennsylvania State University*

Seymour Evans, *New York University*

Joseph M. Cronin, *Harvard University*

David S. Seeley, *Public Education Association, New York*

Paul E. Peterson, *University of Chicago*

Laurence Iannaccone, *Ontario Institute for Studies in Education*

Walter I. Garms and James A. Kelly, *Teachers College, Columbia University*

James W. Guthrie, *University of California at Berkeley*

Robert J. Schaefer, *Teachers College, Columbia University*

Contents

xi

3

4

5

6

7

xiii

8

The Urban Principal: Man in Transition, *Seymour Evans*, 133

9

The School Superintendent in the Crucible of Urban Politics, *Joseph M. Cronin*, 145

10

11

12

13

**Financing Urban Education, *Walter I. Garms
and James A. Kelly*, 255**

14

City Schools in a Federal Vise, *James W. Guthrie*, 273

Toward Improved Urban Education

Introduction

The chapters of this book were written by different men from their own viewpoints. While this presents a variation in writing style, it is a major strength of this text. Indeed, no one author could have, or at least should have, undertaken this work. It is also immediately evident that no single institution or geographical area was able to produce the authors necessary to compile this work. Each chapter topic was selected for its relevance to the problems of urban schools and its author chosen because of recognition of his study, research, and experience in his area of interest.

There is criticism of urban education in this work but forward movement begins with a frank admission of the problems of the present and a new approach for the future. All of these authors are educators who work and live in urban centers. They are concerned not so much with what was or is (although of necessity they describe that) but rather with what might be. When their criticism seems harsh it stems from their strong concern; if their suggestions appear challenging it is because they believe our nation and its educators capable of meeting that challenge if it is recognized.

The continued use of the word "urban" in this text and the frequent reference to the educational disturbances in New York City are necessary. Clearly, the problems brought out in this book are general to metropolitan education, including suburban areas and even occasionally touching on the more rural areas. However, "urban" is the shorter term and is generally understood to include the elements of the metropolitan area. As to the excitement in New York, the events there appear to have captured the interest of educators everywhere, in somewhat the same way the Russians' launching of Sputnik did. Much can be learned from study of the events in New York. However, a closer examination of the chapters of this book will reveal an application and interest in many other metropolitan areas of the nation as well.

In Chapter 1, Harry J. Hartley, Head of the Department of Educational Administration, New York University, takes up what is perhaps the most frequently ignored area of modern administration: the philosophic basis of administrative decision-making. A recognized scholar in school administration, Hartley purports what he terms "the humanistic imperative for urban governance." In this chapter he has provided an insightful and sensitive dimension for urban administration. Utilizing an existential base, the chapter becomes even more enlightening as we recognize that it is commonly held that the student revolt stems from existentialism. Hartley demonstrates a keen understanding of his topic and his pleas are particularly meaningful when we realize that Hartley's best-known area of publication is the economics of education: programming, planning, budgeting systems in education. Those readers who have not known Hartley well may be surprised at the emphasis he places on the philosophic basis upon which all administrative decisions must be made. Readers who have known him will recognize him in this chapter. Student involvement in decision-making will become an increasingly important fact in the lives of urban administrators in the next few years, and Hartley has not only supplied the administrator with a basis for surviving this new phase but of gaining stature as a human being because of it.

The reader is introduced, in Chapter 2, to the nature of education in metropolitan areas by W. Deane Wiley, Dean of the Department of Education, Southern Illinois University at Edwardsville. Wiley was a high school principal in a metropolitan area on the West Coast and then a professor of educational administration in a metropolitan area on the East Coast before becoming dean. Thus, he brings a wide and diverse experience to his treatment of the problem. Wiley proposes considerable freedom for each urban school in order that it can cope with the unique problems of its particular clients. Rejecting the traditional bureaucratic model, Wiley pleads for the flexible master schedule in the hands of a creative principal as a meaningful answer to the problems of urban education.

For the past 15 years one of the most publicized and pressing problems in education has been the desegregation and integration of public schools. Here, as in most instances, urban schools face greater problems than suburban and rural counterparts. Robert Heller, in his role as Director of the Study Council at the University of Buffalo and Associate Professor of Educational Administration, has had a unique opportunity to study this pressing urban problem. In Chapter 3 he discusses the problem, the efforts of various urban school districts to solve it, their successes and failures. His treatment is extensive and insightful.

Perhaps no man better understands (at least from a principal's viewpoint) the problems of parent participation than Stanley Lisser. Lisser was the principal of I.S. 201, New York City, when it underwent what was perhaps the first revolution of community takeover in the United States. This was the *beginning* of the "demonstration districts" in New York City which have captured the spotlight of publicity and national concern over community control and parent participation. The series of events left Lisser without a school to administer. For the last several years he has been an administrator for the Center for Urban Education. No other agency has been more concerned in studying the problems of urban education, and Lisser has played a major role in this activity. If Lisser speaks from a bias (as we all do), he has had several years to reflect on that bias. If the bias remains, it is tempered by his insightfulness and concern for improving urban education. Few are more qualified to speak on this vital topic in Chapter 4 than Lisser, probably because of his bias rather than in spite of it.

In Chapter 5, Tony Baratta discusses decentralization in New York City. As Chairman of the Division of Educational Administration and Supervision at Fordam University, Baratta sits in an advantageous position to view the educational and political maneuvering in that city's efforts to decentralize or prevent decentralization. He has for the most part been factual in this matter, albeit somewhat selective. He clearly supports (although not so passionately as some), the effort to decentralize, while pointing out some of the possible pitfalls.

The problems of urban education are inordinate. Some people suggest decentralization as a panacea to all or at least most of these problems. Chapter 6 provides a somewhat different solution, that of the federated system. Vern Cunningham has long been recognized as a leader in educational administration. He has been a professor at the University of Minnesota and at the University of Chicago. Presently Dean of the School of Education at Ohio State University, he continues in a tradition of contributing to the literature of educational administration with his colleague Ray Nystrand. In their chapter Nystrand and Cunningham present an interesting, provocative and convincing argument for the federated system. Interestingly enough, they do not oppose the goals of decentralization. In fact, they applaud them and offer what they believe to be a more effective means to those ends.

One of the most perplexing areas of the new urban educational administration, and for that matter, all educational administration, is negotiation. Until a few years ago, most administrators and school boards were opposed to negotiating with teachers about any issue. Today negotiating is a fact of life for urban school administrators. Teacher unions and associations are among the most influential groups in policy decisions in urban school districts. In Chapter 7, Frank Lutz, Director of the Division of Education Policy Studies at Pennsylvania State University, discusses the social process of negotiation as it affects urban education. He takes the position that the usual nonpersonal, fiscal-legal approach to negotiations precipitates more problems than it solves. He attempts to present the social and interpersonal aspects of educational negotiations and takes a look at the future of education as it may be affected by the negotiation process.

Chapter 8 presents the urban principal in what is perhaps his number one role in modern urban education, the building administrator of an "educational union shop." Sy Evans was a building administrator in a metropolitan area before becoming a professor of administration at New York University and the director of its Institute for Staff Relations. Evans is well equipped to write on this topic by his experience, training (his Masters is from Cornell's Labor Relations Institute), and his research and publication. In this chapter he clearly presents the urban principal's dilemma and a model, supported by data, for solving it.

As the problems of urban centers become more intertwined with those of urban educational systems, it is increasingly clear that urban education and the chief school officer cannot remain aloof from the politics of urban government. During his years at Harvard University, Joseph Cronin has emerged as a scholar in the field of educational administration. He is personally involved in politics and during the past several years has engaged in the study of the political realities of urban school districts. In Chapter 9, Cronin discusses the school superintendent in the heat of urban politics, exposing the myths and realities of political action of urban superintendents. After reviewing past and present situations, he speculates upon a future where urban superintendents may not head a separate educational-governmental agency; but rather, a department of education within a single urban governmental structure.

Some efforts have been haltingly made to better coordinate the functions of urban city government and educational governance, usually with little or ineffectual results. Likely the man best informed about such an effort is David Seeley. He was the first director of educational liaison appointed by Mayor Lindsay and is now the Director of New York City's influential Public Education Association. Seeley presents his view of why Lindsay attempted to intervene in the educational decisions of New York City and why that attempt ended in disaster. Chapter 10 is unique in books on educational administration. It presents an interesting and controversial topic in an articulate manner.

Chapter 11 continues in the same vein as the previous chapter. Paul Peterson is primarily a political scientist. Much of his work at the University of Chicago has centered upon poverty groups, education, the Office of Economic Opportunity, and the governance of urban education. In this chapter Peterson presents data related to the federal effort to influence urban change, modify poverty, and produce urban educational reform.

Chapter 12 presents an analysis of the governmental patterns at the state level and their effect on urban education. Laurence Iannaccone is recognized as one of the best-informed scholars about state politics related to educational decisions. He has studied at three urban universities in the U.S. and one abroad. In addition, he has served as a professor in universities in four urban centers: on the West Coast, East Coast, Midwest, and Canada. In this chapter he analyzes the rural patterns that dominate state legislatures, the ties linking the educational professionals and school board members into that rural power system. Finally, he describes the effects of this legislative system on urban education.

"If it is a cliché to say that city schools are in trouble, it is also a cliché to say they are in financial trouble." So Walter Garms and James Kelly of Teachers College begin Chapter 13. Both men have centered their careers on the study of fiscal variables related to urban education. Kelly has also served for two years with the Urban Coalition. The authors point to the shifting population and industrial patterns of urban centers and federal fiscal policy as two major factors in the fiscal catastrophe many urban school districts now face. They also review the development of rurally oriented state legislatures. Finally, the authors propose a system of allocation of fiscal resources that they believe would alleviate this potentially disastrous situation.

Following upon the criticisms of federal and state allocation of resources to meet the problems of urban education, Chapter 14 discusses the problems of urban education specifically related to the legislative branch of the federal government. James Guthrie spent a year in the U.S. Office of Education and the last several years in the professorship at the University of California. When analyzing the voting patterns of the legislative branch of the federal government and their allocation of resources, the author finds considerable fault with the present trends. He concludes that "the magnitude of the urban crisis is such that a large measure of the direction and coordination of our efforts and the resources for those efforts must come from the federal government."

Teachers College, Columbia University has been recognized throughout the twentieth century as one of the outstanding institutions in the country that is fundamentally concerned with education. Its present dean, Robert Schaefer, is one of the most articulate, sensitive, and scholarly men in education today. In Chapter 15 he speaks his views of how the urban university and urban public education are related and how each may assist the other in making our cities more livable.

Finally, the Editor has attempted a concluding statement. This is not intended as a summary, for the authors have expressed their points of view far better than could the Editor. Rather, the final statement reflects the Editor's point of view, influenced at least in part by the knowledge his contributing authors have shared with him and with the readers of this book.

1

Humanistic
Existentialism
and the
School Administrator

Harry J. Hartley

Introduction

The primary purpose of this essay is to formulate a complement, or perhaps an alternative, to the present scientific-empirical-systemic approach to administrative conduct. More specifically, subsequent paragraphs describe *existential humanism* and show how it may be an appropriate philosophical basis for contemporary urban school administration. Major sections include: 1) underlying assumptions; 2) existential philosophy; 3) four major existential writers; 4) existential implications for urban administration; and 5) behavioral manifestations of an existential administrator. Advocacy of an alternative approach, such as existential humanism, should not be misconstrued as a rejection of current management science techniques and strategies.

There is no quarrel between the humanities and the sciences. There is only a need, common to them both, to put the idea of man back where it once stood, at the focus of our lives; to make the end of education the preparation of men to be men, and so to restore to mankind—and above all to this nation of mankind—a conception of humanity with which humanity can live(1).

We are moving into an age where, it seems, nearly any man can be replaced by a machine. The worth of human beings is decreasing in direct proportion to our technological progress. Deeper values have given way to material strength, and the result is urban wastelands.

Underlying Assumptions

The contemporary urban school administrator who espouses humanistic values is a spiritual leader in an age of disbelief. However, he may be part of an advance guard that is capable of creating new life styles for the urban school leader of tomorrow. It is an exaggeration to relate current urban wastelands and the decay of cities to public policy made by short-sighted technocrats. But it is fairly obvious that the present administrative era is one in which we venerate scientism while barely tolerating humanism. Urban education no longer exists to produce men prepared for life in a society of men. It exists to prepare men as specialized experts who can readily gain professional or industrial employment. The latter can provide specialized answers, whereas the former can formulate liberating questions. The danger in overemphasizing the latter is that it may lead to the congealing and eventual self-destruction of urban society. Our cities have been built and rebuilt not with human purposes in mind but with technological means at hand. "A curious automatism, human in origin but not human in action, seems to be taking over(2)."

Administration is on the threshold of a systems era in which policies are being developed by means of techniques such as PPBS, PERT, input-output analysis, operations research, cost-effectiveness analysis, and so forth(3). The intricate problems of our time can be analyzed immediately with computers, but what to do with these analyses is a persistent dilemma. Recent advances in technology and science far outspace any comparable advances in human wisdom. Systems analysis, as a derivative of general systems theory, is a substantial improvement over previous administrative methodologies. However, systems analysis is more a mode of thought than a mechanical tool. Too often, urban analysts focus upon efficient means (such as program budgeting) rather than noble ends (such as human purposes) as they plan school programs for city children.

There *is* a wisdom lag. Unfortunately, some of the urban schools that use systems analysis have tended to emphasize *saving* at the expense of *accomplishing*. The need exists in ghetto schools, for example, for *uneconomic* allocations of resources. It is necessary to "waste" money on noneconomic values that reflect our social conscience. Social conscience in the arena of urban polity is intertwined with existential humanism.

Educational administration has many philosophical dimensions and it is possible to relate contemporary schools of thought to urban school officials. Philosophy involves the study of questions, and the individual who assumes the awful burden of responsibility of providing educational leadership is confronted with questions arising from seemingly insoluble problems.

Any attempt to link existentialism with educational administration is based upon the premise that the former may be conceived as an educational philosophy. It is sufficient to assert that existentialism is one of the competing theories in education, and thus little attempt is made here to repeat what readily can be found elsewhere in foundation texts and journals.

Professionally-oriented administrators occasionally may be criticized for studying academic philosophy in a somewhat nontechnical manner. However, a characteristic of existential philosophy that distinguishes it from analytical schools of thought is that ". . . the existentialist has not relinquished philosophy's traditional audience—namely, everybody, regardless of any technical competence, philosophical or other . . ."(4). Furthermore, any question pursued to its beginning or its end becomes a philosophic question, even though the individuals involved may not be aware they are engaged in philosophic dialogues. Thus, the administrator who rejects philosophical inquiry and the humanistic side of education may ultimately discover that his position is not unlike that of the French Revolutionist who proclaimed, "The mobs are in the street. I must find out where they are going, for I am their leader."

The phenomenon of administration may be viewed as the product of a particular school of philosophy, namely, realism, which is based upon the Aristotelian doctrine of forms. Administration is principally an attempt to order and regulate some process, and the goal of a realist is a fixed, orderly, and regular cosmic process. As a field of study, administration has not yet reached the level of reflection. It is still in a pre-reflective era inasmuch as there have been relatively few attempts to include the humanities in the preparation programs of future administrators. Admittedly, administration is becoming much more sophisticated, as attested by the incorporation of knowledge contributed by the behavioral sciences and by the fairly recent development of conceptual frameworks in the area of administrative theory; but it is still more closely related to custom than to thought. The role of the educational administrator is not unlike that of Plato's ruler of the state, because both are leaders of the human community. Many of the moral and social problems unresolved by our society are being delegated to the public school, i.e., integration, social justice, societal goals, educational equality, intellectual freedom, religious affairs, moral ideals, etc. The ultimate responsibility for solutions to such problems frequently resides with the administrator, who being short of divinity, requires many of the intellectual qualities which were necessary for the philosopher-king.

If the school administrator of today is pursuing ideals of clarity, simplicity, sincerity, and goodness, he must deliberately examine alternative propositions before engaging in practical courses of action. One such set of propositions is the philosophy of existentialism.

Existential Philosophy:
An Historical Consciousness

Existential thought is frequently designated under the rubric of existentialism, but most philosophers are careful not to interchange the two expressions. Existential thought is the broader term and suggests the lack of a systematic, unified doctrine or school. For purposes of simplicity, the term existentialism will be used herein, but it might be argued that this label ought to be abandoned altogether. Existentialism is not easily reducible to any simple set of tenets because it contains several widely different revolts against traditional philosophy; it represents a basic divergence from analytical and logico-rational philosophy in terms of the nature of reality and in the approach philosophy should employ in discerning reality. More a mood than a systematic theory, it is characterized by a great faith in human intentness and potentiality.

Existentialism questions the very presence of a fixed, immutable reality, and it is staunchly opposed to the tradition of classical philosophy—from Plato to Hegel—which seeks eternal, universal truths primarily by means of the objectivistic rational intellect of man. The rejection of conventional values by existentialists has led many critics to call it a philosophy of complete nihilism and utter despair. On the other hand, existentialism is perhaps the most humanistic and appealing movement in modern philosophy. At one time or another almost everyone has reflected upon such major existential themes as the sources of agony, despair, suffering, detachment, dread, anxiety, neuroses, guilt, anguish, care, pain, freedom, absurdity, injustice, cruelty, love, kindness, abandonment, alienation, suicide, death, authenticity, the nature and limits of reason, existence and essence, the triumph over adversity, self-realization, God, and the relationship between the individual and society.

Because existentialism contains a distrust of reason, it is frequently accused of being anti-intellectual and irrational. It stands in opposition to the scientific conception of the world which presently dominates the United States in our Age of Analysis. In fact, existentialists appear to be unequivocal in their rejection of the method of science; their basis is that we have stopped *living* our lives in favor of *knowing* our lives. They consider existence a mystery and something exclusively human; truth is regarded as subjectivity and priority is given to the categories of the irrational(5).

Existentialism differs from other schools of philosophy because it is based on the belief that human existence precedes essence. Traditional philosophies have always assumed the priority in time of the essence (unique qualities; blueprint) of man over his existence (act of being). The existentialist reverses this assumption by affirming: "We first are; then we attempt to define ourselves. Man is the great contingency; his essence is not given. His very specialness lies in his ungivenness"(6).

Man is a builder, whose life is spent in the project of constructing himself and achieving liberation from his self-imposed slavery. He is an unfinished product and he is ultimately responsible for each of the choices made in his lifetime. The highest good is individuality, even though it is somehow wretched, revolting, and miserable. Existential man is thrown into the world, and although he is abandoned to a life that ends in death, he strives for authenticity by becoming an ascetic of the spirit. The Idea of Man is not yet completed, for we help formulate this Idea with our lives and with our freely-made choices. In fashioning myself, I am fashioning MAN, although there is no absolute conception of man. I invent my own morality, for I have freedom of choice and am not coerced by others. Life is viewed as its own reward. This value theory emphasizes free-expression through such things as painting, dialogue, sculpture, literature, and music; and it is based upon emotional sources.

Four Major Existential Writers

It is interesting to observe that most of the living "existentialists" have repudiated this label, and it has been suggested that the only feature these writers have in common is a marked aversion for each other. The intellectual ancestry of existentialism is usually traced to Soren *Kierkegaard* (1813–55) of Denmark, who was a Protestant of sorts. He regarded it as his mission in life to defend true Christian life against its distortion by the church, and he was concerned with how one can advance from unauthentic being to authentic being. He stressed the morbid aspects of human life and implied that individual man is being engulfed in the mass of men. Kierkegaard rejected ". . . the senseless accumulation of knowledge. He wanted to discard the superfluity of knowledge, in order that we may again learn what it means to live as a human being"(7). His dislike of rational thought is illustrated in two statements: "Whoever wants to be a Christian should tear the eyes out of his reason," and "Reason is a whore."

Friederich Wilhelm *Nietzsche* (1844–1900) of Germany, related metaphysics and ethics to the moral crisis of Western civilization. He concluded that belief in God is no longer tenable in the modern world: "God is dead and we have killed him." He opposed the maxims of bourgeois society and believed that in society, man loses his authentic self and sinks into a general mediocrity. He developed the popular concept of a "Superman," or Overman, who represented something of a man-god. When man acts "morally," he is only following the precepts of society and thus remains at the herd level. To be truly an individual, man must dare to be immoral, like Nature. He rejected the notion that man is made in the image of God and asserted that man is essentially free in defining himself. The freedom to produce possibilities is creativity, the highest form of which is self-creativity.

Martin *Heidegger* (born in 1889) is a German who believes that the whole history of human thought and existence has been dominated and characterized by man's understanding of *being*. His writings are based upon the consideration of such metaphysical concerns as "Why is there anything at all, rather than nothing?" and "What does it mean to be?"(8). Methodically, Heidegger analyzes the concept of *dasein* (similar to human existence) in respect to its temporal and historical character. He attempts to penetrate the origins of being and pleads for a return to metaphysical considerations.

Probably the most influential and best-known existentialist is Jean-Paul *Sartre* (born in 1905), who has contributed greatly to French philosophy and literature and who rejected the 1964 Nobel Prize for literature. Both he and Heidegger have been greatly influenced by Edmund *Husserl* (German, 1859–1938), who provided them with the phenomenological method (descriptive analysis of subjective processes). Sartre distinguishes between the two major divisions within existentialism, Christian and Atheistic, and he states: "Atheistic Existentialism, of which I am representative, declares with greater consistency that if God does not exist there is at least one being whose existence comes before its essence, a being which exists before it can be defined by any conception of it. That being is man or, as Heidegger has it, the human reality"(9).

Sartre's many philosophical essays and books, novels, plays, literary criticisms, and autobiography (*The Words*) have made him a kind of conscience in modern French thought. In his autobiography, Sartre attacks the roots of self-deception and hypocrisy and lashes out at the very elements that contributed to his character—heredity, religion, family, and the bourgeois confidence in culture. As was the case with the other writers discussed above, the dialectical development of Sartre's thinking makes it easy to describe him briefly but difficult to represent him adequately. Because paradox and irony constitute intrinsic elements of existential methodology, there is little sacrosanctity in some of the writings.

Others who might be classified as existentialists are Martin Buber, Gabriel Marcel, Miguel de Unamuno, Simone de Beauvoir, Albert Camus, Maurice Merleau-Ponty, Franz Kafka, and Paul Tillich. Some writers have interpreted by means of existentialist themes the writings of Dostoevsky, Freud, Goethe, Shakespeare, Rilke, Toynbee, G. Allport, Maritain, and others.

Because existentialism is philosophy in its most subjective and individualized form, one might assume that it would find favor in our modern world. Many writers, artists, intellectuals, and professional educators (G. Kneller, V. C. Morris, and T. Brameld, among others) have been influenced by, and contributed to, existential thought(10). Even the so-called "hippie movement" has been defined as a somewhat degenerate form of existentialism for the weak-minded and weak-willed, although it differs from continent existentialism. Recent university student revolts and the "New Politics" certainly have existential overtones.

Existential Implications
for Urban Administration

The educational administrator is *not* a philosopher. He is a philosophizing person of practical affairs who transforms the theoretical elements of his thinking into an operational context. For the existential urban administrator, this transformation might be more easily observed by describing characteristics *not* associated with him. This is not unexpected, for he is the embodiment of a non-systematized philosophy which rejects much of the traditionalism of American education. His leadership style represents deviant behavior, for he is providing spiritual leadership (humanistic roots) during an age of disbelief (positivistic influence). The existential leader sustains a strong moral paradox, a fervent belief both in legitimate human hope and in the limitations that existence places implacably upon every human hope. As such, he is an existent self who reflects upon the most extraordinary, intense emotional experiences involved in expanding the selfhood of others through education.

A basic principle of Sartre states that as a man chooses he is choosing for humanity. Applying this to the administrator, we can easily see his burden, for in choosing and making decisions he is choosing for all. He reflects the human predicament and the anguish of freedom. He must base decisions on intuition and finite knowledge within which human lives are enclosed. There is a denial of universals and formal categories and the choices must be formulated singularly. His intuitive insight results from affective experiences such as anguish and from an understanding of the human condition; 'to be' means to be engaged in choosing and personal appropriation, and existential knowledge provides the basis for authentic choice. Assuming that man's freedom is the foundation of ethics, the "good" decision is one which the administrator makes freely on behalf of self-fulfillment.

The existential administrator is the counterpart of the Persian prophet Zarathustra, whom Nietzsche described in *Thus Spoke Zarathustra* as a liberator of mankind. Nietzsche's prophet aided men in freeing themselves from their self-imposed tyranny and attempted a restructuring of the world out of chaotic ruins.

In reflecting upon the fundamental presuppositions of his work, Zarathustra underwent an existential transformation and became a higher man (Overman). His existence, his life in solitude, and his creation of new values were the result of an assessment of old values; he created a new essence on the basis of a prior existence that was justified by the inner necessities of the life of the Overman that he was. Zarathustra, as a leader, provided for man's possibility to overcome himself by asserting that man will be nothing else but what he makes of himself. The price that this leader pays for his beliefs may be isolation, but since human existence involves abandonment anyhow, this voluntary isolation may be a cheap price for the results obtained.

Educational administrators are frequently depicted as organizational change-agents who incorporate meaningful innovations into the social processes of education. If they are influenced by existentialism, they must begin their consideration of betterment with critical reassessment of the basic present structure. Schools are formally organized along the Weberian pure-type models of rational bureaucracy. The curriculum is also formally structured and priority is given to the method of science in presenting the content of the behavioral, social, and natural sciences. There is a trend toward increased objectification of students in regard to the importance attached to such things as class rankings, grade point averages, intelligence quotients, standardized exams, automated teaching methodology, and even educational research which dehumanizes the subjective nature of man. *Man is becoming merely a datum.*

The existential administrator is the faint beacon of light which flickers in the darkness of educational scientism. He is a sometimes misunderstood provocateur of humanism resisting the growing tide of educators who have turned upon man as an object of knowledge (*en-soi*). If positivism succeeds in knowing about the self completely, it will drive out *pour-soi,* or selfhood. Men will merely exist as objects, like chairs, rather than as subjects possessing emotions, feelings, and passions which defy rational analysis. Granted that knowledge has objective, social aspects, but thought is subjective and individualized, and the school should encourage both knowledge and thought.

The administrator, like Zarathustra, must create new humanistic values out of old, and define a new educational essence. Sallust once remarked, "Every man is the architect of his own fortune." The individual who administers an urban educational institution is the architect of each of the persons assigned to his organization. His power is commensurate with his responsibility.

Education represents a form of power, ". . . more powerful than any other agency on earth, . . . the one generative force potentially great enough to combat all degenerative human forces"(11). This statement and one to follow by Professor Brameld are significant for students of administration. It was Brameld, in 1950, who provided the foundations of social reconstructionism (a form of modern progressivism) in education. In 1965, he modified his position in view of contemporary influences. After analyzing such patterns of thought as scientific humanism, objective idealism, dialectical materialism, supernaturalism, and existentialism, Brameld chose to identify himself with the latter: "The reconstructionist philosophy of education . . . is the philosophy of existential humanism"(12).

Underlying the existential leader is the concept of irrationality which provided the foundation for George Bernard Shaw's contention that all progress depends on the unreasonable man. In a description of leadership qualities, Shaw once remarked that a true leader is an unreasonable man who persists in trying to adapt the world to himself while the reasonable man adapts himself to the world. Such a person is the existential school superintendent.

A list delineating some of the behavioral elements of an existential educational administrator is presented here. This outline is both tentative and exploratory in nature. Not only do the elements overlap, but their framework contains intentional leaps from pre- to pro-scription and from area to area (teaching, curriculum, organizational structure, student counseling, etc.). The import of this approach is to be found in the totality of the 20 components rather than in the isolated items.

Behavioral Manifestations
of an Existential Administrator

1. Resist positivistic methodology which formulates decisions solely on the basis of quantitative analysis. Management science, including such techniques as operations research, statistical decision theory, systems analysis, and linear programming, assists the human decision-making process, but is in no sense a substitute for it.
2. Use intuition as a major basis for decision-making. Recognize the positive role of intuition which implies self-knowledge and familiarity with the area involved. This might be a form of "romantic rationalism."
3. Emphasize the humanistic tradition insofar as this contributes to the expansion of an individual's selfhood. Reject absolute nihilism and lead the organization in such a manner that human freedoms are implemented and expanded.
4. Reject the senseless accumulation or superfluity of knowledge that attempts to describe MAN (universal conception) rather than men as particularistic individuals. The concrete, diverse aspects of human separateness are stressed.
5. Encourage the Socratic method of teaching, in which the instructor serves primarily as a midwife in eliciting knowledge from the learner.
6. Advocate a curriculum related to social and personal real-

ity which includes such humanistic elements as the arts, moral philosophy, great books, and individualized programs of study.

7. Liberate students and teachers from restrictions upon learning imposed by the doctrines of traditional educational philosophies.

8. Encourage liberal "free-thinking" in which each person assumes responsibility for his choices, feelings, emotions, and entire life. Unconstrained emotional responses for each person are sought. The choices must be meaningful—something important and "real" for the student.

9. Show concern for the extraordinary—for the most intense emotional experiences related to administering an educational organization.

10. Avoid sources of impersonality and alienation in student-faculty-administrator-community relationships. In contrast to the detached form of analysis by the linguistic philosophers is the emphasis on involvement and participation in the concrete concerns of human life found among the existential practitioners.

11. Encourage interpersonal confrontation of professional and nonprofessional personnel. Individuals work in a social environment which should be an expression of community (not merely collectivism). The individual cannot become human by himself, for self-being is only real in communication with other self-beings.

12. Refute supervision and coercion of personnel by external standards. Supervision criteria should be formulated from within the organization by its members.

13. Promote education as a source of freedom. Freedom is a necessary basis for human creativity and intellectual growth. Education, including history, should be used by students to change the course of history away from Cacotopia towards something more human.

14. Express a commitment to openness rather than to teleological closed-ended systems and procedures. Man is always what he is yet to be; his acts are contingent upon his decisions, which should be freely made.

15. Oppose organizational patterns of bureaucracy, which are based almost solely upon the Weberian element of rationality. A purely rational social organization such as a school is undesirable because it ignores the nonrational aspects of social conduct. Neo-Weberian models, such as Blau's "other-face of bureaucracy," are more suitable for schools than Weber's pure-types.

16. Develop a unique leadership style which, in terms of one well-known social system model, might be described as more

idiographic (emphasis on individual need-dispositions of subordinates) than nomothetic (emphasis on institutional sanctions and role-expectations of subordinates).

17. Promote an attitude of "fallibilism" in the school. Individuals and human knowledge are never absolute but exist on a continuum of uncertainty and of indeterminacy.

18. Resist the scientific temper of pragmatism which permeates American public education. Science unites us only as intellectual beings, not as human beings. Existential truth is infinitely more than scientific correctness.

19. Initiate existential counseling techniques into the school program. These are related to existential psychoanalysis and psychotherapy techniques from psychology; they emphasize nondirective approaches to the counseling of students rather than behavioristic, client-centered methods.

20. Oppose selected elements of control by the various levels of government which tend to increase the constraints upon individual decision-making. This is not a plea for the "local control" concept as such, but it does imply a need for some autonomy of local districts.

These 20 existential dimensions might be summarized by formulating four dominant themes and relating each item to one of these themes:

A. Emphasize self-expression for each individual (items 2, 3, 5, 6, 8, 9, 13).
B. Oppose externally based determinants and sanctions (7, 12, 14, 15, 16, 20).
C. Resist quantitative assumptions that deny human separateness (1, 17, 18).
D. Create conditions in which interpersonal communication and social selfhood are encouraged (4, 10, 11, 19).

Conclusion

A major difficulty with transposing existentialism into practice is that our culture tends to extol the worth of social intercourse, group activity, group norms, and socially acceptable behavior. Our conceived values may include a desire for individuality, but our operative values generally do not reflect such a belief. Those who advocate the extreme individuality of existentialism in the schools could easily become the objects of severe criticism.

Many educators are characterized by their adherence to tradition and fear of change. If one were to construct a continuum with traditional values at one end and emergent values at the other, the educators who are in a position to bring about change (such as administrators and boards of education) probably would be located on the side of the traditional values. This is unfortunate, for the mutual impact of school and society is so profound that these unimaginative administrators can wield an influence far beyond their immediate confines. The burden of proof is upon those who would introduce existentialism into public education. It must be shown that this is an improvement over present dominant patterns of thought.

The acceptance by an individual of the position of school administrator might appear to preclude the possibility of existential thought. However, the broad restrictions of the role can be accepted by the occupant if his choice is uncoerced and he is given the freedom to administer in a meaningful and creative manner. He brings with him a unique personality, particular need-dispositions, emotions, and an individualized style of leadership. Education is characterized by fixed ends and varying means. It is this premise that enables one to conceive that the restrictions that limit an organizational leader are broad enough to permit individual discretion to operate.

In the vanished past of not too many years, the power of urban school administrators was nearly as unlimited as an absolute monarch. Today, with demands for decentralization, community-operated schools, increasing teacher activism in policy areas, and other issues, the urban administrator is a much-harried man with an increasing sense of powerlessness. Some claim that it is an ungrateful job for which the duties, sacrifices, risks, and anguish seem altogether disproportionate to the rewards. One is tempted to describe city school officials as the fallen women of Europe have been described: ". . . the eternal priestesses of humanity blasted for the sins of their people." School officials are no longer priests, but whenever a crisis arises, they are certain to be criticized by all sides. Perhaps a greater concern for humanity will restore administrative prestige in the eyes of an extremely sensitive, discontented, and demanding public constituency.

Existentialism was included in several recent examinations of the relationship of philosophy to educational administration(13), and it may someday exert more influence upon this professional field. Student demands may transform administrative values. The seeds of existentialism that were present in the 1950's on college campuses grew to new proportions in the 1960's and are likely to mushroom in the 1970's. Students at Berkeley, Columbia, and other campuses brought about administrative reforms that will also affect lower education. Students today are trying to be genuine, authentic people freely choosing their own behavior, attitude, and mode of living. "Existentialism means, to students, being different and it offers them a change from the morass of conformity, boredom and the meaningless competitiveness in which they see so many of their elders caught"(14).

Compassion and intellectual curiosity are essential ingredients in the makeup of the men who lead our urban schools. In education, the chief school officer is the ultimate chooser and he stands alone in assuming responsibility for specified areas of the human condition. Existential humanism helps to make man more human, and this is the true vocation of a school administrator.

Notes

1. Archibald MacLeish, "The Great American Frustration," *Saturday Review,* July 13, 1968, p. 16.

2. Ibid., p. 14.

3. For my interpretation of the systems perspective, see Harry J. Hartley, *Educational Planning-Programming-Budgeting: A Systems Approach* (Englewood Cliffs, N.J.: Prentice-Hall, Inc., 1968), 304 pp.; "Twelve Hurdles to Clear Before You Take on Systems Analysis," *American School Board Journal,* Vol. 156, No. 1 (July 1968); "PPBS: The Emergence of a Systemic Concept for Public Governance," *General Systems,* XIII (1968).

4. Stanley Cavell, "Existentialism and Analytical Philosophy," *Daedalus,* 93, No. 3 (Summer 1964), 947.

5. For an interesting treatment of traditional rationalism examined in the context of existential phenomenology, see John A. Mourant, "Thomistic Existentialism," *Essays in Philosophy,* ed. J. M. Anderson (University Park, Pa.: Penn State University Press, 1962).

6. Van Cleve Morris, *Philosophy and the American School* (Boston: Houghton Mifflin Company, 1961), p. 74.

7. F. H. Heinemann, *Existentialism and the Modern Predicament* (New York: Harper Torchbook, 1958), p. 40.

8. Martin Heidegger, *An Introduction to Metaphysics* (Garden City, N.Y.: Anchor Books, 1961), chap. 1.

9. Walter Kaufmann, *Existentialism from Dostoevsky to Sartre* (Cleveland: The World Publishing Company, 1956), p. 290.

10. The three existentialist classics are probably Soren Kierkegaard, *Concluding Unscientific Postscript,* Martin Heidegger, *Being and Time,* Jean-Paul Sartre, *Being and Nothingness.*

11. Theodore Brameld, *Education As Power* (New York: Holt, Rinehart and Winston, Inc., 1965), p. 8.

12. Ibid., p. 80.

13. Robert E. Ohm and William G. Monahan, *Educational Administration—Philosophy in Action* (Norman, Oklahoma: University Council for Educational Administration, University of Oklahoma, 1965), pp. 70 and 75; Orin B. Graff et al., *Philosophic Theory and Practice in Educational Administration* (Belmont, Calif.: Wadsworth Publishing Company, Inc., 1966), chap. 10.

14. Robert Baust, "The Inner World of Today's College Student," *Education Synopsis,* XIII, No. 1 (Winter 1967–68), 39.

2

The Structure
of Education
in the Urban School

W. Deane Wiley

Introduction

Looking to the suburbs or the city, one of the most striking characteristics of the school is the almost pathological pursuit of curriculum standardization within school districts. Given a school district with more than one elementary school, junior high, or high school, it is not possible to avoid a picture of similarity of program offering which essentially denies a curriculum tailored to the clients of any individual school. It may be that quality education must be redefined by urban educators as something other than having all of the high schools in a system running in step, or at least giving the semblance of running in step. Certainly those focusing attention on urban education have seldom accepted the "democratic offerings" argument as tenable in the face of demonstrated lack of quality.

The purpose of this chapter is to propose that a given secondary school must be allowed to break out of the curricular bureaucracy in which the urban high school finds itself and be allowed, within wide limits, to pursue a program of quality distinctly designed for its clients. The pursuit of a program tailored to meeting unique needs will challenge a succession of organizational values now held by most school men in different hierarchies of importance. This chapter will attempt to discuss some of the challenges which might predictably occur in the implementation of severe structural change involving the basic elements of learning.

Change and the School

The literature presently shows the urban school inundated with investigations of the change process. A lexicon of change terminology has rapidly worked its way into the speech of school administrators and those who comment on schools and school administrators. Yet, agreement on the contextual format of these concepts is vague and disparate. Practically speaking, where may the school organization turn to find operational concepts for the "change agent"? The New York City school organization has a formal "Office of Innovation." Are those working in that office, by definition, change agents? There is a consistent demand for designing organizations with "built-in change mechanisms," yet organizations tend to continue to respond to the research concepts supporting "steady state" and "organizational equilibrium" descriptors.

There is a growth of research (Carlson, Miles, Goldhammer, et al.) that points the finger at the school superintendent as the major change agent, advocate, or innovator (one apparently takes a choice with impunity). Yet, George Spindler sets forth the case(1), argued further by Art Gallaher(2), that the superintendent is traditionally managed by the client system and that this system is not "apt to permit advocacy as part of the administrative role."

Despite the looseness of concept development, and despite the arguments as to who will invent, advocate, and adopt, it still appears that change will take place. Even if no better argument is set forth for change than that it appears to take place less on a planned basis than as a "happy accident of coincidental factors," school organizations will and do change. If one assumes that urban schools are in such a condition in their effects on children that *any* change must be better than the status quo, then a search for *what* rather than who is equally relevant for change discussion. As a matter of fact, the *what* is an area for discussion that is fraught with peril! Here lies the contentious heart of education. Polarize it between the liberals and the conservatives, the progressives and the traditionalists, or the disciplines and the life-adjustments, the *what* of education is very closely allied to change in terms of *how*.

The Bureaucratic Model

The past 15 years (with a good deal of acceleration during the past five) have called into question the typical hierarchical pattern of traditional bureaucratic organization for the public school. The steady and insistent demand of teacher organizations to be involved in what has historically been preserved for administration is but one of the sources of pressure. The student body of the high school is rapidly becoming restive in its traditional role as captive client in the educational supermarket. The parent system seems, in many communities, to be increasingly restive under the reins of traditional patterns of administrative cooptation. Since the work of Roethlisberger and Mayo, students of organizational theory have consistently questioned the Weberian model for organizations. Concepts of collaboration, colleagueship, (McGregor, 3) decisional participation (Lewin, 4; Allport, 5), and interpersonal competence (Argyris, 6) demand not only new styles within the organization but new structures as well.

Yet, for all of the literature, the traditional bureaucratic model flourishes nowhere in a grander manner than in the public school system. The constantly demonstrated interchangeability of the human parts of the school organization is Taylorism carried to its most illogical ends. The constant demand of the urban school organization to serve the iron law of oligarchy bleeds the effort of the organization into system and sub-system maintenance to a degree that is tolerated only because of the governmentally created and supported monopoly of the service offered.

Efforts to change the urban school structure through manipulation of the governmental structure are consistently frustrated by politics on the part of interests which seldom seem to have education of the nation's youth as their major goal. The apparent inability of urban school leadership to retool its machinery to conform to the rules of a very different scene is little less tragic than the counterforce this leadership often tries to create in the name of sacred and historical tradition. This counterforce is aided immeasurably by a national public that views education generally as "something that happens" in a school if a child behaves himself and is clean.

Despite the pessimism one might assume from the foregoing, there are islands of change growing up in our educational sea. Some school districts are beginning to create structural change in the school organization by a direct attack on restructuring the learning process. This restructuring has led, and will continue to lead, to a rearrangement of the functional properties and potency of the traditional bureaucratic hierarchy. In addition, the restructuring is causing collaboration, colleagueship, participation in decision-making, and the development of interpersonal competence to emerge as organizational realities rather than as abberations within the traditional bureaucratic mode.

Structure and Learning Process

In the commentary on urban education being recorded by the lay press, there is only the most oblique reference to major change in the structural components of the learning process. Mario Fantini and Gerald Weinstein devote all of their last chapter, "The Challenge," to a proposal of serious learning impact(7). To implement their program will demand major structural change in the learning process. Hilda Taba and Deborah Elkins(8), while apparently placing their basic faith in the "beautiful" teacher, nevertheless assert that compensatory education is no substitute for changes in the structure of education itself. Arthur King and John Brownell observe that, "In an effort to design a school that has *optimally favorable characteristics for learning,** the internal organization of schools has received considerable experimentation and is very likely to receive more"(9). The structural elements of learning include, in large part, four major variables: teacher competencies, student needs and desires, physical facilities, and time. Each of these variables should be capable of wide manipulation by the building principal and teaching staff. If the major variable of all structural components is perceived as the curriculum, these four variables and their interaction will provide the real structural constraints on the curriculum of any given school.

School men contain all of these variables in the term Master

---

* Italics added.

Schedule. The master schedule is a major responsibility of the school principal. However, its theory and construction is taught in few, if any, administrator preparation programs. The principal's ability to construct a master schedule showing imagination and ingenuity is rarely if ever mentioned in an interview leading to employment as a principal. In fact, it is not difficult to discover high schools where the principal is not very involved in the construction of the master schedule, having delegated it to a vice-principal as an onerous and time-consuming task. Despite the cavalier manner in which it continues to be treated, the master schedule is:

> . . . to the high school principal as the musical score is to the concert director, for in either case a soundly planned program, harmoniously and tightly knit in all of its component parts, will determine the effectiveness of the individual and his organization. . . . Indeed, the importance of the master schedule can hardly be exaggerated. It abstracts, in words and numbers, the essence of the school. For a given school year, it sets forth in precise detail who is going to do what for every period of every day in the week. Subjects, students, instructors, classrooms are all assigned. From a close study of a master schedule, a canny reader can learn much of a school: the programs it offers; the constraint or freedom that affects the student's choice of courses; the school's position on the spectrum that runs from ultra-conservative to radical; its size, resources, shape—even its philosophy(10).

The master schedule is not a difficult area for empirical investigation. Its effects are felt daily by students and teachers, and if it is "bad," vocal remonstrances are easy to evoke. It also has a good deal to say about the implicit values placed upon curricular programs. In the early 1950's an unpublished investigation of more than 500 high school master schedules suggested that the two most important subjects offered in the American high school were band and physical education. These two subjects consistently vied for first place in the master schedule, not as a function of the principal's value system but as a matter of scheduling difficulty—which in fact gave them the highest priority value in the schedule.

To destroy the formal master schedule, therefore, results in no small challenge to those educational values held most dear by large numbers of teachers, parents, and principals. This destruction is, however, proceeding on a scattered front throughout the nation. The major problem is that this front is almost exclusively in the suburbs. The urban school system, while consistently urging the expenditure of a greater and greater number of dollars, has been the most intractable in attempting a vastly different approach with the dollars it has. Large city school systems, for example, have consistently taken highly qualified teachers into schools so structured, in terms of variables noted above, that the finest teacher is beaten by the institutional conformation within a short time. Yet if a teacher is given an opportunity to carry the curriculum to a student in a manner that denies the nonsense of the formal master schedule, the opportunity for real change becomes a possibility.

Variable Vs. Traditional Schedule

Compare for a moment the rationale between a traditional master schedule and the variable class schedule being developed in some schools today:

Traditional Schedule

A. One day cycling—such a schedule repeats itself every day of the school year.
B. Standard length periods of time—each period meets for the same number of minutes regardless of the subject matter involved.
C. High levels of control over students—all students are assigned to class, with the exception of lunch, from the time school begins until it is finished.

The Variable Class Schedule

A. There are no standard lengths for periods. Classes meet for a length of time determined by what is being taught, and how it is going to be taught, during any particular class meeting.
B. Students are not in formal class arrangements or study halls for all of their learning experiences.
C. Teachers meet students in both formal and informal groupings throughout the time cycle.
D. A concept of facility use concerns itself with what and how a subject is to be taught in any given facility at any given time.(11)

The rationale for a variable master schedule requires the urban school to divest itself of the protective cloak of historical tradition and answer some stern questions. Some of these might be:

1. With the computers existent in most urban centers, why have they not been employed in implementing a variable master schedule at secondary levels?
2. What is the educational justification for employing the Carnegie unit as a measure of learning?
3. What is the educational justification for the apparent insistence that a quality high school program consists of six subjects, viz; English, history, mathematics, science, foreign language, and physical education?
4. What educational rationale exists to support each class being offered the same amount of time as every other class?
5. What educational argument(s) can be advanced to support a learning group being one teacher and 30 students in a classroom, five or six periods a day, every day of the year as the only or "best" organization for learning?

These questions and many others have been asked in more than 100 suburban schools. The answers have resulted in the use of some form of variable class master schedule. Urban schools, on the other hand, have not yet begun to answer many of these questions. Perhaps their most serious stumbling block continues to be the conformity with which the total educational program is viewed. The present apparent inability to view each of 100 high schools in the same district as having unique constituencies, and therefore unique needs, stultifies any real educational advances for their clientele.

The inability of the urban central headquarters to see this uniqueness is not necessarily an implied argument for decentralization. However, the consistent refusal to recognize the uniqueness may leave decentralization as the only viable political weapon to relieve the frustration of the client system. The view of uniqueness is also not a demand that urban systems plunge into an experimental area fraught with the peril of causing greater condemnation than what is presently being generated. The implementation of a variable class master schedule is long out of the experimental phase. At least two nationally known computer programs are available to urban districts. Well over 100 high schools have operated with these programs for more than five years, and these may be visited as models. The market place has no dearth of consultant aid to any school district desirous of exploring the concept more fully.

A Learning-Structural Rationale

While each high school must essentially develop its own educational rationale for the implementation of a variable class master schedule, early users of these schedules appear to have developed a commonality in some basic areas. Robert Bush and Dwight Allen summarize a list of seven basic assumptions all or part of which seem to have been carried out in most schools(12). The two most fundamental are:

1. Each subject when properly taught will include four basic types of instruction:
   a. Independent and individual study
   b. Small-group instruction
   c. Laboratory instruction
   d. Large-group instruction.
2. Class size, length of class meeting, and the spacing of classes ought to vary according to the nature of the subject, the type of instruction, and the level of ability and interest of pupils.

The following assumptions are suggested as pertinent in turning from the standard master schedule to a computerized modular variable schedule:

1. Some experiences and learning will be common to all students in all subject areas:
   Technique: a. Large-Group Instruction
2. Some experiences and learning will be unique or individualized for specific students in any subject area:
   Technique: a. Independent study
                b. Open laboratories and clinics
                c. Small-group discussion
3. Some experiences and learning for some students will be more in-depth in some curricular areas:

Technique: a. Individualized Independent Study
            b. Directed Readings Programs
            c. Teacher-Assigned or Student-Initiated Independent Study Projects
4. Learning Experiences and instruction will require variability throughout the school day, week or year to include:
            a. class size,
            b. instructional time,
            c. staff,
            d. school facilities and resources.
    Technique: Utilizing a computerized, modular, variable scheduling program.
5. The learning experience is founded upon a curriculum which is concept-oriented or concept-centered. Fundamental concepts are identified within each subject matter area and becomes, then, the basis for structuring the curriculum and expected learning activities for all students within a curricular area.
6. A curriculum is developed which offers achievement opportunity for all students regardless of *assumed* ability or *assumed* learning potential.

The rationale presented above demands, besides gross structural change, sophisticated knowledge of the three major modes of instruction, i.e., large-group, small-group, and independent-study concepts. It is, after all, the ability of an individual school to manipulate and control these three structural components that is suggested as efficacious for implementation by the urban school. There is little argument left to support a continued refusal to implement the educational concepts of variable class scheduling. Each of the large urban school systems should designate and support within their educational systems pilot high schools aimed toward complete implementation. Given the vast cultural and environmental learning opportunities which exist outside the inadequate urban school building, a variable class schedule in an urban setting is predictive of expanding real learning far beyond the walls of the formal classroom. The "field trip" becomes an individualized learning experience. The "assembly," the study hall, the 50-minute class, the five-minute passing period, the clanging of bells, the 30-pupil classroom mode, and many other cherished myths become identified for the anachronisms which they in fact are.

Those learning experiences which the vigorous and imaginative teacher has been unable to carry out because they "upset the schedule" become part of a variable class schedule and not destructive to the "other teacher's" plans.

Conclusion

There is presently a question in the minds of many as to how the urban school, especially the inner city schools, will survive the present criticism concerning ineffectiveness and irrelevance. Competing school systems have been suggested by some; billions of dollars in aid is the answer of others; better teacher training is another of the myriad suggestions. The purpose of this chapter has been to suggest that competing school systems will probably be structured very much like the schools with which they are designed to compete. Millions, if not billions, of dollars have already been and are in the process of being consumed by urban school systems, with little discernible difference in the quality of the learning process. Teacher training is as much shaped by the institution it serves as it is shaped by the collegiate institution, the institutions being in fact blood brothers under the skin.

While it is not intended here to imply that urban schools do not need money or better teacher training, it *is* strongly contended that more money and better teachers plunged into the institutional rigidity that characterizes urban organization for instruction holds little if any promise for substantive change.

This conclusion places the highest value on the institutional impact of learning designs. Further, it contends, without compromise, that the flexibility and variability offered by large-scale computer systems, presently available to all, hold the major promise for imaginative manipulation of the prime variables that comprise the teaching-learning process.

Notes

1. George Spindler, ed., *Education and Culture: Anthropological Approaches* (New York: Holt, Rinehart & Winston, Inc., 1963), p. 238.

2. Art Gallaher, Jr., *Change Processes in the Public Schools,* Center for the Advanced Study of Educational Administration (Eugene, Ore.: University of Oregon, 1965).

3. D. McGregor, *The Human Side of Enterprise* (New York: McGraw-Hill Book Company, 1960).

4. Kurt Lewin, "Group Decisions and Social Change" in Theodore M. Newcomb and Eugene L. Hartley, eds., *Readings in Social Psychology* (New York: Holt, Rinehart & Winston, Inc., 1947).

5. Gordon Allport, "The Psychology of Participation," *Personality and Social Encounter* (Boston: Beacon Press, 1960).

6. C. Argyris, *Interpersonal Competence and Organization Effectiveness* (Homewood, Ill.: Dorsey Press, 1962).

7. Mario D. Fantini and Gerald Weinstein, *The Disadvantaged: Challenge to Education* (New York: Harper & Row, Publishers, 1968).

8. Hilda Taba and Deborah Elkins, *Teaching Strategies for the Culturally Disadvantaged* (Chicago: Rand McNally & Co., 1966).

9. Arthur R. King, Jr. and John A. Brownell, *The Curriculum and the Disciplines of Knowledge* (New York: John Wiley & Sons, Inc., 1966), p. 119.

10. Judith Murphy, *School Scheduling by Computer, the Story of GASP* (New York: Educational Facilities Laboratory, 1964), p. 1.

11. W. Deane Wiley and Lloyd K. Bishop, *The Flexibly Scheduled High School* (West Nyack, N.Y.: Parker Publishing Co., 1968), p. 1.

12. Robert N. Bush and Dwight W. Allen, *A New Design for High School Education: Assuming a Flexible Schedule* (New York: McGraw-Hill Book Company, 1964), p. 8.

3

Desegregation,
Integration,
and Urban Schools

Robert W. Heller

Introduction

One of the most important, yet difficult, tasks ever to confront public school educators is that of providing all students with a quality education within a racially integrated or racially balanced educational system. Presently, the problems of racial integration are most acute in urban schools where the percentage of nonwhite population is rising rapidly, with a corresponding decrease in the white population. It will not be long before the nearly all-white suburban and rural school districts in the nation are forced to face their social responsibilities and begin to undertake the complex process of racial integration of their schools. If children are to receive a full education, they cannot be deprived of significant contacts with groups that represent American society and comprise the adult world. Pupils educated in racially segregated classrooms are hampered by unrealistic experiences of life. The role of the school is to prepare children, be they white or Black, for adult life; this education cannot take place under the existing artificial conditions(1).

Since the 1954 U.S. Supreme Court Decision—*Brown vs. Board of Education of Topeka*—the nation has been charged with the responsibility of desegregating its schools. Much effort has been expended in eliminating the injustices brought about by *de jure* segregated conditions. However, much still remains to be done in correcting the conditions resulting from *de facto* segregation. *De facto* segregation is viewed by many as the number one problem facing urban school systems today.

In the past, a serious impediment to progress in overcoming the problems associated with *de facto* segregation was that of recognition by responsible authorities that it did, indeed, exist at all. It appears unreasonable today to believe that this is any longer the case. The problem now consists of convincing citizens that segregation harms children and in inducing educators to take steps which will result in eliminating segregation, regardless of whether it is the result of intentional, *de jure,* or unintentional, *de facto,* circumstances.

Two rather serious consequences appear to be emerging from the attempts to educate the culturally and economically deprived and minority-group children in American cities. The first deals with a polarization in the thinking of those concerned with the problems of providing quality education to all children(2); the second, the more serious of the two, is the appearance of an increasing number of people supporting a separatist movement in American society, a condition which we must never allow to exist if there is to be hope for maintaining our democratic society.

The polarization of thinking stems from one group of educators supporting compensatory education for the children of the poor and minority groups as the vehicle for overcoming educational deficiencies resulting from their segregation in the ghetto. The other group, while recognizing that compensatory education may be of some value, are committed to ending *de facto* segregation and eliminating ghetto conditions. The latter group is not convinced that merely upgrading the educational experiences of students within the confines of a compensatory educational program is sufficient for preparing ghetto children adequately for success in later life. Children raised and educated in the ghetto come to believe that it is their world, and they cannot be divorced from this environment merely through compensatory education. Supporters of this viewpoint argue that *de facto* segregation barriers must be eliminated. Their position was strengthened by the appearance of two government reports of great significance to education, *Equality of Educational Opportunity,* describing a study directed by James S. Coleman under the auspices of the U.S. Office of Education, and *Racial Isolation in the Public Schools,* the U.S. Commission on Civil Rights Report(3). Both reports contain data which support negative findings on the value of compensatory educational programs for minority youth(4).

The methods which urban school districts are using to provide quality education vary. Some of the districts are completely committed to a comprehensive compensatory educational program, even if it results in maintaining *de facto* segregation patterns. Other urban school districts are moving ahead with plans and programs designed to end *de facto* segregation and ultimately bring about a racially integrated school system.

Patterns of Urban Centers

During the past two decades the population pattern of urban centers has changed. Most central cities have experienced a loss of population or are just barely maintaining their population levels. At the same time, the more mobile middle and upper middle-class whites have been fleeing to the suburbs for housing, but return to the city for many services which their tax dollars no longer support. Those remaining behind in the cities are, for the main, the less educated, poorer, nonwhite Americans, who are being joined by a substantial number of in-migrants. These new residents have little or no understanding of how to deal with city living, frequently do not possess skills applicable to city life, and demand services from the city to which they do not contribute tax dollars.

Despite population declines in most of the nation's urban centers, public school enrollments have increased. Fourteen of the 15 largest urban school systems, with a minimum of 500,000 city population, experienced an increase in the number of school-age children from 1950 to 1960. Nonwhite students represent the greatest percentage of the increase. Many of these cities, meanwhile, have had a decrease in the number of white school-age children(5). In addition, most central cities have large private and parochial school enrollments where whites constitute the vast majority of the student body. This results in a substantial drain of white students from the public schools and contributes to *de facto* segregation(6).

The unique pattern of segregation within the public schools of this nation has resulted in a phenomenon that makes it increasingly difficult to racially integrate schools. While segregation of schools is quite common, the urban areas have the most highly segregated schools. The 1960 census revealed that two-thirds of all Americans reside in our metropolitan areas. Contrasting this with the figures from 1900 revealed a changing population pattern in the metropolitan areas. At the turn of the century approximately half of the Black population residing in metropolitan areas lived in the central city. By 1960, however, eight of ten Blacks in metropolitan areas were residing in the central city. The white population in central cities in 1900 included about six of every ten living within the metropolitan areas. This had changed by 1960 to more than half of the white metropolitan population residing in the suburbs(7). The report of the United States Commission on Civil Rights further points out that, in 1960, over 79 percent of the nonwhite public school enrollment was in the central city schools(8).

Racial segregation of schools is most prominent in central city schools where the largest concentrations of Blacks are found. New York State illustrates this vividly. In the Bix Six Cities (Albany, Buffalo, Rochester, Syracuse, Yonkers, and New York City) 47 percent of the public school pupils are nonwhite, compared with five percent in the rest of the state(9).

Looking at segregation patterns in 75 cities, the Civil Rights Commission Report reveals that over 75 percent of the Black students were in elementary schools whose enrollments were over 90 percent Black, while at the same time 83 percent of the white students were in nearly all-white suburban schools. This is equivalent to nine of every ten Black elementary school children attending majority Black schools(10). The Commission report further reveals that the pattern of segregation holds true regardless of the school district size, proportion of Black-white students, or geographical location of the urban center(11). What has been developing, particularly during the past three decades, is a pattern of segregation throughout the United States that has no clear boundaries and significantly intensifies in urban areas.

In 1965, 200 communities with a 1960 nonwhite population of one thousand or more were surveyed. These localities covered a 19-state area and accounted for 75 percent of the Black population of the North. The 1,100 schools in these 200 communities had nonwhite enrollments of 60 percent or greater. Approximately 80 percent of the segregated schools were located in New York, Michigan, Illinois, Pennsylvania, Ohio, and California. Three-fourths of those schools were concentrated in six great cities: New York City, Detroit, Chicago, Philadelphia, Cleveland, and Los Angeles(12). However, the existing political, legal, and social structure of these major cities makes it virtually impossible to integrate the school systems prior to drastic changes taking place.

Efforts to decentralize schools in the central cities, although gaining in popular support, are not resulting in the establishment of school districts which can develop, maintain, and support integrated schools. John Everett elaborates on the well-intentioned efforts of the American liberal who sees the decentralization issue of our city schools as a step toward bringing the community and school system together as partners in the educational program(13). Citing New York City as an example, he points out that the proposed 33 school districts in the decentralization plan will result in 33 homogeneous communities which do not represent the typical heterogeneous mixture of American communities. This type of community goes contrary to the American way of life. As Everett states,

> One of the purposes of the American public school system is to weld people of diverse backgrounds into a nation with common goals, common ideals, and common aspirations. The glory of public education in America is that it was able to take the children of immigrant parents and teach them not only a common language but also to forget the historic hatreds of the bloody battlegrounds of the world(14).

The decentralization of large city school districts is only one issue within a complex city educational bureaucracy that is wracked with problems, most of which have some bearing upon any ultimate process of desegregation and integration.

One such problem, and perhaps the most important, is the scarcity of fiscal resources. The availability of adequate local financial resources to city school districts has been declining. State and federal monies are increasing at a relatively rapid pace but these funds, even when combined with local tax monies, are not sufficient to meet the needs and demands of large city school districts.

The per-pupil expenditure patterns of central city and suburban school districts have changed drastically during the past few decades. In 1957, the central city spent $310 per student as compared to $303 in suburban school districts. In 1967, the central-city per-student expenditure was $414, but the suburban expenditure had risen to $559. Adding to the significance of these per-pupil expenditures is the fact that in 1964 the median income for central-city Blacks was $4,463 in comparison to $7,212 for central-city whites(15). The financial burdens of central cities are increasing at a time when their educational problems are becoming most acute as they strive to educate a rapidly changing clientele. Adding to this, of course, are the problems caused by the shrinking tax base of central cities with a corresponding increase in demands for the tax dollar, not only by the educational enterprise but by all branches of the city government.

Segregation and Its Effects

Segregation, as defined by sociologists, ". . . is a condition that tends to exclude or minimize association between groups, restricting the relationships that do occur to subordinate-superordinate roles"(16). In educational settings, varying classifications are used for identifying segregated schools. A popular method used in many city school systems is the 90–10 ratio. Once the percentage of one racial group reaches 90 percent, the opportunity for meaningful association with other groups becomes minimal. This ratio, which has had wide acceptance, holds that:

> Schools whose student body is less than 10 percent Negro will be classified "white" segregated schools; if less than 10 percent of the student body is white, the schools will be considered "Negro" segregated schools; the remainder will be referred to as "integrated schools"(17).

The 90–10 ratio and other static ratios of this nature do have some drawbacks and limitations which must be recognized by those employing them. This was shown in the application of this ratio to some school district data which revealed little significant difference than when used with intervals of 80–20, 70–30 or even 99–1(18).

Mary Ellen Warshauer and Robert A. Dentler have developed a procedure they term the Interval Method because it places segregation levels in terms of range of percentages. The Interval Method stipulates,

> . . . that a school is ethnically segregated if it contains more than *two times* the community population proportion of a given minority group. A school may also be defined as segregated if it enrolls *less than half* the proportion of a population group characteristic of its community(19).

This index is useful because it clearly identifies the "critical point concept" which is the status ratio of a school. Once the critical point has been revealed, that is, where the proportion of minority group students is more than two times the proportion of this particular group in the community, the status of the school descends rapidly for middle-class groups and they begin, in increasing numbers, to remove their children. This steps up the process of increasing the percentage of minority group children into the school—which most probably will eventually result in segregated educational conditions.

Regardless of the index used to measure the degree of segregation, it is generally recognized that segregated conditions do indeed exist. Segregated schools, whether they be white or Black, result in conditions that provide unequal educational opportunities.

Two research efforts stand out as the most significant in dealing with the effects of segregated education upon children. The reports, *Equality of Educational Opportunity* and *Racial Isolation in the Public Schools,* are the result of rather massive research efforts funded through federal agencies. The former study, commonly referred to as the Coleman Report, is a highly technical statistical report on the effects of segregation on children from minority groups.

Coleman and his associates gathered extensive data from more than 3,000 schools, representing 650,000 students in grades one, three, six, nine, and twelve. More than 60,000 teachers, several thousand principals, and hundreds of superintendents of schools responded to the questionnaires and interviews. The broadest conclusion one can possibly draw from the findings is that American public education remains largely unequal in most of the nation. Or as Daniel Moynihan has so ably stated it, "The American educational system as it now operates is turning out seriously unequal citizens"(20).

Moynihan scrutinized the Coleman report and offered five major findings with interpretive comments:

1. . . . the educational achievement of 'racial' minority groups in the United States is grievously below that of the white majority with the significant exception of Chinese-Americans.
2. . . . there does not appear to be any significant degree of discrimination in the quality of the school facilities provided minority children. This is not the same as saying that the school facilities are equal. They are not. But one has the distinct impression that where inequalities exist, they can be explained better by the nature of the urban and rural environment than by any internal functioning of the school system itself.
3. . . . that despite our convictions to the contrary, it does not appear that the quality of school facilities, as we now conceive of the subject has any very powerful differential effect on student achievement.
4. . . . this is something we have always known, but somehow in the United States try to forget—is the all powerful fact of social class, or if you prefer the term, social stratification. In specific terms, this means the family background of the individual student, and the family background of his fellow student. . . . Because race is the single most inclusive . . . determinant of class in the United States, I shall argue that Coleman's data represents the most important demonstration of the absolute necessity of racial integration in education that has ever been assembled.
5. . . . concerns the elusive question of motivation. . . . American children have learned to like school, and to expect it to be a primary source, even *the* primary source, of their own social mobility. . . . I believe it is now well known that in this area Coleman found that a sense of control of one's own destiny was far the best predictor of performance(21).

Christopher Jencks summarized his perceptions of the Coleman Report by drawing three general conclusions:

1. The present public school system in America is doing nothing to narrow the gap between Negroes and whites. If the gap is narrowing at all, the credit must go to forces outside the school system.
2. The appropriation of more money for ghetto schools will probably accomplish little or nothing since those schools which have introduced expensive instructional innovations have shown little improvement in the achievement levels of their students.
3. Closing the gap between Negroes and whites would require radical changes in the present system of matching teachers with students and students with one another. Barring truly open housing, mixing classes as well as races, equality of opportunity would require the abandonment of the neighborhood school concept(22).

The Coleman Report elaborated instances of segregation as well as achievement differences among various minority groups, with the emphasis upon Blacks. The findings on student achievement levels have quickly found their way into educational reports and legal discussions, and have been used to support, both pro and con, policy positions in education. The finding which focused upon the relationship of pupil achievement to characteristics of schools are presented here as representing the "typical" type of data found in the report:

1. Socio-economic factors bear a strong relationship to academic achievement. However, when these factors are statistically controlled, it appears that differences among schools account for only a small fraction of the differences found in pupils.
2. Schools do make a difference for pupil achievement in this respect, the achievement of minority pupils depends more on the kind of schools they attend than does the achievement of white students.
3. Variations in the facilities and curricula of the school appear to account for relatively little variation in pupil achievement insofar as this is measured by standardized tests. Any variation that does exist makes more of a difference for the minority pupil.
4. Teacher quality shows some relationship to pupil achievement. Again, teacher quality seems more important to minority achievement than that of the majority.
5. Perhaps one of the most significant findings is that pupils'

achievement is strongly related to the educational background and aspirations of the other students in the school they attend. Coleman summarizes this in his statement,

> If a white pupil from a home that is strongly and effectively supportive of education is put in a school where most pupils do not come from such homes, his achievement will be little different than if he were in a school composed of others like himself. But if a minority pupil from a home without much educational strength is put with schoolmates with strong educational backgrounds, his achievement is likely to increase(23).

The U.S. Commission on Civil Rights Report includes much data which parallels that found in the Coleman Study. However, it does go beyond simply pointing out areas of concern for educators, and makes important recommendations for alleviating many of the present unfavorable social, educational, and economic conditions. The recommendations are followed by a brief summarization of supportive rationale. The recommendations include the following:

1. Congress should establish a uniform standard providing for the elimination of racial isolation in the schools.
2. Congress should vest in each of the 50 states responsibility for meeting the standard it establishes and should allow the states maximum flexibility in devising appropriate remedies. It also should provide financial and technical assistance to the states in planning such remedies.
3. The legislation should include programs of substantial financial assistance to provide for construction of new facilities and improvement in the quality of education in all schools.
4. Congress should provide for adequate time in which to accomplish the objectives of the legislation.

(5–6) The Commission recommends . . . that the President and Congress give consideration to legislation which will:

5. Prohibit discrimination in the sale or rental of housing, and
6. Expand programs of Federal assistance designed to increase the supply of housing throughout metropolitan areas within the means of low- and moderate-income families.

(7–8) In addition, the Commission recommends that the Department of Housing and Urban Development:

7. Require as a condition for approval of applications for low- and moderate-income housing projects that the sites will be selected and the projects planned in a non-discriminatory manner that will contribute to reducing residential racial concentrations and eliminating racial isolation in the schools.
8. Require as a condition for approval of urban renewal projects that relocation will be planned in a nondiscriminatory manner that will contribute to reducing residential racial concentrations and eliminating racial isolation in the schools(24).

A summarization of the major findings in the Commission's report relative to conditions of segregation and racial isolation and the resultant effects upon the education of children includes the following:

1. In racially isolated schools, Negro students typically do not achieve as well in school as white students.
2. The social class of a student's schoolmates strongly influences his achievement and attitudes. This relationship between a student's achievement and the social class composition grows stronger as the student progresses through school.
3. Negro students are more likely to have teachers with low verbal achievement than white students.
4. The longer Negro students are in desegregated schools, the better their academic achievement and attitude. The relationship between achievement and social class composition of a school grows stronger as the student progresses through school.
5. There is also a relationship between the racial composition of schools and the achievement and attitudes of most Negro students which exists when all other factors are taken into account:
   a. Disadvantaged Negro students in school with a majority of equally disadvantaged white students achieve better than Negro students in school with a majority of equally disadvantaged Negro students.
   b. Differences are even greater when disadvantaged Negro students in school with a majority of disadvantaged Negro students are compared with similarly disadvan-

taged Negro students in school with a majority of white students. The difference in achievement for 12th-grade students amounts to more than two entire grade levels.

c. Negroes in predominantely Negro schools tend to have lower educational aspirations and more frequently express a sense of inability to influence their futures by their own choices than Negro students with similar backgrounds attending majority white schools. Their fellow students are less likely to offer academic stimulation.

d. Predominantly Negro schools generally are regarded by the community as inferior institutions. Negro students in such schools are sensitive to such views and often come to share them. Teachers and administrative staff frequently recognize or share the community's views and communicate them to the students. This stigma affects the achievement and attitudes of Negro students.

6. Racial isolation is self-perpetuating. School attendance in racial isolation generates attitudes on the part of both Negroes and whites which tend to alienate them from members of the other race. These attitudes are reflected in behavior(25).

The data reported in the Commission's Report are too massive to report here in detail. However, this brief summarization does present a rather clear picture of the adverse educational conditions that come about from racially segregated schools. More important, perhaps, is the data which support the educational advantages resulting from children attending racially integrated schools.

Approaches to Desegregation of Schools

Improving ethnic balance is different from successfully integrating schools; however, the former is often the first step toward achieving true integration. Jacob Landers supports this position when defining the concept of integration:

> The mere juxtaposition of children to result in physical propinquity does not necessarily result in meaningful or improved educational experiences. Better ethnic balance may be achieved, but integration is a far broader concept involving the very essence of good education and the basic foundations of American democracy(26).

Presently most efforts toward bringing about racial balance in schools are programs of desegregation. Most school districts have found the road to both desegregation and integration a frustrating one. The frustration is compounded when one realizes that school desegregation has become practically impossible in some of the largest cities. Urban schools appear willing to try almost every approach suggested to bring about desegregation and eventual integration of their schools.

In some school districts, however, authorities realize it will not be possible to make significant gains in the near future, and consequently are attempting to improve education under present somewhat-segregated circumstances. An example of this type of effort is the Banneker School District in St. Louis, Missouri, which views desegregation as an ultimate goal but has meanwhile developed a program for promoting quality education under segregated conditions for 14,000 youngsters. Basic to this program for quality education is not only a reassessment of the administration, but also the upgrading of teaching techniques, recruitment of competent staff, and the involvement of the community in activities of the school(27).

Most urban school systems, however, are attempting to develop programs of desegregation that have immediate gains in the belief that conditions are such that they cannot look to the future for solutions to many of their problems. School authorities, therefore, often give the appearance of struggling to find immediate remedies or approaches to desegregation. Often an approach that is innovative and appears to have promise for one school system has already been tried and rejected by another. It is difficult to assess why school authorities in the one district have selected a tried-but-less-promising approach abandoned by another school district. Perhaps they have added a new "twist" or have reason to believe conditions in their community and school system are significantly different. Failure to adequately establish avenues of communications among school districts also looms as a plausible explanation for these conditions.

It is sometimes difficult to assess the progress educators have made in bringing about long-range programs of desegregation that promise eventual meaningful integration of city schools. Present efforts toward integration appear to be somewhat limited in scope and oftentimes resemble "last ditch" efforts to patch up immediate crisis situations. Few long-range, systematically-developed programs of integration appear to be developing.

Open enrollment, school pairing, central schools, bussing, and school closing are a few of the more prominently utilized programs which are designed to bring about desegregation of schools. This is by no means a complete listing of the approaches, but in view of the rather extensive usage of these five, each will be discussed briefly.

Open Enrollment

Open enrollment is a plan designed to allow students to attend schools, usually of their choice, outside their own attendance areas. It has been used mainly in the larger city school districts. Two kinds of schools usually participate in the open enrollment plan: first, those which are overcrowded, have a large nonwhite student body, and are located in or near the core area of the city; second, those schools located in the peripheral areas of the city in white neighborhoods and where classroom space is available.

As a vehicle for promoting desegregation and integration of schools, open enrollment has not been particularly successful. Only token numbers of students have taken advantage of any opportunity to transfer to another school. School district officials have also been reluctant to promote open enrollment as a program for integration and frequently do not stipulate racial criterion as necessary for participation. Some city school districts, such as Buffalo, New York, and Newark, New Jersey, give priority to students transferring from predominantly Black schools(28).

Open enrollment programs have not received enthusiastic endorsement from either the Black or white community. Oftentimes there is a great deal of hostility exhibited at the onset of open enrollment plans. The white community often shows intense resistance in the early stages but frequently comes to eventual acceptance. The Black community has never been particularly supportive of open enrollment as it lacks promise for meaningful integration. Parents in New York City have responded to open enrollment, as described here, while the white parents separately resisted the program when initially introduced but have gradually showed some acceptance. On the other hand, the Black parents have generally remained indifferent to the idea(29). This Black indifference stems from several factors, such as the travel inconvenience to students, increased cost of transportation, and a general belief that open enrollment plans do not lend themselves to long-term programs of meaningful racial integration of schools.

School Pairing

Princeton Plan   School pairing involves the merger of attendance areas of two or more schools serving the same grades and in close proximity to one another. It was introduced in the Princeton, New Jersey, public schools in 1948. Princeton officials merged the attendance areas of two elementary schools and assigned all students in grade K-5 to one school and all students in the remaining grades, 6–8, to the other school. This merger resulted in Princeton elementary schools sharing the black student population and eliminated the predominantly Black schools (30).

The Princeton Plan has been used by a number of school districts and has resulted in bringing about desegregated schools of varying degrees. Smaller cities have appeared to most frequently utilize the plan. New Haven, Connecticut(31), paired two of four junior high schools and Coatesville, Pennsylvania(32), desegregated its elementary schools using the pairing technique.

A 5,000-student suburban school system in Inkster, Michigan, paired its schools to promote desegregation. This school district is somewhat unique in that the school board and almost 90 percent of the faculty are Black. The student population is 80 percent Black and two schools contained over 75 percent of the white students. Pairing of schools resulted in a better balance of students and a rather unusual school organizational pattern, with four primary schools (grades 1–3), two middle schools (grades 4–5), one intermediate school (grades 6–7), one junior high school (grades 8–9), and one senior high school (grades 10–12)(33).

Central Schools   Closely aligned with the Princeton Plan is the concept of central schools. This differs from the central school concept as used in rural and suburban school districts, often on an intra-school district basis. Central schools, normally developed in communities with a large number of schools are designed primarily for improving the ethnic balance of schools by making the entire school district a single attendance area for all students in particular grades. Segregation that might have developed through residential patterns of a community can be overcome on a grade-by-grade basis(34). Berkeley, California, combined three junior high school into a single attendance zone. All seventh graders go to one school, all eighth graders to another, and all ninth graders to a third school(35). As a result of converting the three junior high schools in Berkeley to city-wide attendance areas, the schools in 1965 were 38 to 47 percent Black, whereas in 1963 one of the junior high schools was majority Black(36).

In New Jersey, two school districts, Teaneck and Englewood, utilized the central school plan. In Teaneck, prior to 1964, six elementary schools were all white, one was majority-Black, and one was 40 percent Black. To promote desegregation, the majority-Black school was converted to a central sixth-grade school serving all children in the community. The students in the lower grades were assigned to the previously all-white schools. In the elementary school with a 40 percent Black population, the attendance area was expanded to include greater numbers of white students. A somewhat similar situation occurred in the Englewood community where two of the five elementary schools were majority-Black and the other schools were nearly all-white. To improve the racial composition of the schools, beginning in 1964, all sixth-grade students were assigned to a single school and the other elementary schools were changed from K-6 to K-5 schools. In 1966, the district added a second central school. Both of these schools now house the fifth- and sixth-grade students, with the other schools handling the K-4 grades(37).

Bussing

Transporting of students by bussing them from their segregated neighborhood schools to predominately white schools is a technique many urban school districts have employed as a means of promoting desegregation. Two forms of bussing are most prevalent: bussing within a school district and bussing across school district boundaries. Both forms have come under heavy criticism from white and Black groups. However, experience has shown that the fears of both groups are unwarranted. This is particularly true of the white parents who fear that the achievement level of the children will suffer as a result of the influx of culturally and economically deprived, low-achievement youngsters. Preliminary research data now reveal that advantaged children continue to achieve at the same levels as they did prior to initiation of the bussing plan, while the disadvantaged child's achievement level rises. Most bussing plans are being conducted on a modest basis, and result in only token desegregation of the receiving schools. In addition, the bussing is provided only on a one-way basis, i.e., within the central cities or central cities to the suburbs. Suburban children are not being bussed to the central cities specifically for improving ethnic balance of schools.

Rochester, New York; Boston, Massachusetts; and Hartford, Connecticut, operate bussing programs from the majority-Black core schools to neighboring suburban school districts. Cooperation of the central cities' neighboring communities has been an essential variable in putting the bussing plans into operation. Oftentimes this has not been without problems. State, federal, and private foundation funds have been used to support various aspects of the programs.

West Irondequoit, a Rochester suburb, agreed in 1965 to accept 25 first graders from selected racially imbalanced Rochester schools. Of a student enrollment of 5,800 in West Irondequoit, only four were Black. The initial plan was modest but offered a beginning. Each year since 1965 the number of students has increased. Other suburban school districts had now begun cooperating in the bussing program with the Rochester schools, and by 1969 eight public school districts plus eight private and parochial schools were bussing 744 children from racially imbalanced Rochester schools. Most of the inner-city children come from lower middle-class families. The Rochester School District pays the tuition and transportation costs(38).

It is also interesting to note the events associated with the election of school board members in the West Irondequoit School

District during this period of time. Bussing has become the central platform issue during school board elections with anti-bussing candidates gaining seats on the board. By 1968, the majority of school board members had become "anti-bussing," a classification based upon their publicly stated position during school board elections. However, this majority of so-called anti-bussers did not terminate the bussing program, but rather reduced the yearly quota of new students to 12 from the previously agreed upon figure of 25. In spite of this action to continue the program, though on a reduced basis, the majority of the board has once again changed. During the school board elections in the spring of 1969 three vacancies were filled by moderate candidates who did not oppose bussing.

Boston currently has two bussing plans, METCO (Metropolitan Council for Educational Opportunities), which is privately run by citizens; and Operation Exodus, operated under the direction of the school district. METCO bussed 220 inner-city children to seven suburban schools in 1966. In 1968 the figure had risen to 916 students and 28 suburban schools. This program, organized by private citizens from Boston and surrounding communities, is financed through a Federal grant and the Carnegie Corporation(39). Operation Exodus busses over 1,000 children to schools outside their neighborhood school district within the City of Boston(40).

Hartford, Connecticut, has designed an experimental program known as Project Concern to determine what influence integrated classes and extra services have on inner-city children bussed to the suburbs. Two hundred and sixty-five deprived children from Hartford were bussed to 33 schools in five Hartford suburban school districts in 1966. These 265 students represented only a fraction of the more than 25,000 Blacks residing in Hartford. By 1969 the number of students increased to 1036 and 15 suburban school districts. This project is being financed jointly by funds from the state and federal governments, private foundations, and local monies(41).

Other bussing programs, most of which generally follow the pattern of offering desegregated educational experiences to limited numbers of inner-city children, are in operation in scattered communities throughout the country. Philadelphia, Portland, Buffalo,

Oakland, Denver, and Seattle are just a few of the major urban centers which operate bussing programs. Most, however, are rather limited and involve only a small fraction of their disadvantaged core area children.

School Closing

Urban school districts have found that one of the most effective ways to promote desegregation of schools is to close down or phase out selected core area schools which are highly segregated. Oftentimes these core schools are badly in need of repairs, understaffed, and generally deprive children of the necessary environment conducive to learning.

Since most urban school districts have utilized this technique, it is not necessary to describe in detail the process. However, one school district warrants a brief discussion because of the way in which it approached desegregation using the school closing idea(42).

School officials in White Plains, New York, developed a school closing program which also provided for evaluation of the plan. This suburban city of 55,000 inhabitants, located 20 miles from New York City, built a new all-city comprehensive high school large enough for all students and converted the former high school building into a junior high school.

In April, 1964, the school board adopted a racial balance policy that stated there would be no school in the community with more than 30 percent Black enrollment or less than 10 percent. This plan was implemented by the opening of school in September, 1964.

The Board of Education voted to close the Rochambeau elementary school in the inner city because the Black student body was approaching 63 percent. The pupils were reassigned to the district's remaining ten elementary schools, which were predominately white. Transportation was provided for K-6 pupils living further than 1.5 miles from the schools to which they were reassigned. Approximately 20 percent of the 4,500 elementary children in the school district were reassigned and nearly 500 pupils had to be transported to their new schools.

Beginning in September, 1964, White Plains initiated an evaluation of its racial balance plan. School district officials were interested in finding the answers to questions such as, "What has happened to the achievement of children who live in the neighborhoods adjacent to the receiving schools?" and "What has happened to the achievement of children from the inner-city schools?" These questions are partially answered in the evaluation report prepared and released by the Board of Education:

> . . . the achievement of neighborhood children has not been adversely affected by the presence of center city children in their school. Rather the data suggest that the achievement of these children is, in many respects, better than the pattern shown by the control group which was composed only of neighborhood children attending these schools prior to the Racial Balance Plan(43).

> The study of third grade achievement of center city children who entered first grade in 1964, in an integrated situation, seems to indicate that this group is achieving slightly better at third grade than did the center city children who spent first and second grades in segregated schools(44).

In each case achievement was based on scores received on Stanford Achievement Tests administered during the first two weeks of October in each of six years, 1960 to 1966. The report points out that the criterion for pupil selection in each group does not lend itself to completely unbiased research methodology. However, the data are important enough to suggest positive statements for the racial balancing program. In this rather limited setting, desegregation appears to have had no adverse effects on the performance of either minority or majority children.

Alternative Organizational Structures

The organizational structure of most urban school districts has resulted in patterns which are rather rigid, highly bureaucratic, and not particularly conducive to innovations designed to facilitate programs of desegregation. Recently, two innovative organizational approaches used as vehicles for desegregation of schools have been receiving increased attention from educators and other social scientists. The two approaches are the middle-school and educational-park concepts.

Middle-School Concept

While there still exists some confusion as to what educational rationale brought about the present middle-school movement, it is generally recognized by proponents of school desegregation as a promising innovative organizational structure.

The middle school is an intermediate school specifically designed to better meet the needs of children, particularly those entering or progressing through adolescence. It can be easily adapted to provide for a variety of instructional innovations with a curricular program which best serves children whose intellectual, social, physical, and emotional needs are quite similar.

The question of what grades should be included in the middle school has not been resolved. It is important that as much flexibility as possible should be provided. Ultimate decisions relative to grade structure rest with each school district, which best knows its students' needs and schools' curriculum. This author perceives the middle school as encompassing grades 5, 6, 7, and 8, with a curriculum providing for advanced placement, remedial placement, and overall more responsible placement of pupils than is now being done in most school district organizational patterns which include a separate intermediate facility.

New York City and Buffalo are adopting the middle school plan of grades 4–4–4 as a means of effecting eventual racial integration. Buffalo plans to use the first four-year sequence to preserve the neighborhood school concept and begin integrating the children at the second four-year sequence, the middle school(45). New York City is developing middle schools to promote quality education in an integrated environment. The plan calls for replacing all junior high schools with middle schools by 1972(46).

Many other urban school districts are in the process of developing plans for middle schools. The rationale to support this movement varies with each district. However, it appears that many urban school districts justify their middle-school involvement by its value as a vehicle for promoting racial integration(47).

Educational Park

The educational-park concept has come into existence as a plan designed to promote equal educational opportunity and as a vehicle for promoting quality integrated education. It is a plan which attempts to provide both these variables in a modern, comfortable, aesthetically pleasing environment.

J. Alan Thomas supports the position that educational quality based on adaptability, innovativeness, attractiveness, and comprehensiveness is best achieved through an educational park. He perceives the educational park as promoting quality and integrated education(48). Max Wolff views the educational park as a vehicle through which the community can approach solutions to the critical problems of today's society, one of which is integration. The educational park, serving as the community's cultural center, will bring children and adults together and promote sound intergroup relationships(49).

While much is being written about the virtues of the educational park, to date no complete educational park in an urban school district has come into being. However, the educational park is in the planning stages in a number of urban areas. The concept of the educational park has no rigidly set meaning. School districts planning educational parks are designing them based upon their particular needs and available resources.

Pittsburgh is in the stages of planning a 60-million-dollar school building program which includes the development of educational parks. Site selection will be based upon developing parks in regions of the community that offer the best promise for integration of schools. A target date has been set for early in the 1970's, with the initial phase for the implementation of the educational parks based upon the creation of large new high schools and conversion of most of the present high schools into middle schools. Each of the new high schools will house between 3,000 to 5,000 students.

The high schools will eventually become the core of a school subsystem serving 15,000 to 20,000 students in a continuing educational program of elementary, middle, and secondary schools. Five of these educational parks are planned to replace Pittsburgh's 22 secondary schools as well as several elementary schools(50).

In East Orange, New Jersey, a city of 70,000 in close proximity to New York City, the campus-plan educational park is under development, with the entire city school system to become one integrated educational-park complex. This school system of 10,000 students has a Black student population of approximately 70 percent. The educational park will include a K-4 lower school, a 5–8 middle school, and a 9–12 secondary school(51).

The city of Syracuse in upstate New York is also planning to develop educational parks in the form of public elementary campus-plan schools. Each campus complex will replace older elementary schools in the surrounding vicinity and is intended to minimize the adverse effects of *de facto* segregation. Four campus schools, each consisting of several satellite schools with 500 pupils and clustered around a central core facility, are planned. The first educational park campus, projected for 1970, will have eight satellite schools of approximately 520 K-6th grade children in each school. The satellite schools are designed to preserve the neighborhood school concept while bringing children from various neighborhoods in the community together on the same educational site. Each satellite will be a neighborhood school with the children traveling to and from school together on the same bus.

The elimination of *de facto* segregation is one of the prime purposes for developing the educational parks. However, the core of each campus is to be shared by all students from the eight satellite schools and will contain such facilities as science and language laboratories, libraries, art and music rooms, an auditorium, gymnasium, educational television center, guidance suite, health center and cafeteria(52).

Numerous other urban school districts are in the process of talking about, studying, and planning educational park complexes, including such cities as Berkeley, New York City, Albuquerque, St. Paul, and Buffalo. To move into the educational-park plan is by no means a simple process, and much planning is needed to overcome such obstacles as adequate financing, transportation difficulties, increased staff, large site acquisitions, and the development of sound school community relations programs to educate citizens as to the community's gains when moving to the educational park plan.

Conclusion:
The Ultimate Aim—Integration

This discussion has focused upon the process of racial desegregation of urban schools. The purpose has been to present a broad overview rather than narrowly define one or two sub-areas for detailed analysis. Hopefully, the reader has emerged with a broader understanding of how school authorities and other interested individuals and groups are approaching the problems created as a result of *de jure* and/or *de facto* conditions of racial segregation.

Let me close this discussion by making a clear distinction between the concepts of desegregation and integration, which are all too often, and mistakenly, used synonymously. Desegregation, as used here, is defined as the process of bringing individuals, particularly children, of varying social, economic, and ethnic origins together in the public schools. Integration goes beyond this to include the critical variables of respect, understanding, and acceptance as human beings on an equal basis.

Desegregation often becomes one of the initial phases in a program designed to bring about racial integration. It is much less difficult to desegregate a classroom, school, or school district than it is to meaningfully integrate them. The process of integration is very complex and oftentimes necessitates changing values, attitudes, and patterns of behavior. Racist attitudes and behavior are learned and a program of stressing new, more liberal values and attitudes may be necessary for most citizens, both young and old, prior to initiating programs of racial integration.

One very serious drawback in our efforts to bring about racial integration stems from the relative vacuum within which we operate. The educational enterprise is being treated as an isolated social system divorced from the other social systems which form the larger system, society. If other social systems are not striving to bring about racial integration, then how can schools succeed? A child leaves his segregated community in the morning to attend a desegregated school only to return to his segregated environment in the evening. Other members of his family have similar experiences at their place of employment, as they shop for food and clothing, and when seeking recreation. Members of minority groups who are isolated from other subsystems of the community find it difficult to become enthusiastic with the efforts being advanced in schools.

The integration of Black and white Americans cannot be accomplished in an isolated fashion. Rather, it will require the combined financial, technological, and human resources of the total community working together. The economic, educational, political, industrial, and other social subsystems of society are integrally related to one another, and the problems of one subsystem are often the problems of others. Such is the case with racial integration.

Schools, and in particular urban schools where racial problems are presently most visible, will only achieve limited success in their efforts to promote racial integration. Lasting racial integration of our total society will not come about until all its subsystems are truly committed to working toward this goal.

Notes

1. Jacob Landers, "Integration in the Major Metropolis," in *School Desegregation in the North*, eds., T. Bentley Edwards and Frederick M. Wirt (San Francisco: Chandler Publishing Co., 1967), p. 261.

2. Nathaniel Hickerson, "Integrated Vs. Compensatory Education in the Riverside–San Bernardino Schools," in *School Desegregation in the North*, eds., T. Bentley Edwards and Frederick M. Wirt (San Francisco: Chandler Publishing Co., 1967), p. 117.

3. Both of these reports are must reading for all those concerned with the educational process. The U.S. Commission on Civil Rights Report, *Racial Isolation in the Public Schools*, Vol. 1 (Washington, D.C.: Government Printing Office, 1967), cites the Coleman Study in deprecating the role of compensatory education for disadvantaged children and advocates in its place a national "racial balancing" law for schools. The Coleman Study, *Equality of Educational Opportunity*, Office of Education Report OE-380001 (Washington, D.C.: Government Printing Office, 1966), supplied much of the data found in the Civil Rights Commission report.

4. For a detailed review of the Coleman Study, see Robert W. Heller, "The Coleman Report Revisited," *Urban Education*, Vol. 4, No. 1 (April 1969), pp. 41–54.

5. Michael D. Usdan, "Some Issues Confronting School Administrators

in Large City School Systems," *Educational Administration Quarterly,* III, No. 3 (Autumn 1967), pp. 220–21.

6. An example of this is Syracuse, New York which had a public school enrollment of 30,844 for the 1967–68 school year. The parochial school enrollment was 14,000 students. Negroes constitute 19 percent of the public school enrollment and 2 percent of the parochial school enrollment. See *Process of Change—The Story of School Desegregation in Syracuse, New York,* U.S. Commission on Civil Rights, Clearinghouse Publication No. 12 (Washington, D.C.: U.S. Government Printing Office, June, 1968), p. 1. Also see "A Plan for Accelerating Quality Integrated Education in the Buffalo Public School System," The State Education Department, Albany, New York (August 19, 1966), Chapter II, p. 2., where it is pointed out that in 1965 there were 31,900 white children in the parochial schools within the city of Buffalo compared to 50,165 white students in the public schools. The total public school student population in the city of Buffalo for 1965 was 73,-083 *(Salary Study, 1965–66,* Western New York School Study Council).

7. *Racial Isolation,* op. cit., p. 11.

8. Ibid., p. 3.

9. *Program 1969* (Conference of Large City Boards of Education of New York State, October 1968), p. 17.

10. Ibid., pp. 3–5.

11. Ibid., pp. 6–8.

12. Robert A. Dentler, "Community Behavior and Northern School Desegregation," *The Journal of Negro Education,* XXXIV (Summer 1965), pp. 258–67.

13. John R. Everett, "The Decentralization Fiasco and Our Ghetto Schools," *The Atlantic,* Vol. 222, No. 6 (December 1968), pp. 71–73.

14. Ibid., p. 72.

15. Alan K. Campbell, "Educational Policy Making Studied in Large Cities," *The American School Board Journal,* March 1967, pp. 18–27.

16. Mary Ellen Warshauer and Robert A. Dentler, "A New Definition of School Segregation," in *The Urban R's,* eds., Robert A. Dentler, Bernard Mackler, and Mary Ellen Warshauer (New York: Frederick A. Praeger, Inc., 1967), p. 6.

17. Ibid., p. 7. The definition of this ratio, as noted by Warshauer and Dentler, originally appeared in the report of the Advisory Panel on Integration of the Public Schools, "The Hauser Report," *Report to the Board of Education* (Chicago: Board of Education, 1964).

18. Ibid.

19. Ibid., p. 12.

20. Daniel P. Moynihan, "Education of the Urban Poor," *Harvard Graduate School of Education Association Bulletin,* XII, No. 2 (Fall 1967), p. 4.

21. Ibid., pp. 4–7.

22. Christopher Jencks, "Education: The Racial Gap," *The New Republic,* Vol. 155 (October 1, 1966), pp. 21–26.

23. The Coleman Study, op. cit., p. 325.

24. *Racial Isolation,* op. cit., pp. 209–12.

25. Ibid., pp. 202–204.

26. Landers, op. cit., p. 251.

27. Samuel Shepard, "Instructional Planning for the Urban Settings," in *Urban School Administration,* eds., Austin D. Swanson and Troy V. McKelvey (Beverly Hills: Sage Publications, Inc., 1969), pp. 109–122.

28. Robert L. Crain, *The Politics of School Desegregation* (Chicago: Aldine Publishing Company, 1968), p. 116.

29. Landers, op. cit., pp. 272–73.

30. *Racial Isolation*, op. cit., p. 142.

31. "Desegregation—10 Blueprints for Action," *School Management*, Vol. 10, No. 10 (October 1966), p. 106.

32. *Racial Isolation*, op. cit., p. 142.

33. Martin Buskin, "How Schoolmen Are Handling the Hot Ones—Integration, Innovation and Negotiation," *School Management*, Vol. 11, No. 6 (September 1967), p. 64.

34. *Racial Isolation*, op. cit., p. 142.

35. Robert J. Havighurst, "These Integration Approaches Work—Sometimes," *Nation's Schools*, Vol. 80, No. 3 (September 1967), pp. 73–75.

36. *Racial Isolation*, op. cit., p. 143.

37. Ibid., pp. 142–43.

38. Havighurst, op. cit., pp. 73–75. See also Robert E. Lamitie, "Voluntary Enrollment by City Pupils in Suburban Schools," *The Quarterly*, Vol. XX, No. 4 (June 1969), pp. 4–7.

39. Bernard Bard, "Brooklyn's Bus to Equality," *Saturday Review*, Vol. 50, No. 7 (February 18, 1967), p. 79. See also Austin Swanson and Donald Carson, "The Costs of Improving Racial Balance in the Buffalo Metropolitan Area," *The Quarterly*, XX, No. 4 (June 1969), pp. 8–15.

40. "Roundup Report: How Schools Meet Desegregation Challenges," *Nation's Schools*, Vol. 78, No. 5 (November 1966), pp. 62–72.

41. Bard, op. cit. For a two year evaluation report of Project Concern in Hartford, see Thomas W. Mahan, *Project Concern 1966–1968* (Hartford, Conn.: Board of Education, August 1968).

42. Much has been written about the White Plains, New York, program of desegregation. See especially, "The White Plains Racial Plan Evaluation," A report published by the White Plains Board of Education, 1967; "Achieving Racial Balance: The White Plains Story," *School Management*, Vol. 12, No. 1 (January 1968), pp. 45–49; and K. A. Beavan, "Racial Balance in Schools—New York Experiment Fails," *The Times Educational Supplement* 2738 (November 10, 1967).

43. "The White Plains Racial Plan Evaluation," op. cit., p. 18.

44. Ibid., p. 35.

45. "A Plan for Accelerating Quality Integrated Education in the Buffalo Public School System," op. cit.

46. William A. Cuff, "Middle Schools on the March," *The Bulletin*, National Association of Secondary School Principals, February 1967, pp. 82–86.

47. For a discussion of the rationale supporting the middle school concept see Robert W. Heller, "Needed: A Rationale for the Middle School," *New York State Education*, LVI, No. 4 (January 1969), pp. 35–36.

48. J. Alan Thomas, "The Secondary Education Park: Value Synthesis in Urban School Systems," *Administrative Notebook*, XIV, No. 3 (November 1965).

49. Max Wolff, "The Educational Park," *The Quarterly*, Western New York School Study Council, XIX, No. 1 (October 1967), p. 4.

50. Sydney P. Marland, "The Education Park Concept in Pittsburgh," *Phi Delta Kappan*, XLVII, No. 7 (March 1967), pp. 328–332.

51. The East Orange, New Jersey education plaza plan is discussed in *Racial Isolation in the Public Schools*, op. cit., as well as in James E.

Mauch's "The Education Park," *The American School Board Journal,* CL (March 1965), pp. 9–11.

52. *The Campus Plan,* A Report on a Feasibility Study for Elementary Construction in Syracuse, New York, 1967. For an excellent discussion of the total process of planned desegregation in the Syracuse Public Schools see *Process of Change—The Story of School Desegregation in Syracuse, New York,* op. cit.

4

Community Control: A Case in Point

*Stanley P. Lisser**

Introduction

Teachers, supervisors, principals, and other professional educational personnel have consistently stated that the effective participation of parents is necessary in the educational process. School personnel and the small cadre of parents who organized parent-teacher associations and similar groups have been concerned about the limited participation of parents in school affairs. These groups have sought methods and techniques to obtain a broader base of parent participation in the educational process. The desire and interest for parent participation is common to both the metropolitan and suburban school systems. Yet, during the past few years, the nature of parent participation in urban school systems has caused fundamental stresses which have created a need for a reexamination and clarification of the whole concept of "parent participation" in the public schools. The same professional educators who were calling for parent interest and involvement seem to be appalled by the contemporary style of parent involvement. This may be because the issue of participation has become interrelated, at least in the large metropolitan areas, with the question of

---

* Mr. Lisser was principal of I.S. 201, New York City, in 1966, when that school attempted to open.

political control of the educational system—a style of control that would require a realignment of the traditional relationships(1).

Although controversy and confrontation have always been a part of public education, the controversies and confrontations of today differ from those of previous years in at least one significant way. In the past, controversies centered on the *process* of education. Parents and community leaders attempted to influence education decision-making, but usually accepted the basic power structure within which the decisions were made. Today the focus of the struggle is on changing the institutional structure. Only after the structure is changed to provide for increased community control will the question of changing the educational process to improve reading scores, for example, be undertaken. The issue over a change of structure in New York City has taken the form of decentralizing the public educational system. However, this issue is not confined to New York City; other metropolitan school systems are beginning to experience the same stresses, as well as the contentious issues of the extent to which parents should participate in and control the schools.

Community Control

In order to understand this new phenomenon of "community control" of education, it is necessary to examine the events surrounding the opening of Intermediate School 201 in Harlem, in New York City. The bitter 1966 conflict over this school brought the issue of "community control" into the open. The opening of this five-million-dollar school plant, which was supposed to be modern and innovative, served as a catalytic agent for a massive *local* struggle, with citywide implications. Reverberations of this struggle are being felt in New York City. The contest sparked financial grants from the Ford Foundation for three demonstration districts in local community control: I.S. 201, The Two Bridges, and Ocean Hill-Brownsville. These have been focal points of controversy since their very establishment. How and why did a community reject I.S. 201, a new modern educational structure? What new definitions of parental participation resulted from this controversy? Lastly, what are the guidelines for future parent participation in education which professional educators must consider?

The controversy surrounding the opening of an intermediate school in East Harlem, New York City, represented a significant turning point in the methods and objectives of local community groups. The attack began to center on the political structure of education rather than on its process. It was at I.S. 201 that a sustained struggle surrounded and enveloped an individual school for the first time. In the past, unhappy claimants had attacked the central Board of Education headquarters to demand system-wide changes. But dissatisfaction with the public schools of New York City resulted in the change of tactics at I.S. 201.

The essential core of the educational problem in New York City, and all other large urban centers, is that the public schools have been unable to fulfill their basic function of providing effective education for the majority of children who attend. Without seeking to cite many indices of this failure, the published scores of children in the commonly accepted measures of academic achievement, e.g., reading and mathematics, bear sad witness to this failure. The problem has other ramifications because this academic failure is intensified in areas of the city which are economically deprived, while success rates are much greater in the middle-class areas of the city.

The 1954 Supreme Court school integration decision, while directed at *de jure* segregation, focused attention on the *de facto* as well. This latter form of segregation was prevalent in New York City and other urban centers. Civil rights groups held school authorities responsible for eliminating *de facto* segregation even when residential segregation was the cause of the problem. These facts had been known for years; the Franzier report, published in 1935 after the Harlem riots, described, in detail, the sad litany of the failure and obsolence of the Harlem schools. However, in the 1950's education occupied a growing and more central role as the primary contributor to the future economic well-being of the then disadvantaged persons. Nonskilled positions for the uneducated were disappearing and school failure doomed an individual to economic failure in a society which increasingly demanded academic proficiency for all types of employment.

Participatory Democracy

Concurrent with the growing dissatisfaction with public education in New York City in the 1960's was the rebirth of the concept of participatory democracy as a means of resolving the economic, political, and social problems of the poor. The advocates of participatory democracy argued that people with less income, less education, and holding less desirable occupations needed to develop skills to become politically effective. Participatory democracy was further encouraged by the legislative requirement of the Economic Opportunity Act of 1964 that community action programs be developed, conducted, and administered with the *"maximum feasible participation of residents in areas which members of groups served"*(2). The Office of Economic Opportunity, the agency which was to administer the poverty program, asserted its belief in participatory democracy in its community action workbook. This stated that a "promising method" of implementing maximum feasible participation was to "assist the poor in developing autonomous and self-managed organizations which are competent to exert political influence on behalf of their own self-interest"(3).

The precursor in New York City of the involvement of local community poverty organizations in education occurred with the Mobilization for Youth (MFY) organization, centered on the Lower East Side. Mobilization for Youth was not only concerned with the solution of problems which existed in its local area, but also with the involvement of the community residents in the solution and the demand for the solution of citywide problems.

At this time MFY had hired eleven full-time professionals to their community development staff as well as twelve full-time indigenous organizers and another ten part-time workers. When an individual on welfare assistance did not receive the benefits for which he was entitled, an organizer would "call (or help the client to call) the investigator and insist upon immediate action." They encouraged the formation of the Council of Puerto Rican Organizations of the Lower East Side and the Negro Action Group. Financial and staff assistance were given to these and other organizations which enabled them to bring residents to consider "public-school problems, police brutality, housing, and civil rights." The groups supported by MFY participated in the

March on Washington in 1963 and in voter registration drives. Mobilization for Youth, after having stimulated residents to demand improvements in the local schools, encouraged residents to participate in two school boycotts. Similarly, rent strikes were used to demand improved housing for the poor. Mobilization for Youth had indeed become a flow channel for the demands of the poor(4).

Among the social agencies in which federally-funded poverty organizations attempted to obtain greater involvement of community residents in New York City was the educational system. In New York City, the decision-making power in education was centered in a citywide Board of Education and the central Board of Education professional staff. Local community residents and local agencies and organizations could attempt to influence the central board through petitions, demonstrations, and other means. However, no formal structures were provided for effective local participation in the determination of policy, nor was there important policy-making authority delegated to the local communities.

By January, 1964, local school principals on the Lower East Side began to complain about the use of public tax funds to support MFY's "full-time paid agitators and organizers for extremist groups." They objected to being "constantly harassed by demands made upon them by splinter groups that do not represent the majority of the parents in their schools." The principals were reacting to demands by local parents for the ouster of a principal from one of the local schools. They were also reacting to the increased activity of some parents which they ascribed to the activity of MFY workers. In August, 1964, MFY was accused by the *New York Daily News* of having "communists, subversives, and left-wingers as members of its staff." Mobilization for Youth survived a prolonged investigation and continued as an organization (refer to Peterson Study for a more detailed treatment). It survived despite the fact that the New York City Mayor's office was not considered to be friendly to this organization. The survival of MFY indicated that "Wagner (Mayor of New York City) and Screvane (Deputy Mayor), simply did not have the resources for eliminating threatening organizations"(5). Contrary to the structure in other large cities, the local community poverty organizations were developing in New York City with a local freedom of program choice not subject to a veto of elected city officials. In addition, the local poverty organizations obtained representation on the citywide council against poverty.

The educational authorities in New York City did not see the wider implications of the disputes on the Lower East Side. Local community poverty organizations, operating independent of the influences from City Hall, were able to organize parents on a local community level to demand improved services in their neighborhoods. The protests could be centered on local school conditions and on individual schools. By the time the struggle evolved at I.S. 201, this development in participatory democracy would lead to demands for local community control of the I.S. 201 educational facilities.

Threads that Wove Community Control

Several events occurred between the time of the Lower East Side protest of 1963–1964 and the opening of I.S. 201 in September of 1966—events which further crystallized the frustrations of the minority group communities *vis a vis* the educational authorities. This specifically made it possible for new community poverty organizations in the East Harlem area to help parents organize and contest the opening of I.S. 201. It evolved into a testing ground for the advocacy of "community control" of the schools. This advocacy emerged from frustration and was not the result of a carefully designed campaign.

Minority Dissatisfaction

Three threads which merged into one strand of community control are apparent in an analysis of the events. The first thread was the growing dissatisfaction of minority groups with the educational system. Basic to this were the deficiencies mentioned before, such as widespread academic failure and failure of the central educational authority to implement any policies which made a significant dent in changing the student population and the *de facto* segregated schools. Citywide achievement tests administered by the Board of Education indicated great academic failure, and the number of *de facto* segregated schools in New York City increased between 1958 and 1963.

The struggles to improve education were led by citywide organizations such as the NAACP, CORE, Urban League of New York, and other local civil rights and community organizations. Integration of the schools was one of the demands of these groups. The tactics of the coalition led to citywide boycotts of the school system. On February 3, 1964, an unprecedented boycott of the New York City public schools resulted in an absence of 464,361 pupils, or 44.8 percent of the total enrollment(6). In order to find some resolution to these problems, and suggest new policy guidelines for the New York City Board of Education, the then New York State Commissioner of Education, Dr. James Allen, established in March, 1964, the State Education Commissioner's Advisory Committee on Human Relations and Community Tensions.

The recommendations of this advisory committee emphasized organizational changes in the structure of the school system in order to achieve maximum desegregation. The implication was that accompanying curriculum changes would also lead to academic excellence. The report essentially called for the creation of a system-wide 4–4–4 structure. *De facto* segregation was accepted to some extent in the elementary schools. However, the middle schools (grades 4–8) "should be so located as to provide *for as many* children as possible an experience in an integrated school. Shuttle buses were to be used to reach these middle schools." The report also called for comprehensive high schools and the establishment of educational complexes "to promote communication between faculty, parents and administrators"(7).

Our proposals do, we trust, make plain the fact that substantial forces must be reckoned with the redirected if desegregation is to be achieved. If these proposals are adopted and implemented we are confident they will effect some immediate desegregation. More importantly, they would help prevent an increase in the rate of segregation within the schools. To accomplish this, however, they would have to be introduced promptly, progressively, and in an ever more extensive network during the next five years(8).

The report assumed that these changes would take place through the existing citywide Board of Education. It did not call for any major changes in the political structure of the public school system. It did recommend educational complexes which would have provided greater parent participation. The Board of Education accepted some of the major recommendations of the Allen report (May, 1964), and the proposed 4–4–4 reorganization was adopted as the policy of the New York City schools.

Site Problems

The second thread in the weaving of the confrontation at I.S. 201 now became apparent. The planning for a school facility in New York City, from the recognition of the need for the building to the actual opening of the unit, was a long process which extended over a period of five to ten years. The junior high schools of Harlem and East Harlem were overcrowded. In 1958, the Board of Education chose a site in East Harlem for a new junior high school which was to alleviate existing and projected overcrowding in the area. It is important to note that this initial decision, which set in motion seemingly irreversible bureaucratic steps of action, preceded the installation of the reform Board of Education in New York City. The 1962 reorganization of the Board resulted in greater responsibility being assigned to local district school boards in New York City, and the installation of a new superintendent of schools from outside the New York City educational hierarchy.

The 1958 site selection also preceded the emphasis of the 1964 economic opportunity act on the participation of local poverty constituency in policy-making. Procedures in 1958 emphasized only the participation of the office of the borough president and professional educational staff at the Board of Education. There was very minimal provision for eliciting community opinions and reactions. Even with this minimal provision for community opinion, the then-existing local area school boards of the area, Local School Boards 10 and 11, warned against the East Harlem site for I.S. 201, saying it would make integration of the school impossible. However, concerted community action was difficult because the proposed site fell into the borderland between two school districts administered by two different field superintendents, and as a result, authority for the school shifted from district to district. Therefore, the school remained on the planning boards, and site acquisition proceeded.

The New York City Board of Education, as mentioned, had adopted as policy certain key aspects of the May, 1964, Allen Committee report: specifically, the proposed grade reorganization of the schools. In 1965, J.H.S. 201 was already under construction. The school unit had been planned and physically designed as a junior high school. However, that same year, the school was designated as I.S. 201, an *intermediate school,* serving grades 5–8, to implement the Allen Committee recommendations. The city-wide Board of Education apparently did not see any contradiction between the key sentence in the Allen report that "middle schools should be so located as to provide *for as many children as possible* an experience in an *integrated school"*(9) and the designation of 201, at a physical site in the center of a Black and Puerto Rican ghetto, to serve as the first new intermediate school of the city. The newly revitalized local school board, composed of parents and community members, questioned the feasibility of making I.S. 201 an integrated school. The community members received the impression that the Board of Education had promised that the school would be integrated, although specifics of a plan to integrate the school were not discussed. Community members were on record as demanding an integrated school. Opposition to the site—where construction was proceeding—had also been voiced. The Board of Education may well have believed that once a bright new physical plant was ready to open, in contrast to older, over-utilized school plants, the demand for utilization of the school would overshadow demands for compliance with promises to provide an integrated school. None certainly envisaged the extent of the confrontation which was to occur.

Community Action

At the same time in 1965 when the Board of Education designated I.S. 201 as an intermediate school, the third thread, the growing role of community action organizations in the East Harlem area, became apparent. The influence of citywide politics and the coming mayorality election of 1965 in New York City resulted in planning grants to competing O.E.O. poverty organizations in the East Harlem area that summer. Planning grants were made to East Harlem Tenants Council, primarily an organization made up of Puerto Ricans, and to MEND (Massive Economic Neighborhood Development), an organization with a chiefly Black constituency.

I.S. 201 was scheduled to open in September, 1966. Throughout the year, the two poverty organizations, which only had planning grants, were locked in a bitter dispute as to which organization would be declared the official community action agency, and as such, receive full funding—one million dollars to implement their programs. In early 1967, after the public confrontations over I.S. 201, MEND was declared the official community action agency for the community.

Of the two organizations, MEND played the more dominant role in the confrontation. It is important to understand the philosophy of this organization, even though it was not an openly avowed protagonist in the many facets of the 201 struggle. A succinct summary of the philosophy of MEND is stated by Paul Peterson:

> . . . the MEND staff provided one of the most effective flow channels for neighborhood demands that was observed. The stimulator's task was to locate needs of people and help to solve them, individually or collectively. As MEND's executive director remarked, "Our main objective is to get the people involved in solving their problems. . . . It is more important to get the people involved in the process of getting the street light fixed than getting the light fixed itself." The stimulators handled housing complaints, aided in problems with the welfare department, activated the local PTAs, and planned a voter registration drive(10).

In addition, a little-noticed paper delivered by Dr. Preston Wilcox (consultant to community organizations in the East Harlem area) at the dedication of the Community Association of the East Harlem Triangle, Inc., raised for the first time the proposition of local community control of schools in New York City. He said that:

> If one believes that a segregated white school can be a good school, then one must believe that a segregated Negro and Puerto Rican school, like I.S. 201, can also be a good school. We must be concerned with those who are left behind and who will be left behind even if the best conceivable school desegregation program should be implemented.

Wilcox continued his rationale:

> If it is true that the public school system can do no more than it is already doing, then the communities of the poor must be prepared to act for themselves. The residents of the ghetto must seize the opportunity to assume a leadership role in the education of their own children, just as they must become involved in the direction of all programs set up to serve their needs. In this they claim only a chance to exercise by some of those outside the ghetto . . . an instrumentality (must) be developed which would assure minority group parents of direct access to the channels of informed opinion and power(11).

Wilcox suggested that a school-community board for I.S. 201 receive the veto power over all staff selection for I.S. 201, review the curriculum, and hire people to serve as school-community linkers.

The question of the intervention of local poverty-funded organizations in educational affairs, as initiated by the MFY, was once again raised. The issues were not only educational reform and the integration of schools, but equally important, the process by which these reforms and changes would be accomplished.

These implications of the struggle over I.S. 201 were not recognized by the citywide Board of Education, or even the local school personnel. This concerned expanding the concept of parental participation to include their participation in the determination of school policy and the inclusion of local federally funded poverty organizations in the struggle. To a large extent, dichotomous goals were merging among the contestants, but the opening of I.S. 201 provided a common ground. The local poverty organizations were interested in the development of participatory democracy and the building of grassroots support for their organizations. The two key poverty organizations in the East Harlem area, MEND and East Harlem Tenants Council, were both on temporary financial grants and were vying for permanent recognition, and its consequent financial support. The Board of Education was concerned with opening a new school with innovative educational programs, and if possible, integration of the school population. Integration appears to have been a secondary goal of the central Board of Education, although it was the primary goal of the local community. The educators wanted parental participation, but within the traditional framework. A serious redesign of the delegation of authority was not envisioned.

Convergence and Confrontation

The direct convergence of these forces, and the ensuing confrontation, took place in September, 1966, when I.S. 201 was to open. The specific details of the struggle and the events which led to the climax in September, 1966, are not germane to this account. The official opening of the school was delayed about two weeks, and the school opened without any surface change in the authority roles of the protagonists. However, new coalitions had been created, and the dominance of local organizations in the school struggle, as opposed to the traditional role of the citywide organizations, was apparent. Although the struggle involving I.S. 201 was led by local parent and community groups, the assistance of MEND should be noted.

Peterson outlines MEND's role in the following:

> . . . perhaps the most significant undertaking that MEND staff became involved in during the first year of its existence was related to its concern over local educational policies. Through activating PTAs at a number of local schools, they had increased pressure on school officials to respond more adequately to local needs. Receiving the greatest notoriety was the boycott of independent school 201, a new air-conditioned school located on the border between East Harlem and Harlem. With the assistance of MEND staff, residents demanded that the school be integrated by busing in white students. When the

school system refused to grant this request, the residents demanded community participation in decisions affecting school policy, including the selection of teachers. The parents negotiated with school officials and representatives of the mayor, demonstrated in front of the school, and forced the temporary removal of classes to another school. They initiated a public dispute between Mayor Lindsay and the school board over the handling of the problem. While they were not granted such extreme demands as the dismissal of the principal on the basis of race alone, they did win recognition as participants in decisions affecting the school. As of September, 1966, it remained unclear as to how much influence over school policy the parents would be granted. Nevertheless, the dispute and the recognition won by the parents was the most significant political action stimulated by the community action program in any of the three cities(12).

It had been demonstrated that tax-funded local poverty organizations could and would help to organize parents in local communities of New York City. These groups, with their local-based constituencies, helped to shape and significantly redesign the priority of issues in public education in New York City. The debate and dialogue were no longer confined exclusively to integration and the creation of quality education. The vehicle to reach eventual goals became community control. To a large extent, the goal of community control and/or decentralization became the focus of the struggle, on the assumption that community control would, through its institutionalization, bring about improvement in the educational process.

Although the local war over I.S. 201 seemed to have been lost in September, 1966, the Board of Education created, in June of 1967, three experimental school districts to develop the concept of decentralization in New York City. The Mayor's Advisory Committee on the decentralization of the New York City schools, with McGeorge Bundy as chairman, was appointed April 30, 1967. The report issued by this group on November 9, 1967, *Reconnection for Learning—A Community School System for New York City,* triggered the debates and actions that enveloped the New York City system, and resulted in the passage by the State Legislature of the Decentralization Law of April, 1969.

Thus, in New York City, the development of policies to increase parental participation in the educational process has become intertwined with the question of community control and/or decentralization. However, this development is not restricted to New York City, but is also evident in other major cities of the United States, such as Philadelphia; Boston; Los Angeles; St. Louis; Washington, D.C.; Detroit; San Francisco; and Chicago. These cities have begun to explore and implement significant changes in the educational decision-making process without the explosive confrontations that occurred in New York City. The role of the tax-funded poverty organization has not been as powerful in the other cities as it has in New York City. However, there may be a reshaping of such organizations' role in other large metropolitan centers.

The design of guidelines for greater parental participation in the educational process cannot be divorced from the larger question of community control and/or decentralization. The specific definitions of the latter two rubrics have not been developed, and the debate over these issues is not as precise as it should be.

The struggle over community control in education is directly related to those seeking a redistribution of power in other services such as police, medical, and welfare. This struggle means the preservation of the present status quo or a redistribution of power. However, the resolution of the fundamental issue of community control would not automatically resolve the question of parental participation in the educational process. When a new structure is obtained, or the struggle is resolved, the problem of parental participation in the educational process of the local school may still remain. As we anticipate the future of decentralization, we must at the same time consider the question of student participation in the educational process.

Parents' Role in Education

The question of the parents' role in participation in the educational process of the local school is still an undefined quantity. We have the fairly standard suggestions to parents that they read to their children; supervise homework assignments; take their children on trips to museums, theaters, and cultural places; closely monitor their children's progress in school; and participate in school workshops and other programs to better understand the program of the school. However, these recommendations do not define the responsibilities of the parents as participants in the education of children.

Another aspect of the problem is that conditions vary from school to school within a school district, and just as certainly from school district to school district. What is needed is not a set of abstract and formal recommendations for parent participation, but a new kind of dynamic process of continuous parent-school interaction which eventually will shape the responsibilities of the parent according to the realities of each school and neighborhood. Unless such programs are developed by local schools and individual school districts, the parents' lack of awareness of their responsibilities will persist.

This is not a procedure through which isolated groups can develop a pattern for all schools. This is a process which must take place in individual schools, and the involvement of parents in the process is crucial. In order to effectively participate, parents in each individual school must work towards these goals:

1. To know intimately the responsibilities and obligations of the local school.
2. To understand their child's school program and its place in the child's educational schedule, and its place within the entire context of education.
3. To learn how to judge the relevance and purpose of academic goals, and evaluate the strategies and techniques that are intended to realize the goals.
4. To appreciate, negatively and positively, a school's atmosphere, structure, facilities, resources, and responsiveness to community needs.
5. To learn how to help obtain adequate academically supportive services for the child.

At the same time, parents should explore ways in which the home can be used to improve the quality of the child's educative experience. They should look into the kinds of home experiences and environments that help educate the child; they should help develop an appreciation for the cultural and ethnic backgrounds of the parents, so the child will come to appreciate the value of his home, and its cultural strengths. Parents should be stimulated to develop a curriculum for home teaching, running parallel to the school curriculum, but geared to children's experiences in the home. The educational responsiveness of the parent, in a sense, depends on the degree to which and the effectiveness with which that responsibility is assumed and asserted.

The strategy to reach these goals would mean that the leadership in the local schools must come from the parents. The parents, through workshops and discussions, should develop their "parent curriculum." This cannot be a process dominated by the professional staff of the school. Parents must call on the professionals for advice and assistance when *they* see the need. From this process, the means for true participation of parents in the educative process of the local school should be developed. The process itself must reinforce the evolution of the partnership between parents and school professionals, with mutual respect for one another.

Conclusion

In brief, the general impression has been created that parental participation in the educational process is synonomous with community control and/or decentralization. When and if this question of political control of education in the large cities is resolved, the question of real parental participation will still remain. The changes in the political structure of the schools will not automatically induce it. However, local community control should create a more positive atmosphere in which to introduce more meaningful parent participation in the educational process. Yet the guidelines for the development of this participation still remain largely undeveloped.

Notes

1. The terms "decentralization," "community control," and "parent participation" are used interchangeably, but it is questionable if there is a common agreement by the professional and lay power contestants about the definition of these terms.

2. *Economic Opportunity Act of 1964* (Washington, D.C.; U.S. Government Printing Office, 1964).

3. Ibid.

4. Paul Elliot Peterson, "City Politics and Community Action: The

Implementation of the Community Action Program in Three American Cities" (Ph.D. Diss., University of Chicago, June 1967), p. 282.

5. Ibid., p. 284.

6. Estelle Fuchs, *Pickets at the Gates* (New York: The Free Press, 1966), p. 73.

7. New York State Education Commissioner's Advisory Committee on Human Relations and Community Tensions, *Desegregating the Public Schools of New York City* (Albany, N.Y.: University of the State of New York, 1964), pp. 28–29.

8. Ibid., p. 30.

9. Ibid., pp. 28–29.

10. Peterson, op. cit., p. 175.

11. Preston Wilcox, "The Controversy Over I.S. 201," *The Urban Review*, Vol. 1, No. 3 (New York: Center for Urban Education, July 1966), p. 13.

12. Peterson, op. cit., p. 176.

5

Decentralization in Urban School Districts

Anthony N. Baratta

Introduction

Decentralization is a relatively recent reversal of the pattern of school system governance in the United States. Decentralization plans and operations, at varying embryonic stages of development and implementation, are reported in many cities such as Boston, Chicago, Cleveland, Detroit, Newark, and Washington, D.C., but more particularly in New York City. Since the greatest amount of activity regarding decentralization has occurred in New York City, this will be the chief focus in the chapter.

The movement toward decentralization in urban school districts is an additional dimension of the principle of diversity of school system governance in our country. Students and practitioners of school administration know that the most potent movement in school district organization has been toward consolidation and centralizations during the past half-century. Witness, for example, that since 1947 approximately 80,000 school districts have been eliminated through consolidation. It is important to note that scant mention was given to the topic of school decentralization in the recent sixty-seventh yearbook of the National Society for the Study of Education entitled *Metropolitanism: Its Challenge to Education*(1). In fact, the fundamental proposition of that serious publication placed high value on metropolitan and regional concepts of school governance.

Why the reversal from centralization toward decentralization? Perhaps the big-city school districts of our country are the point of no return for present school system organization. Maybe the battle against bigness in city school systems is partly attributable to the related social phenomenon in our country against institutional bigness in the business, church, government, industry, and university worlds. Or, perhaps, the tendency toward decentralization is an attempt to arrest the negative outcomes of complex bureaucratic organizations which alienate the common man and ignore "grass roots values." This is held by many to be tantamount to cutting the arteries of American democracy. Large bureaucratic school systems are sometimes criticized because of their 1) rigid hierarchical structures, 2) control by the few, 3) depersonalization of the functionaries, 4) elusive loci of accountability and, 5) unresponsiveness to emerging challenges. Yet, paradoxically, while many big institutions are decentralizing facets of their organizations, there is increased recognition of the merits of business and industrial mergers, and also the establishment of super-agencies in government such as the Metropolitan Transit Authority in New York City. Is it any wonder that issues related to school decentralization are confusing and enigmatic?

Decentralization: New York City Schools in Crisis

During most of 1968, the news about the New York City school decentralization crisis regularly appeared on the front pages of many of the nation's leading newspapers. School decentralization has virtually become a household word in New York City, it has moved to stage-center, and it is no longer merely an academic subject. As a result of the difficulties in the Ocean Hill-Brownsville Demonstration District in Brooklyn, a general paralysis occurred in the New York City public school system during the first two-and-one-half months of the 1968–1969 school year. Newspaper coverage(2) indicated the nature of the crisis, which involved decentralization issues to a considerable degree.

On September 9, the opening day of school, the United Federation of Teachers struck to protest refusal of the local governing board of the Ocean Hill-Brownsville district to reinstate ten teachers it had ordered ousted the preceding May on charges of sabotaging the school decentralization plan or doing unsatisfactory work. The teachers had been cleared of the charges by a trial examiner. The Board of Education branded the strike and ouster illegal. The union also demanded job protection for a group of teachers who had stayed out of the district for several days in the spring to protest the ouster of the ten teachers. After a two-day strike, the union reached agreement with the Board of Education to end the walkout. The agreement provided for the return of the teachers.

The end of the first strike was short-lived. On September 13, the union struck again charging that the Ocean Hill-Brownsville governing board had failed to honor the agreement. The governing board replied that the community residents had barred the teachers from returning to their jobs. Within this second strike period, the Board of Education asked Dr. James E. Allen, Jr., the State Education Commissioner, to intervene. Through the efforts of Commissioner Allen a second agreement was reached and the schools were reopened on September 30.

This second agreement also received a tepid reception from the Ocean Hill-Brownsville school officials. The Board of Education attempted to enforce compliance with the new agreement by suspending the governing board for 30 days and by relieving Rhody McCoy, Unit Administrator for Ocean Hill-Brownsville, of his duties. However, these actions exacerbated the volatile tensions in this demonstration district. Militant and strong partisans in the Ocean Hill-Brownsville district were alleged to have harrassed and threatened teachers, administrators, and observers sent to the district by the Board of Education. On October 14, for the third time in less than six weeks, the teachers union went on strike throughout the city, saying that members had been terrorized and threatened with death at J. H. S. 271 in the Ocean Hill-Brownsville district.

Again outside assistance was sought to help resolve the school conflict. Mayor John V. Lindsay appointed Theodore W. Kheel to head a panel to seek a settlement of the dispute. Within several days this panel discontinued its efforts to assist in a search for such a settlement. Though very little comment was made on the discontinuance of the Kheel panel, it did point out the extremely complex nature of the impasse. Then for the second time Commissioner James E. Allen, Jr. was called upon to settle the strike.

On October 29, 1968, Dr. Allen proposed that a state trustee run the Ocean Hill-Brownsville district. Basically this Allen Plan contained: 1) the appointment of a state trustee for the Ocean Hill-Brownsville district, responsible directly to the State Commissioner of Education; 2) the continued suspension of the Governing Board of the Ocean Hill-Brownsville district until its return is deemed proper by the Commissioner; 3) the opportunity for the Unit Administrator and all principals of the Ocean Hill-Brownsville district to serve if they assured the Commissioner that they could serve under the direction of the state trustee; 4) that the 79 UFT teachers return to regular teaching assignments in the Ocean Hill-Brownsville district, and 5) that all schools in that district would reopen. The city anxiously awaited the resolution of the strike. It hoped that the Allen Plan or some other proposal might be acceptable to the central Board of Education, the UFT, and the Governing Board.

By the end of October, 1968, the United Federation of Teachers had struck the school system three different times. The primary issue set forth by the Governing Board of the Ocean Hill-Brownsville Demonstration Decentralized District in Brooklyn was its demand for community power and control of the schools. A key proposition of this control was the Governing Board's demand to fire or transfer out of the district teachers whom they judged incompetent or decentralization saboteurs. They demonstrated their power, practicing the principle of accountability, by the May 9, 1968 action of ousting ten teachers from teaching assignments. The United Federation of Teachers struck because it judged the ouster of the ten teachers a violation of due process of teachers' rights, and an attempt to break the teachers' union. As the crisis intensified, other issues and charges began to emerge including those of anti-Semitism, white racism, and Black extremism.

This crisis in the New York City public schools was an indication of the seriousness of the emerging concept of school district organization. For the moment, the decentralization movement is experiencing its share of birth pains in New York City. Also, because of the confusion and ineptness regarding the role of the

Governing Board, an unnecessary and tremendous crisis has alienated the important teacher organization. Perhaps the school decentralization movement will experience a temporary set-back. However, this observer notes, the decentralization pattern of governance may be the most important single concept of school governance to be emphasized in the last quarter-century, particularly if it advances the life of Black Americans. This, however, must be accomplished within the legal framework of our society so that the civil and human rights of all Americans are protected.

Purposes of School Decentralization

The goals of school decentralization become interwoven in many complex social, political, human, and educational dimensions. An obvious purpose of school decentralization is to alter the structure and control of school government from one large, dominant, and central locus of authority to smaller, separate, and diffused units. Several fundamental aims expected in a decentralized system, as analyzed and discussed from pertinent documents, literature, and opinion on the subject, will be treated in this section.

A Legal Definition of Purpose

New York State Senate Act 4622 passed on March 30, 1967, although originally devised to increase state aid to New York City, provided a succinct rationale for school decentralization.

> Increased community awareness and participation in the educational process is essential to the furtherance of educational innovation and excellence in the public school system within the city of New York. The legislature hereby finds and declares that the creation of educational policy units within the city school district of New York for the formulation of educational policy for the public schools within such districts will afford members of the community an opportunity to take a more active and meaningful role in the development of educational policy closely

related to the diverse needs and aspirations of the community(3).

In addition to postulating the rationale, this law also directed the Mayor of the City of New York to propose a plan for the decentralization of the public school system.

A Policy Statement as Definition of Purpose

Soon after the enactment of New York State Senate Act 4622, the "DECENTRALIZATION Statement of Policy" was adopted by the Board of Education of New York City on April 19, 1967.

> All members of our Board are committed to the principle of decentralization of operations. In a city as large and varied as New York, we believe it is essential to have as much flexibility and authority at the local level as is consistent with our need for centralized standards . . .
> Now the Board proposes to further facilitate decentralization in the districts, in two major directions.
> The first—set forth in the policy statement—confers increased responsibilities, especially in administrative matters, on the district superintendents and principals and the local school boards.
> The second embodies the Superintendent's recommendations, requested and approved by the Board, regarding various demonstration projects that would permit experimentation to determine more effective methods for achieving greater community involvement with different types and sizes of districts(4).

School decentralization as planned by the Board of Education focused mainly on the decentralization of operations. While this plan did not satisfy the vigorous proponents of decentralization, it was perceived negatively by many professional personnel in the New York City public school system. Yet, the second feature of the April 19 policy statement which set the stage for the establishment of three experimental decentralized districts went almost unnoticed. The Ocean Hill-Brownsville Demonstration District in Brooklyn was created through this plan. Ironically, the Board of Education, because it was the "Establishment," could hardly expect to receive kudos for its foresight and courage in establishing the three demonstration decentralized districts. If the press head-lined this type of action it might tarnish the image that the "Estab-lishment" was status-quo oriented. The mass media generally praised the relatively minor role of a foundation as the change agent in establishment of the three demonstration districts.

A Panel's Definition of Purpose

A third major input concerning the potential benefits of school decentralization emanated from the work of the prestigious panel commissioned by Mayor John V. Lindsay to present a school decentralization plan to the New York State Legislature by De-cember 1, 1967. The Panel on Decentralization, announced by Mayor Lindsay on April 30, 1967, was chaired by McGeorge Bundy, President of the Ford Foundation and formerly Special Assistant to President John F. Kennedy and President Lyndon B. Johnson. Other members included Alfred A. Giardino, then Presi-dent of the Board of Education of New York City; Francis Keppel, President and Chairman of the Board of General Learning Corpo-ration and formerly United States Commissioner of Education; Antonia Pantoja, President of the Puerto Rican Forum; Mitchell Sviridoff, Administrator for the Human Resources Ad-ministration of New York City; and Bennetta B. Washington, Director of the Women's Training Centers of the United States Job Corps.

In the letter transmitting the Bundy Report to Mayor Lindsay the Panel expressed the following principles:

> The first premise of this report is that the test of a school is what it does for the children in it. Decentralization is not attractive to us merely as an end in itself; if we believed that a tightly centralized school system could work well in New York today, we would favor it. Nor is decentralization to be judged, in our view, primarily by what it does or does not do for the state of mind, still less the "power" of various interested parties. We have met men and women in every interested group whose spoken or unspoken center of concern was with their own power —teaching power, parent power, supervisory power, community power, Board power. We believe in the *instrumental* value of all

these forms of power—but in the *final* value of none. We think each of them has to be judged, in the end, by what it does for the education of public school pupils(5).

Appearing in the first section of the Bundy Report, the following provides further definition of the purposes of decentralization: 1) to liberate the positive energies of many participants in school affairs; 2) to define more constructive authority and responsibilities of the various parties while at the same time cutting through the myths that are perceived by these parties as frustrating and constricting effective school actions; 3) to open up the system so that all concerned can have more authority and a greater chance to work for better education(6).

Fundamentally the Bundy Panel analyzed the New York City public school district as a system in crisis. The school system was characterized as being over-centralized and thus too removed to meet the changing demands of its pupil population. It said that the system, especially in the ghetto areas, alienated parents and community people; that the combination of over-centralization and lack of parent and community support of the schools contributed to the crisis; and that, consequently, large numbers of children were not learning. The Bundy Panel, therefore, placed high value on school decentralization as the important instrument for the reconnection of learning for children whom the schools were failing.

The Bundy Report became a focal point of discussions, new proposals, and counterproposals for decentralization. By the end of March, 1968, various supporting views and plans were offered by the Mayor of New York City and the Board of Regents of the University of the State of New York (the official name for the New York State Department of Education).

Opposition to the Bundy Proposal

The United Federation of Teachers, the Board of Education, and several associations criticized the Bundy-Lindsay school decentralization proposals. For example, Alfred A. Giardino, President of the Board of Education, indicated that under the Mayor's plan, the Board of Education would propose and the Mayor would dispose money for school operation(7). In effect, Giardino said, the Mayor would significantly determine educational policies. Frederick C. McLaughlin, Director of the Public Education Association, also warned that to grant the Mayor great power for school district funding would be a backward step(8). However, the United Federation of Teachers, Local 2, emerged as the most potent force in opposing the various proposals for decentralization.

Selected excerpts from the *UFT Analysis of the Bundy Report,* indicated a divergent view of this school decentralization proposal:

> The United Federation of Teachers believes that the adoption of the Bundy proposals would irreparably harm the educational system. The Bundy model is based upon a glorification of the old-time rural school structure and is unfit for the greatest urban center in the world. The Bundy model is not decentralization; it is Balkanization. It runs counter to the current trend of enlarging school districts in order to provide both for greater efficiency and integration by narrowing school boundaries to increase administrative costs and reinforce segregation. Finally, the Bundy report ignores the new power and integrity of the professional teacher who will not continue to teach in any school or district where professional decisions are made by laymen(9).

Further, the UFT noted that the Bundy proposal concentrated on the organization of the school system, not on the content:

> . . . We have indicated our differences and offered proposals of our own for structural changes. But the basic shortcomings of our school system are not due to the fact that there are three districts or thirty, but to decades of financial starvation. Insofar as the Bundy report has stressed mere changes in formal structure, it obscures the real problems. What happens to a child in the classroom is what counts. Quality depends upon whether that child gets help when he needs it—not on whether we have one school system or many. To turn over a starved school system to local control is merely a political tactic to shift blame for inevitable failure on a powerless local leadership from responsible city and state officials(10).

Opposition of the UFT to the Bundy proposal for school decentralization was generally dismissed by the strong proponents of decentralization as an expression of self-interest and self-preservation. This observer views this attitude on the part of anti-teacher organization persons as myopic. Teacher militancy during the late 1960's has many analogous correlations to the militancy of the Black people. The UFT has fought successfully in New York City to improve the professional and economic conditions of teachers. These gains came too slowly and too painfully to be wiped out by a drastic, untested alteration in school government. Unfortunately, the antagonists in the fall, 1968, New York City crisis should be allies, because the fundamental purpose of school decentralization is to help children learn more effectively and teachers are the critical element in this learning. In any case, it was the union that effectively defeated the Regents' Plan for decentralization in the State Legislature.

School Bureaucracy: Pro and Con

No paucity of opinion exists regarding the problems of urban education. Rightfully, these problems are quickly related to the quality of school organization and leadership.

Philip Katz, a Chicago principal, wrote "that the present centralized, hierarchical structure is a deterrent to contemporary school systems—and that centralized structure cannot move fast enough or be sensitive enough to changing conditions"(11). He concluded that, "one way to unleash human potential is to give the worker more control over his work environment."

Herbert Thelen in the same periodical commented:

> I think that this unresponsiveness Katz notices may tend to be more marked in centralized than in decentralized organization, but that would be because a centralized organization is more compact, more intra-communicative, and therefore can more easily become institutionalized. It is the degree of institutionalization (fossilization, routine efficiency, rigidity, technical-legal-proceduralness . . .) that Mr. Katz is objecting to, not centralization per se. And, of course decentralization, by making each unit smaller, can greatly facilitate institutionalization of each unit; but their lack of contact with each other will keep them enough out of step to maintain conflict and vitality—which can in turn be used to build or wreck the system(12).

Naturally, differences of opinion exist among educators regarding the pros and cons of school decentralization. The views of two New York City school administrators regarding the New York City Board of Education's *Statement of Policy on Decentralization* of April 19, 1967, illustrated a difference of opinion. Selig Lester, currently a deputy superintendent in New York City, wrote in the *CSA Bulletin:*

> We run the best educational system in the world, but we are not perfect. We have an obligation to seek perfection. If this proposal requires additional effort on the part of the district superintendent, make me a guinea pig; if my principals think they are being downgraded, make them guinea pigs; but I prefer this to having a politician tell me how to do my job. I'd rather be a guinea pig than a lackey!(13)

On the other hand, Simpson Sasserath, a New York City high school principal, in the same *CSA Bulletin* called attention to the argument regarding the bureaucratic nature of the system and also defended the authority of the principal by writing:

> On April 9, 1967, Mr. Hechinger wrote in his column in the *Sunday New York Times:* "The breaking up of a large bureaucracy into a number of smaller bureaucracies is not decentralization. On the the contrary a smaller bureaucracy, because it controls more tightly, tends to run a more rigidly centralized system than a larger, more distant bureaucracy"(14).

Sasserath added that according to Dr. Lester's analysis, "the principal will be the responsible head of his school because the superintendent asks him to be. It seems to me that the principal should continue to have the right to be the head of his school without being asked." The Sasserath view was typical of the concern by many professionals that their work under a decentralized system would be highly constrained under the control and power of lay persons.

The proponents of school decentralization generally imply that such a pattern will remedy the ills of bureaucracy in the large city systems. What are the weaknesses in the centralized bureaucratic city school system that need modification? Educational administrators and leaders must dig into the subject of bureaucracy so that more than superficial responses can be set forth regarding the strengths and limitations of this form of organizational structure. Willard Lane, Ronald Corwin, and William Monahan summarized selected salient dimensions of this type of organization:

> Bureaucracy is a means of organizing work which permits—even encourages—specialization of talent and effort. Specialization creates a need for coordination, which is achieved in a hierarchy of graded authority regulated by rules, and other standardizing, depersonalizing mechanisms. A net result is a highly specialized, standardized, and centralized set of offices bound by depersonalizing rules(15).

Irving Kristol addressed himself directly to the impact of bureaucracy in relation to Black Americans and their espousal of the school decentralization movement in New York City(16). He indicated that it is an accidental occurrence, but an important one, that our large and cumbersome bureaucracies in education, welfare, and civil service play a crucial role in integrating large numbers of middle-class Negroes in American society. He indicated that bureaucracies are, in truth, the best-integrated sectors of American society. Decentralization of these bureaucracies will almost certainly mean disintegrating them. "We shall end up with only Negro teachers in Negro schools, only Negro police in Negro neighborhoods, only Negro social workers handling Negro clients." Daniel Moynihan also cautioned that school decentralization is likely to lead to "segregated bureaucracies"(17).

The National Advisory Commission on Civil Rights Report strongly recommended that administrative obstacles to community participation in the educational process should be eliminated:

> The schools systems of our largest cities have become highly centralized, with decision-making responsibility for a large and disparate population concentrated in a central board of education. While this process has produced substantial benefits —city wide tax base and non-political administration—it has sometimes entailed serious sacrifices in terms of accountability and community participation. What is necessary is to preserve

the worthwhile features present in the existing system while eliminating the liabilities thus far encountered. The objective must be to make public education more relevant and responsive to the community, and to increase support for it in the home(18).

"Tell it like it is!" is the Black man's axiom for getting to the basic reality. When all the verbiage and discussion has been considered concerning the strengths and weaknesses of school decentralization in New York City, the simple question to be raised is, "Does school decentralization in New York City mean the Black control of various districts within the school system?" The simple answer is yes. Black Americans want to control their own life styles with appropriate institutional and governmental legitimacy and support. Black citizens want sovereignty over their own destinies. The school, the most vital institution of a community, therefore, looms high in the priority system for Black community control.

In 1969, a third of the 1.1 million students in the New York City public schools were Black. It is just and consistent with the American democratic system that power and authority must be rechanneled to the Black community. The various Black leaders in New York city have opted eloquently for the "de-colonialization" of the life of Blacks in "central city." The trend toward decentralization and community control of appropriate educational systems is a practical and crucial method of providing legal and governmental power and authority for the Black citizen in the seventies.

Conclusion

The stakes are high in the New York City school decentralization movement because the environment is opportune for positive structural changes in the system. School decentralization is an important movement because its primary end is to make the public school more public. The decentralized school system ought to be a more effective instrument or organization to better the life of all the children and youth of the city. Its strength is in harmony with the democratic way of life. Therefore, the system, whatever the label, must belong to the people, must be easily accessible, and highly responsive to the exigencies of the citizen. A decentralized form of school government has many value dimensions that must be tried.

Notes

1. Robert J. Havighurst, ed., *Metropolitanism: Its Challenge to Education,* The Sixty-seventh Yearbook, Part I, National Society for the Study of Education (Chicago: The University of Chicago Press, 1968).

2. "Day-by-Day Developments in the City's School Crisis," *The New York Times,* October 28, 1968, p. 34.

3. New York State Senate Act 4622, March 30, 1967.

4. Board of Education, City School District of the City of New York, *DECENTRALIZATION Statement of Policy,* New York City Board of Education, April 19, 1967.

5. *Reconnection for Learning: A Community School System for New York City* (New York City: Mayor's Advisory Panel on Decentralization of the New York City Schools, November 9, 1967), p. 1.

6. Ibid., p. 3.

7. M. A. Farber, "Plan to Reorganize City Schools Assailed by Board and Parents," *The New York Times,* February 8, 1968, p. 34.

8. Ibid.

9. United Federation of Teachers, AFL-CIO, Local 2, AFT, *The United Federation of Teachers Looks at School Decentralization* (New York City, 1968).

10. Ibid.

11. Philip Katz, "A Proposed Structure for Urban School Systems," *Phi Delta Kappan,* XLVIII, No. 7 (March 1967), 325.

12. Herbert A. Thelen, "Urban School Systems (A Response to Mr. Katz). *Phi Delta Kappan,* XLVIII, No. 7 (March 1967), 327.

13. *CSA Bulletin,* IV, No. 5 (June 1967), 6.

14. Ibid., p. 7.

15. Willard R. Lane, Ronald G. Corwin, and William G. Monahan, *Foundations of Educational Administration: A Behavioral Analysis* (New York: The Macmillan Company, 1967), p. 207.

16. Irving Kristol, "Decentralization for What?", *The Public Interest* (New York: National Affairs, Inc., Spring, 1968), No. 11, p. 25.

17. Peter Kihss, "Moynihan Deplores Ethnic Quota Idea," *The New York Times,* June 5, 1968, p. 1.

18. *Report of the National Advisory Commission on Civil Disorders* (New York: Bantam Books, 1968), p. 451.

6

Federated Urban School Systems: Compromising the Centralization-Decentralization Issue

Raphael O. Nystrand
Luvern L. Cunningham

Introduction

The question of how city school systems should be organized is of growing interest. Public attention to this matter has been stimulated by reports of events associated with the decentralization or community control experiments in New York City(1).* The fall of 1968 found New York City government and school officials, teachers, and community groups engaged in a struggle over the distribution of authority to make school-related decisions. This became so intense and volatile that some persons believe irreparable damage has been done to the social structure of the city. Other chapters have discussed the merits of community control in considerable detail. The perspective in this chapter is somewhat different. While we acknowledge many potential benefits in proposals for commu-

---

* The terms "decentralization" and "community control" will be used interchangeably to refer to decision-making arrangements which transfer policy-making prerogatives from a central city board of education to neighborhood or community citizen bodies within the city.

nity control(2), we also believe that arrangements for school governance need to reflect the total context in which urban education must go forward. Our approach in this chapter, therefore, will be to discuss, first, the development of public intent in community control and some problems which it would not ameliorate or perhaps would foster. We then will outline a federated approach to school government which would combine the benefits achievable through community control with those made possible by dealing with education in a metropolitan context.

Understanding the Press
for Community Control

A well-known textbook about municipal politics asserts that the primary functions of city government are two-fold: "supplying those goods and services . . . which cannot be (or any rate are not) supplied under private auspices" and "managing conflict in matters of public importance"(3). Recent events in major American cities have raised serious questions about the adequacy of existing governmental structures as means for achieving either of these purposes. Traffic jams, industrial smog, standing garbage, and rising crime rates reflect the growing inability of cities to provide basic public services. Likewise, the inability of most cities to regulate conflict has been demonstrated by the summer riots which threaten to become annual events in many locales. In short, there is considerable evidence that the vast social and economic changes of recent decades have not been accompanied by needed modifications in the machinery of government.

Weaknesses in governing arrangements for urban eduation are as noticeable as those in any other public arena. Shortcomings in urban school services are well known to the clients of these institutions (particularly those in poor, Black neighborhoods). Such deficiencies have been thoroughly documented. Moreover, the growing amount of public conflict over how to upgrade such services has been front-page news across the nation. Conflict marked by the participation of newly aroused but traditionally docile parents, teachers, and students has directed public attention to a search for alternatives to present-day governing arrangements for city schools.

Many current proposals to reorganize urban school system focus upon plans for decentralizing authority. Proponents of these measures say that the fundamental requisite for school improvement is to position the policy-making function for schools closer to the people served by them. The means suggested for doing so range from plans to establish citizen advisory committees for selected building principals to the controversial New York City proposal to subdivide the school system into many smaller districts, each to be controlled by a local board of education(4).

Advocates of community control have several motives. Among them are:

1. Commitment to the egalitarian ethic that citizen participation is in itself a *prima facie* good and to be encouraged in all public arenas.
2. Black militant arguments that Black children are victimized by white bureaucratic school systems.
3. Belief that neighborhood residents can discern particular local needs better than nonresidents.
4. Belief that schools are controlled by a professional bureaucracy which rules in its own interests(5).
5. Such great frustration with the existing structures that virtually any change which can be effected with some hope of success appears attractive.

Notwithstanding the potential benefits (and there would appear to be several) of school decentralization, such revisions in themselves would be insufficient remedy for the organizational ills of urban school systems. Some of the attractiveness of these proposals undoubtedly rests in the hope that they will reduce the conflict level surrounding urban school affairs. By shifting the locus of policy-making from the maelstrom of cross pressures which characterize city boards of education to more homogeneous neighborhood levels, this may in fact occur. However, no matter how pressing the need to manage conflict in urban school systems, this must not be seen as a substitute for the responsibility to provide educational services. While decentralization may bring peace to troubled city schools, there is little to indicate it would lead automatically to improved education. Decentralization, in other words, is by itself no more a panacea than other alleged cure-alls of longer standing, such as smaller classes and compensatory programs. Indeed, it seems likely that decentralization could result in reduced service levels in particular areas of some school systems.

It appears that a considerable amount of the public press to decentralize school policy-making can be explained by widespread mistrust of the public school establishment. For vastly different reasons, leaders in Black and white communities alike have come to distrust teachers' associations, administrators, and boards of education. While their motives differ, their proposed solutions complement each other; both call for a return of local institutions to a more narrow form of local control. In this way the twentieth century push for decentralization presents a double-edged parallel to nineteenth century Populism. Like the Populists, both groups of decentralization advocates attribute their problems to a conspiracy within the establishment and view members of it with prejudice. Among Blacks, this is most apparent in New York where anti-Semitic feelings toward the teachers' union have been manifested in signs and slogans. Among whites, the charge of "nigger lover" and "Communist" has often been directed to school officials. (The Populist prejudice, of course, was anti-Semitic.) Certain segments of both Black and white populations seek redress by returning to past governmental forms, i.e., smaller school districts(6).

Limitations of the
Community Control Strategy

Because decentralization represents a move to an earlier government form, we are skeptical about its potential as a cure-all for urban school ills. Modern cities are complex institutions with problems of unprecedented magnitude. A declining tax base, air pollution, high-rise slum housing, resegregation, and polarizing racial tensions are new characteristics of many major cities. Redress of such problems requires extensive human cooperation. Difficulties in governing these cities reflect political inability to keep pace with such developments by promoting cooperation. To revert to smaller governmental units is to restrict the geographical base for cooperation and thereby diminish the relevance of government to the emerging urban reality of growing interdependence. As Melvin Webber has noted, "We cannot hope to invent local treatments for conditions whose origins are not local in character, nor can we expect territorially defined governments to deal effectively with problems whose causes are unrelated to territory or geography"(7).

Cities are understood best as sites where mutually interdependent individuals and institutions coordinate their activities(8). Interdependence is the hallmark of urban life. There is no place for the self-sufficient farmer of peasant societies. Everyone in the city relies upon a host of individuals, most of whom they do not know, to produce and deliver the food they eat and the clothes they wear, to convey them from one place to another, to provide them with leisure activities, to make possible their gainful employment, and to control their mutual life space in such a way that conflict is minimized. This extensive set of interdependencies extends beyond any individual's neighborhood to the entire metropolitan area.

While urban residents have become increasingly dependent upon persons unlike themselves, they simultaneously have segregated themselves and others in homogeneous neighborhoods. The functionally interdependent city thus has been characterized by growing spatial segregation. Rich and poor, Black and white, executive and laborer live farther from one another and have fewer personal contacts than did their counterparts in less-advanced societies. The tragic irony of urbanization is that, in a society where interdependence is crucial, the mistrust and polarization which stems from lack of association is fed by growing spatial segregation.

Governmental or jurisdictional boundaries in such a society are unnatural barriers which enhance spatial segregation and work against the functional interdependence that is essential to urban life. To encourage social institutions such as schools to limit the associations of their clients to others within a particular jurisdiction is to limit preparation for future interaction with persons who may be different. Put bluntly in this context, proposals to decentralize school systems may allow homogeneous neighborhoods opportunities to extend and intensify hatred and polarization in a society already marked by race and class conflict. Freedom to teach "Black is Beautiful" in the ghetto would be paralleled by liberty to proclaim "White is Right" elsewhere. It is difficult to contemplate how such "Balkanization" of urban school systems could contribute positively to the growing urban demand for human interdependence.

Given the increasing spatial segregation in our cities, efforts to decentralize urban school systems virtually concede the defeat of efforts to provide educational experiences in integrated settings. However realistic such moves might be from political perspectives, it is ironic that they appear almost simultaneously with evidence of the educational benefits of classroom integration(9).

The skeptics who point to the physical impossibility of integrating the schools of Baltimore, Chicago, New York, Philadelphia, or Washington, D.C., have a strong case. But the social composition of most American cities differs markedly from these cities and the few others like them. To press the case for community control in cities where the ghetto is less ubiquitous panders to human prejudice and jeopardizes the possibilities for integrated schooling.

The "metropolitan problem" has been described as one of structuring government to provide services effectively and efficiently to persons who live within different jurisdictional areas of a single metropolitan area. The presence of multiple jurisdictions has led to multiple governmental units and much confusion in attempts to coordinate their services. In the New York City area alone, for example, there are more than 1,400 governments. Similarly there are more than 5,000 school districts in the approximately 220 Standard Metropolitan Statistical Areas (SMSA) in the nation. Clearly the coordination of educational programs alone in almost any one of these areas would be a massive endeavor. But we know that the provision of quality educational programs depends upon more than educators; cooperation from other governmental units (e.g. health, welfare, police) is essential. To date, efforts to achieve such cooperation have met with only small success. (The brief but undistinguished history of local Community Action Agencies, created under provision of the Economic Opportunity Act of 1964, is testimony to this point.) Balkanizing city school systems would enlarge the problem of achieving interjurisdictional cooperation by increasing the number of units to be coordinated.

Still another objection to decentralization is that it could encourage further the inequitable distribution of school resources
across metropolitan areas. This point can be illustrated by considering present differences in the ability of suburbs within the same
metropolitan area to support schools. Median family income
among the Chicago suburbs ranges from less than $6,000 per year
to more than $24,000 per year. Differences in the assessed valua-
tion per pupil available to school systems in these suburbs ranges
from less than $10,000 per pupil to more than $70,000 per pupil.

As would be expected, these conditions contribute to great
differences in per-pupil expenditure levels among the suburbs(10).
The important point is that variations in suburban ability to support public education are paralleled by similar differences among
neighborhoods within the central city. If the city school system
were divided into neighborhood districts with some degree of fiscal
autonomy, variations in per-pupil expenditure among the neighborhood districts could approach the inequities which presently
exist among the suburbs. The consequence would be a decrease in
equal educational opportunities by virtually any definition ac-
corded that elusive concept.

From a fiscal point of view, the type of school system reorganization which seems most necessary is precisely the opposite of
decentralization. City school systems are confronted by a disproportionate and often growing number of students whose educational deficiencies require comparatively expensive treatment.
These same cities, however, are usually faced with a shrinking tax
base and expanding costs of other necessary city services(11).
Recent federal aids notwithstanding, fiscal crises are familiar to
urban school officials. Most of them identify access to an expanded
tax base as the single greatest need of their system. The financial
squeeze has become so severe that at least two major cities, Detroit
and Chicago, have filed suits alleging that present state-aid formulas discriminate against cities.

In essence, one strong argument against decentralizing the
policy-making function for city school systems is that this move
would not mitigate fundamental problems which beleaguer them.
Greater community control probably would not enhance the possibilities of integrating classrooms, cooperating with other agencies
to provide a more educative milieu, or acquiring badly needed

financial support. Indeed, there is some cause to believe that decentralization in itself might impede the achievement of these objectives.

On the other hand, it is reasonable to expect certain positive outcomes from decentralization. For example, local teachers might become more responsive to concerns of neighborhood residents; parents might become more closely involved and supportive of school programs. The question that arises, therefore, is how can the benefits of strong neighborhood involvement be realized within an organizational framework which maximizes the urban resources that can be directed to educational problem solving? Such a framework must meet two criteria. First, it must call upon sufficient human and material resources so that it can facilitate action upon the educational problems of the entire area as well as those of any particular region or subdivision within it. Second, such a structure must offer sufficient inducements so that citizens would be willing to commit themselves to it.

The Alternative: Federation

Federation is the governmental model which most nearly meets these criteria. A federated system is one in which a central level of local government and a series of district governments each have an independent set of powers over the same jurisdiction while a third set of powers is shared by the central authority and each of the district authorities. In the remainder of this chapter we will describe a model system of federated school government which would meet the effectiveness and inducement criteria mentioned in the preceding paragraph. It can be noted that the model is similar in some important respects to other proposals for metropolitan school government(12).

The Metropolitan Area Board

The central governing unit in the proposed system would be a metropolitan area educational board. The question of whether this body would be elected or appointed is tangential to our present concern. What is important is that the jurisdiction of this body would encompass the life space within which the vast majority of interactions by area residents take place. Thus, the geographical boundaries of the district would break down the spatial segregations of homogeneous residential areas and place all citizens of the metropolitan area in the same school system.

The metropolitan area board of education would have total responsibility for school system programs in five areas: capital financing and school buildings; personnel recruitment, certification, and negotiation; special education services; research and planning; and institutional relationships.

The metropolitan district would assume responsibility for planning, financing, and building all school housing for the district. The department of school buildings would be in charge of repairs and renovations as well as new construction. Members of the department would be required to consult with the department of research and planning and with district boards of education in selecting school sites and developing educational specifications.

The second general function of the metropolitan school district would be teacher recruitment, certification, and negotiation. Recruiters for the school system would visit college campuses across the nation to secure the best possible teachers for the district. Placement of this function at the metropolitan level makes it feasible to recruit over a broader territory by sharing travel costs among the various local districts. More important, it means that local districts which, individually, could not afford lengthy recruiting trips would enjoy greater access to good teachers.

The requirement that all local teachers be certificated by the metropolitan area board would insure that all teachers within the metropolitan area met minimum standards. Because considerable effort could be given to recruitment in such a system, minimum standards for teachers could be quite high. The negotiation of salaries and working conditions would be the third personnel function placed at the central level. This would be another step to insure that no local district would receive a disproportionate share of marginally-qualified teachers because of inability to match salaries of other districts. Contracting with teachers at the metropolitan level would also provide an important element of job security to these teachers. As will be noted later, however, it would be possible for any district board of education to decline the services of a particular teacher. Such a person would return to the teacher pool and be subject to selection by another local district.

The third function of the metropolitan area district would be to provide special education programs for the entire metropolitan area. Educating children who are physically, mentally, or emotionally handicapped is very expensive on a per-capita basis. There frequently are not enough children in any particular neighborhood to sustain a high-quality program. Structuring programs on a metropolitan basis would provide an area large enough to support more highly specialized programs than any single local district could afford. In many areas it would be useful to offer vocational and technical education programs on the same basis. The opportunity to share in high-quality special education programs might be appreciated particularly by persons now in small, high-status, suburban districts.

The fourth function of the metropolitan school authority would be in the area of research and planning. The department of research and planning would have several responsibilities:

1. Evaluate the effectiveness of various instructional techniques.
2. Assess social changes taking place and determine their implications for the school district.
3. Maintain up-to-date population projections and develop plans for new school buildings and boundary changes.
4. Assess the adequacy of on-going school programs from a technical standpoint and make this information available to the public as well as to teachers and administrators.
5. Conduct cost-benefit studies to aid local and metropolitan school authorities in allocating resources to various instructional programs.
6. Serve as a district-wide resource for information about the latest developments in educational theory and practice.

The department also would develop a comprehensive data bank containing extensive information about every student and employee, materials in the district, and other components of the total educational program. This information would be available to teachers and administrators for the purposes of developing instructional packages which match students, teachers, and resources, and to aid in other administrative decisions.

The fifth area in which responsibility would be centered at the metropolitan level would be institutional relationships. The responsibility of this department would be to establish and maintain mutually supportive relationships between the school system and other human subsystems in the metropolitan area. Functions of departmental personnel would fall into three basic areas: business transactions, media relationships, and coordinating efforts with other agencies. The business function for the entire school system, including payrolls and purchasing procedures, would be concentrated in this department. While officials in local districts would be free to work with the media as they wished, a public information office would be maintained for the entire system. Personnel from this office would be on call to help local district personnel with communications problems. The task of coordinating school efforts with other agencies would involve working with employment bureau personnel and officials from housing, health, police, and welfare agencies. The implementation of particular programs in cooperation with these agencies would doubtlessly depend upon local school district personnel. However, the development of a coordinated inter-agency approach on a metropolitan level is an important missing link in most locales.

Local Districts

Within the metropolitan district, a series of operating local districts would be established. In ideal terms, each of these districts would be socially, economically, and racially heterogeneous and enroll from 25,000 to 40,000 students. The policy-making body in these districts would be a local board of education, elected by residents of the respective areas. These local boards and the administrators responsible to them would have primary responsibility for all discretionary matters not specifically assigned to the metropolitan district. Perhaps the most important of these would be the selection and assignment of personnel from the group certificated by the metropolitan body. The local boards would select and assign personnel as they wished. Moreover, if they were not satisfied with the performance of particular persons, they could return them to the central pool for reassignment.

Shared Powers

Other important powers of the local boards would be shared with the metropolitan board. These powers would rest in the areas of finance, program development, and accountability. Most of the power to tax would be reserved to the metropolitan board; local districts would be dependent upon the central authority for the bulk of their operating funds. Allocations by this central authority would be on a program rather than a per-capita basis. However, local boards would be given the power to levy a small additional tax within their own districts, with the condition that the revenues from such a tax would go for program improvements rather than teacher salaries. This condition would insure that no district had financial advantage over others in competing for teachers. Local districts also would be free to seek additional revenues from sources outside the school system, e.g., foundations or special state or federal grants. This provision would tend to offset any disadvantage which poorer districts might experience in attempting to levy an additional local tax.

Responsibility for developing educational programs would be shared by the central and local districts. The metropolitan area board of education would have authority to establish up to 80 percent of programming on a metropolitan-wide basis. This district-wide curriculum, however, would be set forth in terms of broad program goals. It would be up to the local boards of education to specify the particular programs which would be used to achieve these goals. They would be able to choose their own texts, materials, and methods of study. For that part of the curriculum not specified by the central authority, the local boards would be free to specify both goals and programs. Local district experimentation would be encouraged.

Each year local boards of education would be required to submit to the central authority a detailed report indicating how the goals of the required curriculum would be implemented and what the goals and programs for implementation in the discretionary area would be. The central board of education, with the assistance of the department of research and planning, would cooperate with each of the local boards to assess the annual progress which had been made in implementing educational goals at the local level. The results of these assessments, as well as program requests of the local boards, would be considered by the central authority as it made budget allocations for the coming year.

The third area in which the central board of education and local boards of education would share authority involves accountability. Local boards would have the authority to hold local teachers and administrators accountable for local program objectives. They could, if they wished, dismiss particular teachers or administrators from their district. On the other hand, the central board would have the authority to hold local boards accountable for the achievement of the program objectives which had been specified. If, in the judgment of the central board, a local board which received the program resources it requested did not make sufficient progress toward its objectives, the central board could request that an assessment council be empaneled.

An assessment council might consist of two members selected by the central board of education, two members selected by the local board of education under review, and a fifth member selected by the other four. The task of the council would be to review the objectives and programs of the local district to determine causes for unsatisfactory performance, and to specify corrective measures. Such measures might include a shift in objectives, a change in program, a shift in funding levels, or reconstitution of the local board of education.

Benefits of Federation

The model we have suggested would seem to have several advantages over present core city-suburban school arrangements or proposals for further decentralization. In the first place, such a model would tend to equalize the resource base available to support students in all parts of the metropolitan area. Second, it would make it possible to provide more adequate services for students who have special educational needs. The common view is that such advantages would be more helpful to city residents than to suburbanites. This surely is true with respect to our largest and oldest metropolitan areas. However, in many newer and smaller areas (here it should be noted that the median size of U.S. metropolitan areas is approximately 250,000), the converse is true. In many areas the greatest fiscal and special education benefits would be to suburban rather than to city residents(13).

Other advantages have been touched upon briefly. The first is that centralized purchasing, testing, and other functions would result in substantial economies. Another is that cooperation among all jurisdictions engaged in social and educative endeavors would be enhanced. Perhaps the most notable advantage is that it would take into consideration the demands for increased accountability and program determination at the local level—which are central to the arguments of decentralization advocates.

Some Serious Obstacles

Despite these advantages, it is clear that there are serious obstacles to the implementation of such a model in American cities. We can mention them briefly as prelude to considering the incentive question. Perhaps the most powerful force working against school centralization is the American ideal of neighborhood and suburbia. Norton Long has said, "The suburb is the northern way to remain separate and unequal"(14). Spatial segregation has increased in our society because people want it that way. Anthony Downs, Jr., has observed that citizens seek "value reinforcing" rather than "value altering" forces for themselves and their children(15). Thus, people seek housing, work, and social and educative settings in which others like themselves are in the majority. This tendency helps explain the popularity of school decentralization and simultaneously poses the most serious obstacle to greater cooperation in the society at large.

A second obstacle is the obvious fact that present inequities in the distribution of resources means that some areas which presently support schools at high levels would see part of their taxes redistributed to benefit children from other neighborhoods. A third obstacle is that the control of public education within metropolitan areas is presently divided among so many jurisdictions. The consolidation of multiple school districts poses complex legal problems and virtually guarantees the presence of a number of professionals who would oppose such a merger.

Having mentioned these obstacles to achieving federated school systems in metropolitan areas, we will conclude on a more optimistic note by reciting some inducements to reorganization which in the long run may enable advocates of federated government to prevail(16).

Conclusion

The first of these inducements to federation is the obvious shortsightedness of the decentralization strategy from the perspective of Black and other community control leaders. Despite the power which decentralization might give Black power enthusiasts to govern institutions in their own neighborhoods, the fact remains that their primary objective is for equality within the broader society, not just their own neighborhoods. To achieve such equality requires participation with whites in institutions. Although Black power advocates may continue to extoll the virtues of community control, progressive thinkers among them surely will be led to seek an institutional rapproachement with "Whitey." Federated urban school systems could provide such an arrangement.

Downtown and ghetto business leaders, real estate operators, retailers, and service establishment entrepreneurs are simultaneously having second thoughts about the profits of dealing with captive ghetto markets. Many of them suffered great losses in the civil disorders which plagued our cities during the mid-sixties. The prospects of community control are enormously threatening to these people, for they envision the possibility of entire neighborhoods mobilized for violence against an alien business establishment. Efforts to defuse the decentralization movement by working through the schools or other "establishment" institutions could be expected to appeal to them.

Both central-city politicians and suburban civic and governmental leaders probably can be expected to become advocates of metropolitan government in the near future. Some central-city leaders presently view community control as a threat to the smooth functioning of their party organization. This theme has been dramatically played out in Chicago where the entrenched machine fought determinedly against The Woodlawn Organization (TWO) and the Blackstone Rangers in a southside neighborhood. In the long range, however, community control in our largest cities is as threatening to suburbanites as it is to central-city political leaders. Demographers recently have become quite explicit about the exact time that many of our largest cities will be dominated by the poor and the Black. Prospects of the control of central services in these cities passing from white hands is threatening to suburbanites for whom the city is the source of their livelihood. Many of them, therefore, can be expected to support various forms of metropolitan government as means of retaining predominantly white control.

Finally, there are many conscientious laymen, as well as leaders in public education and other areas, who are aware of the very real educational benefits to be achieved by reorganizing urban school systems on a federated basis. Many of these persons already have acted in this direction. Metropolitan school organization is already in effect in Nashville-Davidson County, Tennessee; Dade County, Florida; and Fayette County, Kentucky. Preliminary steps to the same end have also been taken in Chicago (Project Wingspread); Boston (METCO); Columbus, Ohio; Louisville; St. Louis; and Kansas City. Further developments probably are to be expected in these and other areas. Moreover, it is not unlikely that the advocates of centralization will receive substantial encouragement from state and federal planners who are cognizant of the need for comprehensive, coordinated approaches to urban problems.

Notes

1. The best known examples are the I.S. 201, Ocean Hill-Brownsville, and Two Bridges governing boards in New York City. For discussion of the New York City events see Wallace Roberts, "The Battle for Urban Schools," *Saturday Review,* November 16, 1968, pp. 57–61; and Maurice J. Goldbloom, "The New York School Crisis," *Commentary,* January 1969, pp. 43–58.

2. We have elaborated the nature of such benefits in Luvern L. Cunningham and Raphael O. Nystrand, *New Forms of Citizen Participation in Urban School Affairs* (Washington, D.C.: The Urban Coalition, 1969).

3. Edward C. Banfield and James Q. Wilson, *City Politics* (New York: Vintage Books, 1963), p. 18.

4. The Mayor's Advisory Panel on Decentralization of the New York City Schools, *Reconnection for Learning: A Community School System for New York City* (New York City: Mayor's Advisory Panel on Decentralization of the New York City Schools, November 9, 1967).

5. Marilyn Gittell, *Participants and Participation* (New York: Center for Urban Education, 1967).

6. Populism is discussed in these terms by Richard Hofstadter, *The Age of Reform* (New York: Vintage Books, 1960), pp. 60–93.

7. Melvin M. Webber, "The Post-City Age," *Daedalus*, 97 (Fall 1968), 1093.

8. For discussion of cities from this perspective see Scott Greer, *The Emerging City* (New York: The Free Press, The Crowell-Collier Publishing Company, 1962).

9. James S. Coleman et al., *Equality of Educational Opportunity*, U.S. Department of Health, Education and Welfare, Office of Education (Washington, D.C.: Government Printing Office, 1966).

10. For discussion of the problem of fiscal inequality see Charles L. Daly, ed., *The Quality of Inequality: Urban and Suburban Public Schools* (Chicago: The University of Chicago, Center for Policy Study, 1968).

11. An excellent review of this problem in metropolitan perspective is Alan Campbell and Philip Meranto, "The Metropolitan Education Dilemma: Matching Resources to Needs," in *Educating an Urban Population*, ed. Marilyn Gittell (Beverly Hills, Calif.: Sage Publications, Inc., 1967), pp. 15–36.

12. Luvern L. Cunningham et al., *Report on the Merger Issue* (Louisville: Louisville and Jefferson County Boards of Education, 1966).

13. Central city-suburban comparisons which indicate that suburbs would profit from metropolitan fiscal arrangements in some standard metropolitan statistical areas are presented by the Advisory Commission on Intergovernmental Relations, *Metropolitan Social and Economic Disparities: Implications for Intergovernmental Relations in Central Cities and Suburbs* (Washington, D.C.: Government Printing Office, 1965). See especially the reference to the distribution of under-educated adults and high school dropouts on p. 26.

14. Norton E. Long, "Political Science and the City," in *Urban Research and Policy Planning*, eds. Leo F. Schnore and Henry Fagin (Beverly Hills, Calif.: Sage Publications, Inc., 1967), p. 254.

15. Anthony Downs, Jr., "Alternative Futures for the American Ghetto," *Daedalus*, 97 (Fall 1968), 1338.

16. These thoughts were prompted by Downs' discussion of public inducements to desegregate American cities, ibid., pp. 1360–72.

7

Teacher Negotiations in Metropolitan Area Schools

Frank W. Lutz

Introduction

Perhaps the area in which urban school districts have provided the greatest, if not the most effective, response to the changing needs of education in urban centers is that of teacher contract negotiations and administration. The demand in this area is relatively new. In 1960 the United Federation of Teachers (UFT) became the representing unit for the New York City school teachers. Since that time the response in urban areas and increasingly in suburban and rural areas has accelerated, involving considerable action on the part of both administration and teachers. Unfortunately the action has not always been analogous with thoughtful planning and effective procedures.

Although teachers have long been organized in collective organizations, it is only recently that they have used this power to force school boards to negotiate with them. This follows the pattern of all public employees. It was President John F. Kennedy's Executive Order 10988 effective January 17, 1962, that clearly established the right of government employees to organize, to be recognized, and to negotiate with management on working conditions(1). Before that order, the right of public employees to organize and negotiate was ambiguous at best.

Since 1960 the American Federation of Teachers (AFT), of which the United Federation of Teachers (UFT) is the New York City local affiliate, has made the greatest inroads into the large urban school districts. Baltimore, Boston, Chicago, Cleveland, Detroit, Philadelphia, Pittsburgh, New York, and Washington, D.C., are examples of large urban school districts presently operating under teachers' union contracts. Four of these school districts— New York, Baltimore, Detroit, and Cleveland—were involved in work stoppages during the 1967–68 school year. In 1966, there were 33 work stoppages that involved 37,400 individuals and resulted in 68,000 idle man-days. In 1967, however, there were 81 work stoppages involving 93,000 teachers and a total of 973,000 man-days of idleness. Nor were union affiliates the only teacher organizations participating in work stoppages. Of the 81 stoppages, only 26 involved union affiliates; 47 involved teacher association affiliates and eight involved teachers who were affiliated with neither group(2).

Pushed by the success of the AFT in major urban centers, it appears the National Education Association (NEA) has itself become militant. It now can hardly be distinguished from the AFT either in its goals or the means it is willing to use to accomplish those goals. Some experts estimated that during the 1968–69 school year there would be between 300 and 400 work stoppages across the nation(3).

This guess, at least at the lower limit, was unbelievably accurate. Rather than 99 stoppages as predicted by the 300 percent estimate, there were actually 94 work stoppages involving 146,000 teachers. Only about one-third of these stoppages involved AFL-CIO affiliated teacher groups, but they accounted for about one-half of the teachers who struck in 1968 and more than half of the man-days idle due to teacher strikes. This discrepancy can be accounted for by the fact that teachers in the larger districts of the United States tend to develop affiliations with unions as opposed to associations and conditions in these cities tend to result in longer work stoppages. Actually there were ten more stoppages associated with NEA affiliates than with AFL-CIO affiliates during 1968.

Total man-days idle due to teacher strikes in 1968 climbed to 2,191,900 days(4). The 1968 average teacher's annual salary was about $7,900. Thus, if we consider a 180 day teaching year, the total loss to the national economy, assuming teachers were not paid for the days they were on strike, was approximately $91,400,000. If the average taxpayer in the $7,800 bracket pays a 20 percent income tax, this would represent a loss to the federal budget of over eighteen and one quarter million dollars, a figure educators would do well to consider when complaining that sufficient federal funds are not forthcoming to assist education. Looking at it another way, if there are 20 pupils per striking educator (not every educator on strike is a classroom teacher) then there would have been over 40,000,000 pupil-teaching days lost in 1968.

Of course not every man-day idle in education results in a lost day of teaching or a lost day's pay. This fact raises other serious questions. In some districts where there are short one or two day stoppages, teachers' salaries are not docked. In one New York City strike the school board continued to pay teachers long after they had left their posts. Not only moral but legal questions must be raised by such a practice. More commonly, however, an hour more or less is added to the school day once teachers return, and it is assumed this makes up for the teaching time lost during the strike. In other cases the school year is extended into the summer months or certain vacation days are forfeited. Occasionally a combination of the above are utilized in order to rationalize the failure to decrease the teacher's salary and convince the public that the children's education has not been harmed.

Such strategies must assume that the extension of the school day in no way affects the pupils' ability to learn or that the lengthening of the school year into the summer or the abolishment of established holidays has unimportant effects on the learning process. These arguments fly in the face of traditional educational arguments which have consistently contended that pupils could only learn and teachers could only effectively teach for a certain number of hours per day. Thus, it has long been assumed that the school day could not be extended without harm to the teaching-learning process. If this is not correct, we might reasonably ask why teachers should teach only five periods per day rather the six or seven. The same question might also be raised about the "sacred" 180-day teaching year. Arguments invoking the plea of preparation and marking effort and in-service improvement of teachers should fall on very questioning ears, unless such activities are scheduled in such a way so as to be reported with greater reliability and validity than they have in the past.

All this does not speak of the possible psychological effect a teacher strike may have on pupil attitudes toward the teacher. Teachers who argue that negotiations and collective bargaining in education benefit children must be prepared to offer much more convincing statements in the face of these data than the platitudes offered in the past. Undoubtedly educational negotiation benefits teachers economically, but it is extremely doubtful if *today's* children benefit from *today's* teacher strike.

Union Control in Urban Areas

While unions seem to have taken command of teacher negotiation and bargaining in the urban centers of the Northeastern quarter of the United States, teachers in cities and metropolitan areas of other regions have thus far preferred to affiliate with the NEA. Los Angeles and San Francisco are the most prominent examples of urban centers operating under the Whittier Act, a state law governing teacher negotiations in California. In these cities, committees of teachers representative of the proportional membership of the teachers in the school district "meet and confer"(5) with administration regarding personnel matters.

Not only have individual school districts been confronted with work stoppages but collective teacher action has occasionally taken on much larger ramifications when supported by teachers in large city and metropolitan areas. Teacher work stoppages have encompassed large areas, counties, and even entire states. Examples during the 1967–68 school year include Michigan, Florida, and New Mexico. In Utah, Oklahoma, Colorado, and Pennsylvania, NEA state organizations have applied "sanctions" on a statewide basis and have requested that teachers from out of state not make application for teaching positions within these states. Again, however, it is largely the urban and metropolitan areas that are most affected by such "sanctions."

The foregoing assessment demonstrates the existing demand made upon administration in urban school districts to engage in the administrative function of negotiation. Some school districts are involved in negotiations 12 months a year. Others commit major resources to the negotiation process only at specified times during the year. While these districts must also engage in the administration of the contract, they involve teachers in decision-making through various types of committee structures. Decisions made by the committees are usually excluded from negotiations. This process appears to be the most efficient and effective structure for public education. In either case, however, the demands for increased teacher participation in decision-making and the response to such demands will undoubtedly continue to increase in urban districts. While no foolproof or single guide can be given to cope with these increasing demands, the remainder of this chapter will be devoted to generating ideas and likely directions that will be helpful to the urban school administrator in meeting this new challenge in the administration of public education.

Negotiation as a Social Process

Much of what has been written about negotiations in public education can be classified into three categories: 1) philosophic, 2) descriptive, and 3) operational. Philosophic articles generally review tried-and-true proclamations about public education and the responsibility of teachers, school board members, and school administrators to the education of the children of the United States. While one cannot take exception to such beliefs, they are seldom helpful except at the very general level in providing a sound basis for contract negotiation. Publications dealing with descriptive material fall into two sub-categories: legal descriptions and specific cases where negotiations have either been successful or terminated in impasse. Both types of descriptive materials are useful, particularly when generalizations which can be applied to future situations are derived. Operational literature, generally concerned with the "nuts and bolts" of negotiation, can prove useful to school administration at two levels. At one level there are basic materials needed, data required, the scheduling of meetings and so forth which are necessary in order to engage in the negotiation process. Second, when proclamations of how to engage in the process take the form of generalized principles based upon descriptive data and tested hypotheses, this material becomes not only valuable but essential to the school administrator. When, however, the advice is derived from a single experience or a single situation, it is of no more value than the case study of a single situation.

A fourth category in the negotiation process virtually devoid of publication at this time might be entitled the social process of negotiation. Above all other aspects of negotiation, more important than legality, more important than the personalities involved, more important even than the items being discussed is the fact that a group representing a body of teachers and a group of administrators representing the school board and the school administration are brought together into a single room to engage in the social process of negotiation. As a social process, negotiations are governed by the laws of social psychology and sociology. The norms and group memory of the teachers' group as well as the norms of the administration and the school board play an important role in the negotiation process.

The past history of personnel relationships becomes the forest through which the negotiators must find their way. Yet it is often difficult to see the trees because of this forest, to get at the real problems involved in the negotiation. Such a situation is described by Lewis Coser(6) as unrealistic conflict as opposed to realistic conflict. Coser defines unrealistic conflict as one in which alternatives exist with regard to the object of the aggression. Thus, the object of the aggression may begin by being centered on the use of teacher aides. As one begins to solve the problem, the object of the aggression shifts to the school principal who, in spite of previous agreements, assigned teacher aides in his school in a dogmatic and autocratic fashion. As a solution is sought, the problem shifts to the superintendent or the school board who failed to enforce the original agreement. It becomes increasingly difficult to solve the conflict situation. Realistic conflict is when the alternatives are in the form of solutions to the conflict area. Here the conflict area remains the same and conflict is centered upon alternative solutions to the particular problem. Once agreement can be reached by reasonable people, the negotiation team can move to another situation with the knowledge that they have resolved the first problem.

It would appear that the situation involving teacher contract negotiations often centers in the area of unrealistic conflict. Both teacher organizations and school administrators should be acutely aware of these differences and make every effort to bring the conflict into a realistic conflict situation.

The disciplines of psychology, social psychology, and sociology have provided us with numerous principles relating to the process of negotiation. Many of these principles have been the subject of discussions by other authors. This chapter, however, chooses to focus on a topic of human social behavior heretofore untried in the attempt to understand teacher-school board negotiations. It is based on studies by Charles Loomis(7), Conrad Lorenz(8), and Robert Audrey(9), who have, through their studies of animal behavior, developed the concepts of territoriality and boundary maintenance. Recently these concepts have come into vogue as explanations of human behavior. It is with these concepts we shall deal in an attempt to explain that the activity called teacher militancy, much deplored by school administrators and school boards, is but a phenomenon known to all animals, including the human animal.

Aggression involving belligerent behavior toward individuals is simply normal human behavior; it should be expected and can be predicted. If understood, it should of itself generate no counter-hostility on the part of the other. If such an understanding could be achieved, it would be possible, in this author's view, to settle upon the more realistic conflict of issue resolution rather than the un-realistic conflict of individual hostility and resentment.

Although some behavioral scientists under the editorship of Ashley Montague have recently challenged the idea that aggression is a trait inherited by man from his evolutionary ancestors(10), their case appears no better than the case of those authors previously cited. Professor Sherwood Washburn of the University of California states in reviewing Montague's book:

The view of primate behavior and human evolution presented in Montague's article is as inaccurate and biased as Audrey's.

(The fiction writer who popularized the notion of territoriality.)
The data are simply distorted in the opposite direction. The
gentle, cooperative nonhuman primate is as much a product of
the imagination as the killer ape(11).

The fact is that man throughout his history has always found
himself in conflict with other men over one thing or another. He
has always found it necessary to resolve this conflict in some
manner. Occasionally the method was nonaggressive as with pot-
latching of the Northwestern Indians of North America. Usually
the action was aggressive in nature.

Whether the tendency toward conflict and aggressive behavior
is inherited and must be redirected, as contended by Lorenz, or
learned and must be extinguished and a new response relearned, as
contended by Montague, makes little difference to the thesis presented here. Both are probably correct to some extent. The
tendency to perceive areas of conflict is probably inherited by
humans from their biological ancestors. Being capable of cognitive
processes, humans are undoubtedly capable of learning different
responses to the conflict stimulus. Unfortunately, this has often
been an aggressive response.

All animals, from tropical fish to ducks to apes, are capable of
and do establish certain geographic territories which they hold to
be their own. In a sociological sense, these territories constitute a
condition for social action, for the territories may be contested at
any time by other animals or groups of animals. In the case of
human beings, territory may be geographic and it may also be
cognitive. Thus human beings not only own physical space but
hold that they are entitled to certain prerogatives, rights, and privileges based on their investments, training, and official roles. In the
case of the human animal, these cognitive territories are at least as
important as physical territories. Where the human animal is concerned, even in the case of geographic territory, cognition or
perception about the space is often more important than the space
or the legal title to that space. "Squatter's rights" have often been
upheld in courts of law. Thus, even when another person can show
legal title to a piece of property, if an individual can substantiate
that he has lived on that property in an open and straightforward
way for a period of years, the courts will often decide that he has

some rights to that territory or to some recompense for being dispossessed of it.

In addition, whether or not the courts uphold the "squatter's rights" or not, the individual himself will often defend that territory, not only through legal action but through physical action as well. Human beings exhibit a behavior called boundary maintenance similar to lower animals. Boundary maintenance is an activity or a social process engaged in by individuals and groups in order to defend territory which they perceive they own from encroachment by other individuals and/or groups. Without laboring any further over the facts of animal and human behavior, it appears that human beings as well as lower animals establish territories and defend their boundaries through social and individual action. If this fact is accepted and if we can accept the idea that human beings are at least as capable of establishing cognitive territory as geographic territory, it is now possible to utilize the terms territoriality and boundary maintenance to explain the behavior known as teacher militancy.

For a period of more than 100 years, two trends have been apparent in American public education. The first is the increased training and education necessary for entrance and advancement within the teaching profession itself. At one time it was not uncommon for an individual who had completed the eighth grade to begin teaching in a one-room schoolhouse. Later it was a common practice that teachers should be educated in a two-year normal school. More recently, teachers have been expected to complete a four-year degree program that allowed them to meet state certification standards; often they have been required to have a five-year preparatory program leading to a master's degree. Although still uncommon in general practice, it is the unusual urban school system that does not have teachers with doctorates in the classroom.

The second trend that has been occurring concomitantly but not parallel to the first trend is decreasing teacher autonomy. While the poorly trained, one-room-school teacher was responsible to a school board or committee, he found himself largely responsible for decision-making in all areas of education within his school. He disciplined the students; provided the more detailed course of study, if not the actual selection of subject matter itself; established the daily school calendar; ordered, distributed, and utilized the school supplies in terms of his needs and the budget provided by the school committee; provided the necessary janitorial tasks; and was responsible for guidance and administrative tasks necessary to operate the classroom. As the organization of schools moved from the one-room-schoolhouse concept to the centralized school district with its complex organizational structures, the autonomy of the teacher dwindled. During this period, urban school enrollments and school size rose rapidly. The demand for additional services was often met by the creation of a new role position to which were assigned the responsibilities and authority formerly held by the teacher. Thus, the highly trained urban classroom teacher no longer made the majority of educational decisions regarding the students in his charge. The textbooks used in teaching, the tests for evaluating, the size of his classroom, the number of periods he taught, the disciplining of pupils, the guidance services, the establishment of the curriculum guides are but some of the activities in which the teacher now had minimal, if any, decision-making powers.

Principals, assistant principals, guidance counselors, department heads, and curriculum supervisors now all intervene at the building level. Increasingly, the autonomy of the teacher to make educational decisions has dwindled as his competency to make decisions has increased. This is not to say that there has been a conspiracy to limit the autonomy of the classroom teacher, nor is it contended here that these services might not be best provided by trained experts in these areas. The reasons for these trends and the educational effects are not the topic of this discussion. But the trends have existed and resulted in the occurrence of a highly trained classroom teacher with little autonomy to make educational decisions affecting the pupils in his classroom.

The result of these trends appears to be a highly trained classroom teacher who feels competent to make autonomous decisions in many educational matters. On the other hand, the school board and top administrators generally retain their perceptions regarding their decision-making prerogatives. Besides these two groups of professionals that have historically contended for power in the educational decision-making arena, new groups have emerged. In New York City, for instance, the association of assistant principals is currently a powerful group affecting educational decision-making. There are, of course, the counselors, psychologists, department heads, and others, each of whom now perceives certain decision-making prerogatives as his own. Finally, the union imposes a large and imposing structure which, on the one hand, fights for the rights of teachers while, on the other, limits the teachers' autonomy.

Thus, the individual teacher often feels frustrated in his efforts to provide quality instruction to meet the needs of the urban pupil. Finding himself in a large and powerful teacher group organization, he has determined to utilize its resources to combat what he perceives as an infringement upon his cognitive territorial rights of teaching autonomy. It is often the case that the administration and the board and the teachers all perceive with some justification that they own the same decision-making prerogatives; thus, their cognitive territory overlaps in many decision-making areas. Each tends to defend what he perceives as his rightful territory from the encroachment of the other. This activity of aggression over territory is called boundary maintenance by sociologists; in educational jargon, the term is teacher militancy. It is a normal human behavior, and when understood as such, it can provide the basis for moving the unrealistic conflict of personal animosity to a more realistic conflict which considers the issues and alternative solutions to the issues. The recognition of this sociological fact, along with other sociological principles, can provide the basis for meaningful educational improvement within the administrative function of negotiating.

The Present Crisis:
A Course of Action

Never in the history of the United States has urban public education received so much attention from the American public and never has it faced a crisis so capable of destroying public education as we presently know it in urban centers. Hardly a day of the first month of the 1968–69 school year passed but that the *New York Times* carried a front-page article about the crisis in the city's schools. On November 18 an agreement was reached that enabled the schools to open but, in this author's view, at that time it seemed no real solution and only provided a faint hope of keeping the schools open. Nor was the crisis likely to be limited to New York City. Boston had already shown signs of moving in the same direction. Detroit, Washington, Philadelphia, Milwaukee, and Cincinnati were reported as showing signs of following in the path of New York City(12).

The Ocean Hill-Brownsville dispute during the fall of 1968 was an example of the complex conflict and boundary maintenance activity that educators must quickly learn to contain and solve if urban education is to survive the decade. Although an instance of union contract administration rather than negotiation, it clearly fits the model presented.

The central board was struggling to maintain its control of citywide education. As a concession to Negro groups, which were afforded the support of powerful private foundation funds, the central board had established an "experimental district" in the Ocean Hill-Brownsville area. This local board was attempting to extend its influence and consolidate its gains. The United Federation of Teachers, representing more than 55,000 local teachers, had made significant and steady power gains and was not about to lose any of its newly won territory. Add to this the frustrated, emergent, sometimes violent power of Black militancy and the scene is set for the dissolution of the New York City school system.

Minor skirmishes were fought over the establishment of the "experimental district," the right of the local board to choose principals, the decentralization legislation of the spring of 1968, and the 1967–68 strike against the local district. When school opened in September, 1968, each group was ready to renew the fight. The issue seemed to be what to do about the ten teachers suspended by the local board without regard for the legal procedures specified by the union contract. Looming in the foreground was the decentralization of the city's schools and Black control of ghetto schools. In the background was another question: How could a union that represented all the teachers of the district and had negotiated with the central board and signed a contract governing all of the city's teachers work out specific personnel problems with local decentralized school boards? This was the unsolved problem that had closed the Ocean Hill-Brownsville school for the last weeks of the 1967–68 school year and killed the Regent's plan for decentralization. This was the problem that closed the entire school system for the first 47 days of the fall of 1968–69.

The central board was powerless. First, they assigned the ten suspended teachers to classroom duty, but the local district refused to allow them to teach. In retaliation, the union closed the schools. The central board suspended the local board and then reinstated it and reassigned the teachers to the local schools. This time the local district refused to reinstate not only the ten teachers but 100 others who had struck in support of the issue. The union refused to allow the teachers to be reassigned by the superintendent as many others had been in the past. The local district administrator was relieved and reassigned to headquarters, along with all but one of the local principals. Then the local Black groups demonstrated and one junior high school was closed because of it. The union applauded the action in support of the central board's decision to assign the now 83 teachers to the classrooms of the local district (others had "voluntarily" transferred). When the central board reopened the school and reinstated the principal, the union president again called for a citywide strike. It appeared that *either* the union or the local district could take action either to keep the schools open or closed—but that the central board could not get the schools open.

The main focus of the conflict was first ten teachers, then it was what the local Black groups called the "racist" union, then 100 teachers, then the local board, then the central board's president, then the local district administrator, then seven principals. The focus of the conflict was always a person or group, but it kept shifting. It was unrealistic conflict. No effort at solving the problem of how to operate a centralized union and enforce a centralized union contract in the face of the realism of local district control ever appeared on the surface. If it had alternatives, it could have been stated in terms of courses of action instead of personalities.

A temporary settlement came only after some of the "personalities" were removed. The appointment of a "trustee" to oversee the operation of the local district, a panel to "guard" teacher rights, and the removal of three principals substituted new personalities for the old. Nevertheless, these moves left the real conflict unsolved.

Certainly new territories had emerged for the union and the

local Black community. These overlapped the old prerogatives of the central board as well as the union. The boundary maintenance activities should have been recognized as natural and realistic conflict and negotiation activity should have centered upon alternative solutions. Only in this way will urban education survive the present crisis.

A Look into the Future

Composition of Negotiating Units

One of the major problems immediately facing administrators in urban areas is the question of "Where do principals and assistant principals belong in this area of negotiation?" In a few large, urban, industrialized areas principals and other second-line administrators undoubtedly will affiliate with large and powerful labor unions, as they form local negotiating units. New York City has already begun this trend; hundreds of principals and assistant principals have already organized into a unit affiliated with the International Teamsters Union. In other areas, most likely suburban and rural areas, principals will remain within the same organization as teachers. It is likely, however, (and this is the bias of this author) that principals will remain unorganized if top administration and the school board recognize their responsibilities toward this important group of school administrators. State laws have increasingly recognized the right of public employees to organize in order to negotiate their salary and working conditions. They have not, however, recognized as fact that all levels of personnel are employees and, therefore, if the law were broadly interpreted, all individuals paid a salary by an organization are employees and there is no one left in the management category.

Consider the situation that might develop should principals and assistant principals choose to organize in unions affiliated with powerful national and international labor unions. Take the situation where principals perceived that they owned certain prerogatives regarding decision-making that coincide with decision-making prerogatives which teachers claim as rightfully theirs. Such an item as the suspension of a disruptive child may become a demand upon the board from each union. If principals hold it is their prerogative to rule on such a decision and demand that the board recognize that right in a written contract, and teachers also demand that they, as classroom teachers, have the ultimate right of suspension of disruptive pupils, the board finds itself in a dilemma. If they grant the teachers' demand, the principals might strike in an effort to obtain their demand. Now, the principals, by themselves, probably could not close the schools; but, were they affiliated with the Teamsters Union, Teamsters would undoubtedly recognize their picket line and all deliveries of food, fuel, and supplies would cease. In a short time this would close the schools. On the other hand, if the board acceded to the principals' demands, the teachers might decide to strike; and they have already demonstrated their ability to close urban schools.

Other sectors of American labor have learned to handle jurisdictional disputes and undoubtedly public education can also find methods of handling them. It is this author's opinion that the school board has a right to management in each building just as General Motors has a right to management in each plant. It might be wise for school boards and top school administrators to devote some attention to this problem and through their organizations to petition state legislatures to enact laws to effect a reasonable solution governing public employees and teachers.

Teacher Units

It is likely that, in the future, teacher units will represent teachers from larger areas than they do presently. Rather than organizing in local district units and negotiating with local school boards, it is probable that teacher units will encompass entire counties and often entire states. These larger units will negotiate issues such as salary and school calendar on county-wide and statewide bases. Local decentralized affiliates of these larger units will negotiate minor modifications such as cost of living adjustments, school day modifications and specific grievance solutions. The cost of local districts competing with each other in the matter of salary schedules is driving the cost of education close to the fiscal limits in some school districts. Being forced to adjust their agreement upward to match that reached with the wealthiest and most lenient school district in the county or state will almost undoubtedly require county- and/or statewide negotiation in the near future. However, such negotiations might result in county and statewide work stoppages in public education. These situations, when they occur (and they almost undoubtedly will occur in the future as they have in the past, in spite of state law prohibiting such action) will require fact-finding, mediation, and perhaps arbitration. Such conflict-solving activities will occur at the state level and, in certain circumstances, will become the concern of national agencies such as the U.S. Department of Health, Education and Welfare or the Department of Labor.

Such a situation becomes more feasible upon understanding that the goals and objectives of the National Education Association and the American Federation of Teachers appear to becoming consistently more coincident. Indeed, their methods for obtaining their goals are so similar as to be virtually the same, so far as many people are concerned. Their differences presently exist in the realm of unrealistic conflict. As these differences begin to be brought into the area of realistic conflict, it is likely the National Education Association will merge with the American Federation of Teachers, producing one large national organization representing the majority of teachers in the United States in urban, suburban, and rural settings. Such a group will probably retreat from the present demand to negotiate every educational issue and will concentrate its efforts more specifically on salaries and working conditions. Undoubtedly it will concentrate on large units, particularly state-level units, as it is apparent that funds for education will be provided by the state and/or the federal government rather than raised at the local level.

Contract Demands by Teachers

During the first thrust of teacher militancy the major demand of teachers concerned recognition of their organization as a unit representing the teachers of the school district. Once recognition was gained, the second thrust was to focus upon demands concerning wage and working conditions. With hardly a pause allowing the second phase to be distinguished from the third, teacher groups began to demand the right to negotiate every educational policy and administrative decision made in the school district. Issues demanded by teachers for inclusion in contracts included the number of times the football field would be cut during the season, how soon before a tennis match the courts would be swept, the kinds of lunches served in the school lunchroom, and the method of assigning parking spaced to the teaching staff. In the mind of the creative leader of a teachers' organization, everything was a decision affecting the educational goals of the pupils. Thus, it is presently contended that every issue is negotiable.

Such a contention is patently ridiculous. Administration always has made, and will continue to make, certain administrative decisions in a unilateral fashion just as teachers have made certain educational decisions in a unilateral fashion despite board policy and administrative proclamations. The notion that every individual in an organization can participate in every decision is a utopian dream not only impossible to realize but actually disfunctional to the welfare of the individuals concerned. Thus, it appears that in the future teacher groups will return to concentrating their efforts on the area of wage and working conditions. This area may well include, but will probably not be limited to, items such as the salary guide; length of the school day; determination of the school calendar; the use of teacher aides; released time for preparation periods; availability of teachers' lounges and lunchrooms; assignments and transfers within the system; sabbatical, personal leave, and sick leave; the method of introducing changes, as opposed to the decision to introduce curriculum changes; the method of introducing as opposed to the decision to introduce organizational changes; class size based on weekly teacher-pupil contact rather than maximum-unit size; retirement and insurance packages; and grievance procedures.

School boards are beginning to realize that in the process of negotiation it is possible for the board to make demands upon the teachers. Boards will become increasingly aware of this in the future. Through the negotiation process it is likely that boards will demand a longer teaching year in conjunction with granting the higher teacher salaries that will undoubtedly be demanded. The school year may extend over the 12-month period, utilizing summer months, and may specify vacation periods for employees other than the normal summer months. A longer school day will undoubtedly be negotiated in order to provide special help for pupils on a regular rather than on *ad hoc* basis. There will undoubtedly be requirements for stricter evaluation of teaching performance, and it is not unlikely that there will be an attempt to move toward some incentive pay salary schedule based on production, commonly called merit pay.

Emergence of a New School Organization

The foregoing discussions have hinted at, but not specifically stated, how the school organization may be affected in the future by the administrative process of negotiating. Without question, teacher salaries and administrative salaries will continue to soar. Assuming a maximum level, or at least a limited proportion, of tax dollars that can be spent for education and assuming contract demands will press for smaller and smaller class size in special instructional areas, as well as higher salaries, some new type of organizational structure will be necessitated. It is probable that future administrators will be solely concerned with the management of the educational organization thus facilitating the educational process. The process of education could be handled entirely by highly trained teachers who hold either the educational specialist or the doctorate degree in specific areas. Some teachers would operate as diagnosticians of educational problems while others would operate as the prescribers with regard to curricular areas in mathematics, reading, history, music, etc. Specialists in guidance and counseling would operate within this professional group.

Much of the actual routine involved in teaching, however, would be handled by para-professionals with two years or less of college. Such individuals would give the tests, provide the pupils with materials, mark the tests, help children on and off with their "wraps," handle the audio-visual equipment, and give perhaps 90 percent of the services presently provided by teachers. These individuals would work under the direct supervision of the highly trained teachers, diagnosticians, and specialists. While schools may obtain a ratio of one adult to every ten pupils the actual teacher-pupil ratio may well soar to one in a hundred or one in two hundred.

While such an organization is not a new notion in education, it may be that its realization will be a direct result of the negotiation process. These administrators and school board members who despair of the new teacher militancy and of the negotiation process in education apparently lack the historical perspective of American labor. The introduction of the demands by American workers consistently have produced a better product and a better level of living for our people. While the short-run specifics have often been painful and ugly, the long-run perspectives have resulted in a better life for the majority. It is the contention here that the same will be true for this movement in American public education. Building principals will use the negotiated contract as a help to administration rather than a hindrance. They will use rules initiated by teachers to help the teacher become a better-functioning professional. They will use other rules to eliminate incompetence within the profession. Other rules will be ignored as a benefit to both teachers and education in general, thus providing the basis for sound and cooperative action by individual school staffs.

Conclusion

While the organizational structure envisioned may not be the one that eventually emerges, the organizational structures in American education will be modified in a positive fashion and improve educational opportunity. As a result of the new function of negotiating in American education, there will undoubtedly be more money for public education, improved curriculums in subject-matter areas, and increased competency within the educational profession. Public education will be better in 1980 because of professional collective bargaining negotiations in education.

Notes

1. William B. Vosloo, *Collective Bargaining in the United States Federal Civil Service* (Chicago: Public Personnel Association, 1966).

2. United States Department of Labor, Bureau of Labor Statistics, May, 1968.

3. Jack Star, "Our Angry Teachers," *Look,* September 3, 1968.

4. Department of Labor, op. cit., December, 1969.

5. "Meet and confer" is the phrase used in the Winton Act in place of the word negotiate. This is intentional in the law. It specifically intends to bar the labor connotation of the words negotiate and bargaining. It leaves the school board and administration free to act in a unilateral manner with regard to the final decision.

6. Lewis A. Coser, *The Frontiers of Social Conflict* (New York: The Free Press, 1956).

7. Charles P. Loomis, *Social Systems: Essays on Their Persistence and Change* (New York: D. Van Nostrand Co., Inc., 1960).

8. Conrad Lorenz, *On Aggression* (New York: Harcourt, Brace & World, Inc., 1966).

9. Robert Audrey, *Territorial Imperative* (New York: Atheneum Publishers, 1966).

10. M. F. Ashley Montague, ed., *Man and Aggression* (New York: Oxford University Press, Inc., 1968).

11. Sherwood L. Washburn, "How Human Is Inhumanity," *The New York Times Book Review,* October 6, 1968, sec. 7, pp. 8, 34.

12. Fred M. Hechinger, "Local Control of Schools: A Growing National Issue," *The New York Times,* October 13, 1968, sec. 1, pp. 1, 80.

8

The Urban Principal: Man in Transition

Seymour Evans

Introduction

Until recently, some aspects of public education have been enveloped in a myth of fairy tale-like purity. There seems to have been an idyllic perception of a relationship between children and educators characterized by such terms as *calling, dedication, sacrifice,* and *altruism.* This myth placed the educational institution in a societal vacuum free from external environmental pressures and at the same time cleansed it internally of behaviors found in "other" organizations. Therefore, "education was not in politics nor was politics in education," nor were teachers "employees" and administrators "managers." The result of this lingering perception tended toward a lack of realism about the interaction between the educational system and a rapidly changing society.

Origins of the Role Myth

When viewed from a historic perspective, the origin of the myth of the principal's role becomes evident. In the pre-bureaucratic, pre-urban era, the city grade school was nothing more than a group of "little schools" under one roof. The principal's primary functions were to discipline and supervise and assist teachers whenever necessary. In othe words, the principal saw to it that the teachers implemented the predetermined content, purpose, and method of teaching. The teachers' task was to make the pupils master small daily doses of accumulated knowledge selected by the superintendent. Few, if any, teachers had more than 12 years of formal education. The participation in decision-making was minimal, since the teachers' task did not require the making of decisions and their limited knowledge and training did not enable them to make sound ones. In such a setting, the principal's power of knowledge and power of authority were one(1).

It is from this beginning that the traditional authority of the principal evolved. As school systems grew and the organizational distance between the principal and superintendent increased, each principal, more and more, operated his building in a distinct and separate style, relatively free from central office control. Thus emerged the perception, and in fact the role, of the principal as the educational leader of his faculty and the final authority governing all matters taking place under the roof of his building.

Bureaucratization and Role Modification*

Over the decades, as school systems grew in size, the formalization of procedures became necessary. Indeed, the systems' increased complexity and scope required the coordination of specialized roles. Therefore, it has become the pattern, especially in urban districts, for personnel, curriculum, and materials to be handed down from the central office to the individual buildings.

Thus, today we find many of the principal's former functions restricted, and some instances, totally removed from his jurisdiction. Teachers are hired by the superintendent or a central office administrator in charge of personnel. The principal's latitude in scheduling is limited by "district needs" in the areas of art, music, library, physical education, reading, psychological services, etc. Likewise, district-wide programs originating from the "curriculum

---

* For a more thorough treatment of this subject, see the Bibliography reference for Frank W. Lutz, Lou Kleinman, and Seymour Evans, *Grievances and Their Resolution.*

people" and the demands of the "business office" restrict the principal's freedom to initiate curriculum and materials changes.

Further, the knowledge explosion and the increased level and quality of training and education of teachers have all but eliminated the "teacher of teachers" conception of the building principal.

Finally the formalization of the teacher-principal relationships through bilaterally determined (usually without the involvement of the principals) written contracts has placed limits on the prerogatives and authority of the building administrator. For example, the trend has been for teacher organizations, having won a say in salary and working conditions, to gain entry into the area of decision-making in the formulation and implementation of school policy. The absolute freedom to assign teachers to class and duties, to call meetings, to discipline and dismiss the recalcitrant teacher is no longer the principal's. In the exercise of these functions, he is now accountable to the teachers through the contract.

In spite of the changes that have taken place, the professional literature still abounds with ideal characterizations of the principal's role as the educational leader of his staff. In reality, the unanticipated consequence of the bureaucratization of the public schools has been the dismemberment and erosion of the principal's role. Clearly, the roles portrayed in the literature are dysfunctional with regard to the organizational realities existing in urban school districts today. The building administrator's primary function, for the most part, has been reduced to serving as a communication link between the central administration and the teachers, and that of organizational maintenance. Moreover, the guidelines set down for him at the central office are often unrealistic for his school.

David Lewin in a recent article on the New York City principalship stated it thusly:

> What is important to his superiors may seem to him to be unrelated to the problems he faces daily. Duty-bound to accommodate himself to the directives from above, he sits computerized at his desk, activated by the administrative calendar in front of him and fed data by a well-oiled filing system at his side. The data are carefully cross-referenced, and copies of separate items may be reproduced to be filed under several headings. He is painfully aware that he is part of a machine, and he suffers from the depersonalization that is the curse of every big system(2).

Role Myth and
Bureaucratic Behavior

The myth of the dedicated school marm and the benevolent, kindly, and scholarly principal who loves children and regards them as his sacred trust has served to screen from the public eye and foster the development in urban centers of highly centralized and bureaucratic school systems which are insulated from the community.

In these systems, elaborate selection and cooptation procedures evolved which serve to screen out those who do not display the organization's behavioral expectations. Over a period of time, an even more sophisticated rite evolved, including judgments of grooming, coaching, tests, and interviews. This served to mold and socialize, and those who met the expectations of compliance and loyalty were rewarded by promotion. Such procedures, characteristic of many bureaucracies, are an aspect of goal displacement in which the perpetuation of the organization has become an end in itself. Not only do the procedures guarantee the continued life of the system in its present form, they also provide security and harmony for members of the organization during their tenure.

In the process of maintaining themselves in the larger external environment (as contrasted with the process of internal control discussed above), these bureaucracies have achieved equilibrium through controlled communication and impersonality. Here we have witnessed the use of the cry of "no politics in education" as the device to avoid the influence and pressures of the publics and public officials. The New York City school system illustrates well the use of such a control device. Until recently there has been an absence of well-organized school clientele or publics; newspaper coverage of school affairs had been almost non-existent and sketchy at best; the bureaucracy employed a screening process for selecting school board members; and the board was dependent on the central administration for expertise.

Marilyn Gittell states:

> One could accurately describe the situation in New York City over the past two decades as the abandonment of public education by key forces of potential power within the city. . . . The end result is narrow or closed participation in large areas of

nonvisible decision-making, in which effective influence is restricted to an inside core of top supervisory personnel in the headquarters staff of the Board of Education(3).

Common acceptance of the myth resulted in maximum protection for the bureaucracy's members. Behaviors between organizational members and between members and the clientele which had been rejected as unacceptable by the "outside society" as long ago as the 1930's were still the accepted behaviors within the school systems as late as the 1950's and 1960's.

Irrelevancy of Urban Education

In a sense, the control system of the bureaucracy was "too" effective. Not only did it screen and protect the bureaucracy from its publics, it also curtained off from the incumbents in the organization an accurate view of a rapidly changing society. Therefore, the irrelevancy of the schools. What is more, the typical urban school system is still dominated by rural psychology. This takes place even in the face of these facts: 1) approximately 80 percent of Americans live in the standard metropolitan areas; 2) about 75 percent of all Negroes live in the core cities (most of which are in the North), and are fast becoming a majority in many central cities; and 3) the white middle class has moved to the "respectable urban fringes."

Forbes Bottomly has stated:

> It (the system) perpetuates in children adult fears and prejudices about "outsiders." Its discipline and pass-fail evaluation comes out of a small-town Calvinist cruelty which sends the "select" to heaven and dooms the failures to hell. Its curriculum is white, Protestant, middle class and generally Iowan in its value content(4).

Urban principals generally, despite their protestations, subconsciously reveal this sacred or rural organizational mind-set. They continuously urge and encourage students and teachers to "work hard." They equate learning and labor. Can't learning be fun? They equate self-actualization with work. The "work ethic" is all-pervasive.

Principals and teachers must shed their condescending attitudes toward the new urban clientele who resent it. Principals must acknowledge and account for their personal value orientations and adopt an approach to their jobs that is rational and objective.

Principals increasingly perceive professionals as a different class than employees while teachers are coming to think of the terms as synonomous. Principals should recognize the problems generated by such a difference. They must also accept the fact that urban parents have learned from their suburban cousins. They no longer "keep their place"; that is, send their children to school and then keep a respectful distance from the principal's office.

The foregoing needs seem self-evident. However, the control system of the bureaucracy has been so effective that the principals were the last to realize the dilemma for which they were headed. They have allowed themselves to be caught in a three-pronged vice. On the one side, they feel the squeeze of the teacher organizations restricting their administrative prerogatives; on another are the communities challenging their very existence—challenging not only their appointments, but also their continuation in existing positions (examples: the New York City sit-in in the newly appointed principal's office and the Ocean Hill-Brownsville, I.S. 201 situations); and on the third side is the squeeze of "non-support" from the school boards.

A Different Leadership Style

If the urban principal finds himself in a bureaucracy, belabored by increasing pressures from community groups, students, organized teachers, and a frightened board, how is he to survive? Can he exercise any leadership in public education? If he clings to the old myths the outlook is glum. Given the union contract and the bureaucratic nature of urban schools, he must find a way to utilize these elements to promote leadership rather than frustrate it. In order to assist in the development of such an administrative pattern for urban principals, a research study was recently completed. The following draws from the monograph describing that study(5).

A sociological model developed by Alvin Gouldner(6) was used to account for teacher-principal relationships.

Briefly, it was hypothesized that:

1. Mock rule administration would develop positive sentiment and no tension.
2. Representative rule administration would develop little tension but considerable positive sentiment.
3. Punishment-centered rule administration would result in high tension and hostility.

Other hypotheses were generated from this basic model.

A field study was undertaken to test the model. Two groups of schools were identified, each having a different type of educational leadership climate: peaceful and hostile, respectively. Each group contained one elementary, a junior high, and a senior high school. In each of these six schools, a six-week field study was undertaken. Complementary field observations were done in the office of staff relations and the union office. The research model was generally supported by the data collected. Occasional modifications were made where the data provided reason for such change.

The major factor in "warm" leadership climates and peaceful personnel relationships was the existence of representative rule patterns of administration. While representative behavior—behavior associated with representative rule patterns of administration —took place in schools where hostility was the general sentiment between teachers and administrators, its existence was the exception rather than the rule. Further, while the specific problem was solved without much tension, the general climate seemed to remain one of high tension, perhaps because individuals have memories.

In the schools with representative patterns of administration, informal paths for participation were frequently used, but the formal paths were not abandoned. This openness of formal channels appeared to be an important point. In other schools a climate of tension often was created when the administration felt that scheduled meetings were not necessary because, from its point of view, the teachers had no gripes. Teachers, on the other hand, felt that the administration failed to respond to problems of teachers. Is such a situation the fault of teacher or principal communication? No matter which—the failure to hold required meetings with the union representatives is a *mistake,* even if the union fails to suggest items for the agenda.

Mock patterns of rule administration were observed in both types of leadership climates, though there was more in the peaceful than the hostile. In both, evidence of rule breaking on the part of teachers, aided and abetted by administration, included such practices as the use of school phones for personal business, smoking in certain areas of the building, allowing one person to "punch in or out" for another, and ignoring the use of self-treated sick days as "personal business leave." Perhaps there are too many rules for even the most authoritarian administrator to enforce; thus even the authoritarian occasionally administers in mock fashion.

When mock examples of behavior were observed in warm climates, considerable positive expression about the act was also observed. In hostile climates, however, the sentiment around mock behavior seemed to be, "We'll wait and see." Teachers, like other humans, have memories and their best prediction of administrative behavior is based on the usual behavior of administrators. Teachers in hostile climates seemed not to believe the act of mock behavior, or to be suspicious of it. This resulted in an attitude of, "It can't last—wait and see."

In the field study, punishment-centered administration always created tension and usually hostility. Even in normally warm leadership climates, this was true. While punishment-centered behavior took place in warm as well as in hostile climates, this behavior (not unexpectedly) was considerably more frequent in the latter.

Briefly, two additional important aspects of rule administration emerged from the study. The use of a rule by a principal to mask his authority will reduce tension or occurrence of a punishment-centered behavior. Also, close supervision is usually viewed by teachers as punishment-centered behavior.

It also became clear that all grievances are not personal indictments of administration. Some grievances are brought to alleviate an alleged injustice or infraction of the contract but without intent on the administrator's part. These grievances are brought to a satisfactory conclusion when the relief sought is forthcoming. On the other hand, occasionally the union is seeking to obtain a generalized rule that can be used in playing the "employee-management game." Such grievances are pursued even after individual satisfaction is obtained, until written policy is established.

Finally, it was discovered that principals and teachers perceive the contract's influence quite differently. In addition, variables that have their origins in the socialization process are the ones that account for many of the differences in perceptions within teacher and principal groups.

From the above, the following statements emerged:

1. The most important factor in the establishment of warm principal-teacher leadership climate is the presence of representative patterns of rule administration.
   a. Both formal and informal occasions of representative behavior appear necessary to avoid tension. Most often, the principal who administers a hostile climate sees no need for the formal meeting.
   b. The chapter chairman's meeting with the principal provides an important opportunity for representative behavior and tension reduction.
2. Punishment-centered behavior is to be avoided if one is to avoid tension and hostile feelings.
   a. When punishment is necessary, the principal is well advised to: use a rule to mask his authority; provide a warning before invoking the punishment; be sure the rule and the mandated punishment are well-known and available to all teachers in writing.
   b. The close supervision of a teacher (either face-to-face or through review of written material) is punishment-centered and generates tension.
3. If at all possible, teachers shall establish the rules whose infractions are to be punished, and should devise the punishment (even though administered by principals).
4. Mock rule administration is probably necessary to enable the development of warm climates, but it occurs in hostile climates also. This is probably due to the number and nature of rules in a large urban district. No school can be run by mock administration alone. Thus, the difference is between the mix of representative and mock, or punishment-centered and mock behaviors. The former generates warmth and the latter tension.
5. Considerable attention should be given to the difference in perception of teachers and principals as to the effect of the contract upon principal leadership. Is this chasm due to differences in what the two groups expect in terms of principal leadership? Perhaps teachers really do not know how the

principal has been affected. Regardless of the speculations, the wide separation between the perceptions about the effect of anything as important as the union contract must be of concern to the entire school organization.

6. Finally, running a "tight ship" is not the goal of educational administration and should not be the major goal of the school principal. Further, if it is necessary to use punishment-centered behavior in order to achieve a "tight ship," then it should be understood that tension and hostility between teachers and the school administration will result. While theoretically it is possible that a hostile climate may contribute to the goal of effective education, this should be put as a question not a fact. Another question is: How will a climate of hostility affect the leadership capabilities of the principal? How, in turn, will it affect the teacher-pupil relationship and learning in the school? These are important questions which need answers. Based on this research, a principal can determine the particular rule administration that will result in either hostile or friendly climates between himself and the teachers. The ability to determine this should prove a considerable advantage to a principal in helping him realize his educational goals and administrative philosophy.

Conclusions

It can be stated that the urban principal's position has evolved into one who 1) in terms of the school district, operates from a powerless base; 2) has been stripped of most of his leadership roles by the central administration; and 3) does not participate in the decision-making that affects his position.

What is the urban principal to do? He must abandon the protective womb of the myth that envelops the bureaucracy. He must conceptually grasp the meaning of the societal forces at play. He must come to understand that the emerging norms of society in general, and of teachers and parents in particular, include control devices that are at odds and in competition with the control system of the school bureaucracies. He must accept that conflict is inevitable, as is modification of the system. Further, he must accept the fact that the control system of the educational bureaucracy is, and has always been, a device for the implementation of educational policy determined in a power structure of which he was never a participant. If he is to control his own destiny, if he is to survive, the principal must look beyond the educational bureaucracy for the needed "critical mass" to form a power block which he will be able to use as a wedge between the power blocks of the militants and the decision-making power structure.

Recommendations

Academicians easily state what must be done. It is not so easy for the practitioner-principal to build an effective power block. In some districts principals have reluctantly formed building administrators' negotiating units. Actually, this is an instrument rather than a source of power. The mere formalization of a group, even in states where enabling legislation exists, generates little power. Moreover, it creates an ambivalent and dysfunctional organizational role set for administrators.

How, then, do principals go about creating power? First, they must realize they never have had much power! To equate delegated legal authority with power is an error. A holder of power controls the power source; the receiver of delegated authority does not. Second, the principal must accept the fact that power is never granted nor surrendered willingly. It is a scarce resource that must be taken or created.

The first route, that of taking power, is not feasible for principals at this time. As a group, they lack the basic ingredient of organized "critical mass" to engage in a confrontation tactic. Therefore, they must create power and the recipe is within the potential resources of the principals as a group. They have the relative wealth, energy, size, intelligence, tools, and time. These have been, until now, misused and/or unused resources. Stripping away his protective myth and bureaucratic shield, the principal is under attack. This challenge to his "leadership" can only be answered by developing real leadership through the utilization of their power potential.

For principals to be totally compliant to demands is to abrogate their responsibility and take the easy "out" on the question of accountability. The result is the surrender of leadership. This may create a womb of security for some incumbents who have never exercised leadership. However, the damage done to society would be irreparable. This, however, is only part of the danger. For principals to perceive of their role in education as merely carrying out the mandates of others is to express a willingness to function as amoral instruments of society. This is the antithesis of leadership, or for that matter, of what an educator is. Such is to function as a reactor. An educational leader must be a proactor—controlling, influencing, and causing society to change! If principals allow themselves to become simply the executing agents of others, they will assist in their own destruction.

How, then, might principals go about forming a power block? The key is professionalization calling for a distinct mode of behavior, clear and refined "rites of passage" (i.e., internally controlled formalized training and standards), and most importantly, a *separate* and *exclusive* body of knowledge and skills. As long as the lay public holds that mothering or fathering children endows them with expertise, as long as they believe that to have received an education makes them educators, as long as non-professionals can determine who enters the professional practice, the belief will prevail that all have an equal if not greater say in educational decision-making than does the principal.

Notes

1. Warren Button and Raymond Callahan, "Historical Change of the Role of the Man in the Organization: 1865–1950," in Daniel E. Griffiths, ed., *Behavioral Science and Educational Administration,* National Society for the Study of Education, Sixty-Third Yearbook, 1964, p. 75.

2. David Lewin, "The Changing Role of the Urban Principal," *The Elementary School Journal,* 68, No. 7 (April 1968), 332.

3. Marilyn Gittell, *Participants and Participation: A Study of School Policy in New York City* (New York: Center for Urban Education, 1967), p. 46.

4. Forbes Bottomly, "Some Notes on City School Tensions," *Compact,* Vol. 2, No. 2 (April 1968).

5. Frank W. Lutz and Seymour Evans, *The Union Contract and Principal Leadership in New York City Schools* (New York: Center for Urban Education, 1968).

6. Alvin L. Gouldner, *Patterns for Industrial Bureaucracy* (Glencoe, Illinois: The Free Press, 1954).

9

The School
Superintendent
in the Crucible
of Urban Politics

Joseph M. Cronin

Introduction

It is wise to be careful with the word "crucible," which has several meanings. The short definition—"melting pot"—will not do. Nathan Glazer and Daniel P. Moynihan demonstrated this in their study of New York City ethnic groups, which has implications for understanding the viscosity of ethnic groups in a hundred cities(1).

Perhaps better are the definitions "a place of testing" or "a vessel that will stand great heat." Urban superintendents can more readily agree to these definitions of their work-space.

The study of urban politics has not yet really probed the position of the superintendency. This is due in part to the lack of study of the city school superintendent as a political figure. There has been some consideration of this subject; Alan K. Campbell, for example, has collected several case studies relating to superintendents, among them such situations as the first Benjamin Willis resignation of the superintendency in Chicago and the 1963 search for a new Boston school superintendent.

In general, however, political science studies do not cover the role of superintendents. Edward Banfield's *Big City Politics* is a case in point(2). Inadequate schools are cited as one of five

familiar urban problems that generate conflict, but school problems receive only token coverage. The dozen or so lines on city
school politics in the book hint at desegregation as a major issue
and occasionally cite finance as a problem. Only a short paragraph
on the boards of education and their selection is included in the
summary reports on nine cities. Discussions of how school issues
are handled, of which interest groups care, and specifically, of the
extent to which the superintendent is involved are not presented.

Of course the publication date of 1965 antedates many of the
more spectacular problems facing superintendents; Black Power,
community control, teacher militancy, and strikes were yet to
occur in most cities. Given this perspective, the neglect of superintendents is understandable. On the other hand, one objective of the
present chapter is to remind the observer that the city superintendent has been under pressure, albeit less dramatic pressure, since
the position was established. Support for this view comes from
several sources. For example, Raymond Callahan quotes a prominent nineteenth century board member and journalist:

> The superintendent's position is a difficult one. He is
> the ready target for unreasonable parents, disgruntled teachers
> and officious school board members. In a vortex of school board
> quarrels, he is the first to become crushed(3).

Callahan has traced the "deposing" or "decapitation" of superintendents (even documenting one superintendent's suicide)
from 1895, a year when superintendents almost persuaded boards
to give them complete control over the educational program, to the
present(4). He cites a 1916 judgment that the superintendency
was then "the most hazardous job known to insurance underwrit-
ers" and a 1955 assessment of it as "the most harassing and
ulcer-producing job in public life"(5).

Luvern Cunningham also feels that most sociologists and political scientists "underestimate the role of the chief school officer in
local school politics"; he can cite very few instances of any social
science analysis. Even within the field of education research the
study of boards, of "power structures," and decision-making per se
have been more in vogue than the study of superintendents. Cunningham concludes ". . . the office of the superintendent as well as

the person who occupies the office ought to be central in the study of influence systems and local school district power structures(6).

One way to view the city superintendency is as a study in crisis, the nature of which shifts in each decade. The shape of the crucible varies with the demands of the era and the culture of the city. A second approach is to try to understand the stability and political independence of the position, especially given the pressures on incumbents and the oft-expressed wish by public administrators to merge the superintendency with city government(7). The third approach is to analyze the survival of the superintendency as an illustration of organizational role adaptation, more simply as an example of a creative response to each challenge. Let the discussion begin with the ironic but explicit recollection that the superintendency grew strong only as a result of city school system centralization, a necessary "reform" of the 1890's(8).

This chapter will concentrate on the crisis of one decade, the 1960's, but will examine the superintendency since the era described by Callahan, explaining the durability of the office partly in terms of organizational adaptation, and partly in terms of short-run tactics which exploit the ambiguity of board-executive relationships. To introduce the topic, the phenomena of political independence and centralization will be reviewed.

First, a discussion of just how strong and independent (as an office) the superintendency has become(9). One of the most remarkable survival stories is not that of any particular city school superintendent, but rather of the city school superintendency itself. A parallel professionalized role, that of city manager, was not adopted in many great cities and was sometimes adopted and later abandoned, as in Cleveland and Houston(10).

Sociologists have studied the phenomenon of "organizational survival" and adaptation while others have developed approaches to the study of leadership roles. The city superintendency presents an exacting challenge to those who would explain "role survival." One index of success, albeit superficial, is the periodic and public indication that school superintendents in several cities are paid higher salaries than mayors of the same cities. At one point a Chicago superintendent was the third highest paid public servant in the United States, excelled only by the Governor of New York State and the President.

School personnel lack awareness of the more than 30-year campaign to subordinate schools to other units of government. Political scientists and public administrators in general advocate an end to the separation of city school departments from other city departments. In their plans, school superintendents, instead of reporting to the school board, would report to the mayor and council much as do the city engineer, the chief city planner, and the heads of other major urban departments. One of the most sophisticated versions of such alternative school governing plans was the New York City dream of a "Human Resources Administration," a superagency to coordinate the efforts of social

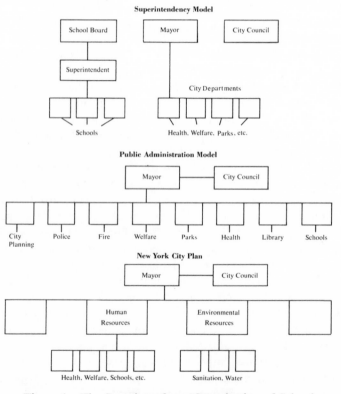

Figure 1   The Superintendency Organization of Schools
and Alternative Models

services such as those provided separately by health, welfare, and education agencies. Such a plan has much to recommend it despite Mayor John Lindsay's difficulties in bringing these functions together. Meanwhile, since the plan was not implemented, the city school superintendent maintains a position of leadership in tandem with the Mayor. The models in Fig. 1 show how elevated the superintendency has remained, as contrasted with the alternative proposals.

Some cities by statute depart from the superintendency model, most often in matters of finance where the mayor, council, assessor, and many others may exact more influence than the programs indicate. In Massachusetts, at least seven cities place the mayor as chairman of the school committee which gives the mayor a much greater potential for balancing resources and for reminding schoolmen of other claims on the city treasury.

This preamble serves simply to mark a phenomenon, that of the success of proponents of the city superintendency in the face of ideological, financial, social, and political pressures. Some of these pressures will be examined in an attempt to understand how men behave as they move into and through this administrative role. One very relevant question is historical—how did the city superintendency acquire the central importance it has achieved?

School Centralization as a Reform

In 1837 the city school superintendency was established simultaneously in Louisville, Kentucky, and in Buffalo, New York. The idea soon spread; the larger cities adopted the role rather quickly during an era when city councils appeared quite willing to allow school boards to strengthen the separate supervision of schools (see Table 1).

But city school boards really were in no position to make the city school superintendent much more than chief advisor on certain curriculum and personnel matters. Most of the larger cities were organized by wards, and ward boards ran the schools in each neighborhood. The ward school boards hired the local schoolmasters, inspected and maintained the school houses, and let contracts

TABLE 1   First Appointment of a School Superintendent

City	Year	Note
Baltimore	1866	(had previously been a treasurer)
Boston	1851	
Buffalo	1837	(1853–1916, elective post)
Cleveland	1853	(1892–1904, an elected director)
Detroit	1855	
Houston	1876	
Los Angeles	1872	
Milwaukee	1859	
New York	1848, 1851	(Brooklyn, Manhattan separately)
Philadelphia	1883	
Pittsburgh	1868	
St. Louis	1839	(three other executives too)
San Francisco	1851	(1856–1923, an elective post)

Sources: Thomas McD. Gilland, *The Origin and Development of the Power and Duties of the City School Superintendent* (Chicago: The University of Chicago Press, 1935); and Theodore L. Reller, *The Development of the City Superintendency of Schools* (Philadelphia: the author, 1935).

for suppliers and materials. The citywide school boards grew in strength as they added four-year high schools and special programs other than those offered by the standard eight-year grammar schools. At the same time, many of the central boards consisted of delegates chosen by the ward boards.

There were various attempts to limit the power of central-city school boards. Callahan has described a plan to replace the city school board with an elected "school director" who alone would appoint the superintendent of instruction(11). Usually, however, efforts at power limitation took other directions; as urban school reformers concentrated on reducing the size of the city school boards, they meanwhile handed over to superintendents the tasks of personnel selection, materials-purchase, and direction of maintenance service, each of which had formerly led to sharp criticism of school boards for spoils politics. Local neighborhood boards were either abolished or reduced to advisory status. Assistants were added to the central staff to help the superintendents visit the schools and coordinate the new services, such as special and vocational education, as they were added.

Reformers insisted that "politics" be separated from the professional functions of school staff selection, supervision, retention, and promotion. Several cities adopted a "board of examiners" function, which paralleled civil service procedures. For example, the New York City reform charter read as follows:

> A board of examiners is hereby constituted whose duty it shall be to examine all applicants who are required to be licensed in and for the city of New York, and to issue to those who pass the required tests of character, scholarship, and general fitness, such licenses as they are entitled to receive(12).

The Bundy panel in New York City admitted that the system supplied outstanding educators, especially during the Depression years when only one of 400 applicants passed the exams to fill scarce teaching posts. But after World War II the supply of teachers shrank without a requisite shift in testing or recruiting procedures. Martin Mayer followed a series of survey reports on the examination system with his own acerbic critique:

> Like the former Chinese gentry, New York school administrators are ranked in a rigid hierarchy of status, achieved through the passage of Confucian examinations which fail to measure either the intellectual or temperamental qualities needed for the job(13).

The centralized personnel system, so effective at drawing the college-trained Irish and Jewish applicants, seemed unresponsive both to the shortages of the 1950's and to prospective Black and Puerto Rican aspirants of the 1960's. By 1967 pressures mounted to return many of the staff selection functions to the local community if not to the school itself.

In matters of finance, many city school systems relied on business managers who enjoyed status equal to that of the superintendent of instruction. Not until the 1960's did St. Louis, Cleveland, and Philadelphia abandon the "dual executive," and much was made of the 1947 appointment of Herold C. Hunt as Chicago's first General Superintendent(14).

Actually, the centralization of executive powers for the superintendent continued—at an uneven pace—well into the 1960's. The important point, in an era that now views "decentralization" as a reform, is that the centralizing tendency was encouraged not only by professionals but by laymen—including businessmen and civic reformers—who wanted vigorous executive leadership for the city school system. Decentralization of some functions, especially curriculum and teacher supervision (much less so in financial matters), was advocated in some cities but that option in 1963 was eclipsed by efforts to press for racial integration, a goal that was generally seen as a system-wide challenge.

This synopsis, a necessary foreshortening of a very complex set of trends, suggests only that for many decades superintendents had to compete first with the board and then with a co-equal business agent for the right to recommend teachers, administrators, buildings, and budgets. In areas where central leadership proved ineffective or inflexible, such as in teacher and principal selection and to an extent in curriculum modification, the reform ideology shifted with the new set of leaders calling for participation and, in fact, for "community control" at a level much closer to parents and pupils.

Superintendent Selection Patterns in Large Cities

Where do school boards find men who will assume the heavy responsibilities of a great city school superintendency? Why do some boards usually search outside the system for a new educational leader while others select local schoolmen? Richard Carlson studied the career patterns of school superintendents and noted a marked tendency for very large school systems to select insiders more often than outsiders (in school districts with a population over 500,000 citizens). He found that school boards usually hire insiders only when the judgment has been made that the schools have been properly administered and no major changes seem necessary. Boards often give outsiders a mandate for change, for expansion of staff and for program innovation. The insiders tend to be paid less, make fewer alterations in the rules, and usually stay in the job longer with little interest in moving. Carlson concludes that the outsider may be more innovative and creative than the insider who simply adapts to fit the office(15).

Superintendents in the largest cities, Carlson speculates, may no longer be looked to for innovation, and potential replacements (e.g., assistant superintendents) for the superintendent's central innovative role can be found in larger school systems. The job may not be so important as it once was (a suggestion not consistent with the preceding discussion of centralization) and the position in large cities may require a heavy public relations burden.

Actually, boards in various big cities behave differently. New York City acts as much like a collection of boroughs in 1968 as it did in 1898 at the time of merger; in a real sense it is an amalgam of four major cities, each with more than 200,000 children, plus the much smaller borough of Richmond (Staten Island). Virtually all of the school superintendents of New York City have risen from within the system. Of the two exceptions in this century, one was the son of an assistant superintendent, and the other served but a brief term during a period of great stress.

Anatomy of a Selection Decision

The patterns of superintendency selection may vary according to the way in which the city school board itself is selected.* The idea of a possible relationship between how a governing board is recruited and subsequent selection of superintendents was tested.

Fourteen boards are affiliated with the Research Council of the Great Cities Program for School Improvement. The cities are Baltimore, Boston, Buffalo, Chicago, Cleveland, Detroit, Houston, Los Angeles, Milwaukee, New York, Philadelphia, Pittsburgh, San Francisco, and St. Louis. Seven of these cities select the school board by popular election; seven use appointments by the mayor, mayor and council, or another group such as a court of common pleas (in Pittsburgh and, until 1965, Philadelphia). The data show that the appointive school boards tend to select outsiders as super-intendents at least half of the time; the elective school board members appoint more insiders by a large overall margin (see Table 2).

---

* This hypothesis grew out of conversations with Kenneth Prewitt, a political scientist at Stanford University and at the University of Chicago.

TABLE 2   The Sources of Great City School
Superintendents 1920–1969 by Appointive
and Elective Boards

Type of Board	Source of Superintendents (Summary)		
	Insiders	Outsiders	Totals
Appointive	20 (45%)	24 (55%)	44
Elective	25 (71%)	10 (29%)	35

$\chi^2 = 5.2$ (significant at the 0.3 level)

(Detail) Appointive	I	O	Elective	I	O
Baltimore	2	4	Boston	6	0
Buffalo	2	2	Cleveland	4	1
Chicago	2	4	Detroit	3	1
New York	5	2	Houston	2	3
Philadelphia	3	4	Los Angeles	4	2
Pittsburgh	3	3	Milwaukee	2	2
San Francisco	3	5	St. Louis	4	1
	20	24		25	10

Source: Joseph M. Cronin, "The Board of Education in
Great Cities; 1890–1964" (Ed.D. diss., Stanford University, 1965).

How can this be? Both types have numerous assistant superintendents and deputies in the wings! Both experience crises of
public confidence and need reform.

One parsimonious explanation grows out of the sheer fact that
elective officials must identify and satisfy a larger and perhaps
different popular constituency for reelection. Voters in large cities
frequently include large groups of public employees, teachers, and
other school workers. Voter turnout in school elections (especially
primaries) is often light and a sizeable bloc of public employees
may decide an election(16). Teachers (and custodians) may pass
the word concerning "our friends" and "our enemies." Recognition
of loyal insiders and the creation of a chain of vacancies is appreciated by ambitious men within. Furthermore, voting data are one
of the few ways to gauge one's popularity with the citizenry (and
staff).

Appointive members can ignore many of the pressures from
within the organization. Other indices of support such as tax or
bond elections count more. Appointive boards have less to lose
politically by virtue of their selection by designation. They may be

freer to seek for the superintendency a man with comparable experience elsewhere, a man with fewer ties to the local school staff constituency.

One test of this explanation of superintendent selection is a case study of an urban school board searching for a new superintendent. The case here summarized only in outline form dealt with a 1963 decision by a large city board of education to conduct a nationwide search for a superintendent.

Many had criticized the school system and its administration during the previous two years. Several daily newspapers ran series on the antiquated buildings and the League of Women Voters released a detailed critique of a teacher recruitment process tailored to the years of oversupply of the 1930's. A "citizens" group in 1961 had sponsored several reform candidates successfully. The mayor, the urban renewal leaders, and the analysts of municipal budgets each voiced criticisms of the schools.

The school board, at the urging of the citizen-sponsored minority, asked a prestigious university professor (a former city school superintendent) to help screen and evaluate the nominees. The most eligible outsiders and many insiders were interviewed and rated by the school board over a period of several months.

The pressure to appoint an outsider became intense at several points during the search and screening process. The newspaper editorials and public utterances of the citizens reform group at times grew shrill. Leaders of the local chapter of the National Association for the Advancement of Colored People stated publicly that they could see no insider who would or could help the urban Negro.

On the other side less was heard publicly, although the president of the teachers' union and other teachers wrote letters to the editor rebutting the assertion that only an outsider could rebuild the school system. The school board members recall that most of the sentiment on behalf of insiders was expressed privately or registered via the school board election toward the end of the search. One of the two citizens' candidates said that close friends questioned the wisdom of his willingness to hire a superintendent from outside the city, and he felt that the reduction in the size of his total vote could be interpreted as the reflection of displeasure at this readiness to reject the claims of "our own" candidates. This school board candidate had himself taught in the school system at one time.

During the summer, racial strife over the schools (lengthy negotiations followed by a boycott and sit-ins) caused the school board to respond defensively to proposals to select an outsider. One member suggested that during such a turbulent time it would be dangerous to experiment with an outsider. Another member expressed the view that it was wasteful to trade educators back and forth because much time was consumed in learning the system; furthermore, why should one rely on the opinions of people in other cities when one had at hand so many informed opinions of how a local educator handles responsibility in his own city?

The behavior of the leading (and successful) insider candidate is instructive. On the one hand, recognizing the groundswell of sentiment for change, he collected program ideas and wrote a lengthy proposal of changes he would make in the curriculum, personnel, and organization of the schools. On the other hand, few of the proposed changes could be interpreted as severe criticism of the incumbent. The point is that this candidate provided a blueprint for "change" which helped those who preferred an insider to reconcile his appointment with the clamor for school system improvements.

The press accounts of the search, of the racial strife, of the turmoil over the schools unquestionably shaped voter opinion on the legitimacy of the search and the extent to which changes were either desirable or tolerable. The working-class voters, and not a few from middle-income neighborhoods, reflected fear at the prospect of forced integration of white children with Negro children at the slum schools of the latter. Some observers feel that this issue made it more difficult to find sufficient votes for an outsider when sentiment gathered for the retention of existing school attendance procedures. The elective board member is quite willing to point to voting data as evidence of mandates either to change or to defend existing arrangements. Racial questions may tend to generate such "mandates."

This case demonstrates the way in which elective board members listen to and interpret voices from the people and from interested parties. It can also be argued that elective boards recruit new board members by a process through which candidates grow accustomed to listening to blocs of voters, including school employees, and other critics, and learn to balance their claims against those of editorial writers and bankers who live in suburbia(17).

Appointive board members may respond to voices and advice of their own choosing as long as the mayor or whoever else appoints them will give them a free hand in their work. Above a certain size (Herold Hunt suggests 200,000 population) perhaps only an appointive board can withstand the pressure to reward the locals(18).

End of an Era: Tenure and Turnover at the Top

Five men, all top executives in a great urban school system, enjoyed their leisurely lunch. Soon they would begin to play cards in the handsome second-floor clubroom reserved for their daily pastime. At about three o'clock, one of the top associates would slip out after explaining to the superintendent and others that someone was coming into the office for an appointment.

The year was 1962. City superintendents had not yet faced many civil rights sit-ins, teacher strikes, or student stalk-outs. New York City, maybe, could already feel the pressure, for the school integration battle lines had formed and the United Federation of Teachers had just won the first collective bargaining election. But Buffalo had had no strikes since 1947, and Baltimore, Boston, Cleveland, Detroit, Los Angeles, Milwaukee, Philadelphia, Pittsburgh, San Francisco, and St. Louis were untouched by teacher turbulence. Nor was it yet clear that city school populations in many of these city systems would so rapidly join Washington, D.C., in becoming predominantly Black.

In 1963, the civil rights movement moved North. Teacher unrest spread, although not for a few years would the American Federation of Teachers win a string of victories. John F. Kennedy was shot. A year later the War on Poverty was declared. Two years later the Elementary and Secondary Education Act took all the remaining moments of leisure away from superintendents with time on their hands. Superintendents like Pittsburgh's Sidney Marland or Philadelphia's Mark Shedd found themselves on one advisory commission after another. A.A.S.A. Presidents Brain (Baltimore) and Spears (San Francisco) found themselves in Washington,

D.C., testifying before Congress on one new law after another. As Bob Dylan wrote, the times they were a'changin.

Before 1963 the job of city school administrators was already more than challenging. Scarcity problems confronted them from every side: few were the cities after 1933 that could raise large chunks of revenue to replace the schools built in the 1875-1900 urban boom. The supply of experienced teachers was shrinking, especially during the 1950's as the suburbs burgeoned. Ford Foundation officials in the mid-1950's recognized the symptoms of decay and "funded" a Great Cities Grey Area program in Pittsburgh, Oakland, and New Haven, to see how schools could be used to reinvigorate aging communities. But the "urban crisis" was not yet a familiar cliché!

Exactly how secure was the urban superintendency before and after 1963? Some of the data reveal that a popular man could stay in the role for a decade or more. Few could rival the tenure of Detroit's popular Frank Cody, superintendent from 1919 to 1942, but job security for others was reasonably free from threats to the jugular.

Consider the long terms of these major city superintendents: Phillip Hickey in St. Louis for 22 years (1942–1964), Arthur Gould in Boston for 15 years (1937–1952), Robert T. Bapst in Buffalo for 13 years (1936–1949), Mark Schinnerer in Cleveland for 14 years (1947–1961), Earl A. Dimmock in Pittsburgh for 13 years (1945–1958), William Jansen in New York City for 11 years (1947–1958), Vierling Kersey in Los Angeles for 11 years (1937–1948), Allen Wetter in Philadelphia for 9 years (1955–1964). Cleveland hired but three superintendents in 41 years (1920–1961); then an NEA report in 1964 complained about having three superintendents in three years.

Not that a few durable giants did not extend their tenure beyond 1964—Buffalo's Joseph Manch from 1957 on, San Francisco's Harold Spears from 1955 to 1967, Milwaukee's Harold Vincent from 1950–1968, and Chicago's Benjamin Willis from 1953 to 1967 (not without terribly public disputes over how Willis should go)(19).

But even before World War II, Milwaukee had Milton Potter for 28 years. Baltimore had David Wegler for 21, Houston had E. E. Oberholtzer for almost the same time span (1924–1945), and

St. Louis, Chicago, and Pittsburgh still others for 12 years or more. A man could stay in office if he wanted, or he could accept a major university assignment. Herold Hunt left Chicago for Harvard in 1953 after 6 years, John Fisher left Baltimore for Columbia in 1958 after 5 years. Both men were at the height of popularity within their cities and within their profession (as A.A.S.A. presidents).

The 1960's were different in many ways from the 1933-1963 generation. Boston's William Ohrenburger (appointed in 1963) could look around the table at the Great Cities Research Council in 1969 and find himself in line to be the "dean" of major city school systems upon the retirement of Manch and Crowther of Los Angeles—by two years his senior. Men still retired, became consultants, or took distinguished professorships or deanships in about half of the cities. The turnover seemed much higher, however, and the reasons for departure much more vivid than formerly: George Brain left Baltimore in 1964 for a deanship following two incidents of physical attacks on his children; William Levenson resigned from Cleveland in 1964 after public criticism from the board chairman, after a racial crisis; Calvin Gross' New York City contract was not renewed by the board, which expected more rapid progress on several complex programs; C. Taylor Whittier's Philadelphia contract was not renewed by the new board whose president, a former mayor, wanted to make his own selection; Laurence Paquin of Baltimore died in office after illness; Fred Gillis of Boston went into mandatory retirement at the age of 70, having accepted the job at age 67 when the committee was deadlocked.

Actually, the number of changes in the large city superintendency was not that much higher than in previous eras. Perhaps it was the "way" a man went—with all the attendant publicity—and not the total turnover(20). Consider the actual number of superintendency selections in 14 "Great Cities" by decade:

Years	Number	Average Number of Appointments per City
1910–1919	23	1.6
1920–1929	15	1.0
1930–1939	12	0.9
1940–1949	16	1.1
1950–1959	15	1.0
1960–1969	18	1.3

It is true that the rate is up slightly in the 1960's—but by less than one-third over the norm. The decade climaxed by World War I was much more turbulent, possibly because that was the era of demand for efficiency described by Raymond Callahan in relation to the cycles of urban reform(21). "Efficiency" is always a popular shibboleth, but superintendents enjoyed longer terms in office after World War I.

But if the turnover rates are lower than conventional wisdom has suggested, the life of an urban school superintendent is nonetheless altered. The era of long lunches, if indeed more than a handful of city schoolmen ever took them, is probably over. The agitation and legislation of the 1960's required a new responsiveness and a reorganization of the superintendency role. Urban superintendents found it necessary to meet specific challenges and at the same time reduce their vulnerability to cries for removal from either staff or community.

The Urban Superintendency: The Organizational Response

Each challenge to the top leadership of city school systems has produced a response in terms of more elaborate staffing of the central administration. One recurring adaptation is the creating of special staff positions such as administrative assistants or directors. New positions tend to follow when new sources of money are provided and/or new demands for programs are made.

The Ford Foundation's Great Cities Grey Area program in several instances gave superintendents lead time of a few years in preparing for new projects. Although most of the superintendents themselves became heavily involved with new urban education ventures, inevitably other staff members had to be brought into the work to help with details of the proposals, program development, and implementation.

Few school systems were sufficiently organized to take a leading role in the "War on Poverty" resulting from the Economic Opportunity Act of 1964. Most cities used other social service agencies or formed new agencies to develop antipoverty programs, many of which involved children and education (tutoring, camps,

Head Start Centers, etc.). An aspect that made it difficult for officials to implement the program successfully was the idea of "maximum feasible participation of the poor"; this was a concept which educational professionals were not at once ready to accept either ideologically or organizationally.

Meanwhile, city school systems faced a barrage of demands for racial equality, sometimes by mail but increasingly in the form of sit-ins, boycotts, and demonstrations by Black citizens' groups —especially in the 1963-1966 period. Only New York City and a few other cities could boast of having wrestled earlier with the civil rights and integration questions; most cities were less attentive or had not been challenged as early and so were relatively unprepared for the crises. Leaders in at least a few large cities were also unwilling to make much of a response.

The Civil Rights Act of 1964 and the Elementary and Secondary Act of 1965 placed new pressures on the urban school superintendent. Staff time was needed to prepare for state or regional Civil Rights Commission Hearings on charges of discrimination in hiring or school zoning and districting. Staff time was needed to prepare detailed proposals for review by state and federal officials. Many hours were consumed by orientation meetings on federal and state guidelines and by subsequent negotiation sessions on the details and revision of proposals.

City school systems rarely have had strong planning divisions except, in some instances, for new school construction. Many of the older cities allowed these divisions to shrink during the war years. These cities built comparatively few new schools from 1940 to 1960. Program planning as a prerequisite to qualification for additional funds was for many a new challenge.

Many city school systems earlier had research offices, but their functions were largely those of statistical data-gathering for state and municipal reports. The new offices created, with titles such as "Assistant for Program Planning and Research," "Director of Special Projects," "Director of Federal-State-Local Relations" included the proposal-writing function which was necessary, especially to comply with Title I and Title III of the Elementary and Secondary Education Act.

Another specialized role created to strengthen the superintendency was that of "Director of Intergroup (or Human) Relations."

The major functions were those of dealing with militant Black groups (or with Mexican-American and/or Puerto Rican groups in a few cities), investigating charges of discrimination, and setting up programs for staff retraining in human relations. Much time and good will were needed as minority leaders argued for fundamental revision of staffing policies, school assignment policies, curriculum, and construction projects.

The Elementary and Secondary Education Act not only made cooperation with parochial schools possible; it mandated mutual discussion of several titles of the act with nonpublic school leaders. City superintendents had to affirm that diocesan school superintendents or their counterparts participated in program deliberation on the needs of the educationally disadvantaged, on school library acquisitions, and in the planning of educational innovations proposed for federal support. Some superintendents shaped as many as 30 or 40 program proposals in concert with nonpublic school leaders; others simply secured the token consent of a bishop or diocesan superintendent and, if state laws permitted, sent over the library books requested under Title II.

The new program and the new problems provoked adaptation in the office of the city school superintendency. The adaptations often required new staff assistants whose major and manifest function was to prepare detailed responses to the external challenges. A latent but vital function was serving as a buffer for the superintendent and his board against new and vocal critics: Black leaders, poverty councils, and those who used the nonpublic schools.

The new aides and directors also enabled superintendents to form *ad hoc* teams to deal with the recurring crises planned by minority group leaders. The teams could not free the superintendent from policy leadership, but they could at least work up the details and communicate with external leaders who above all else felt rage at the lack of school-system response.

During the 1960's teacher militancy also increased, most dramatically in New York City, but also in Chicago and in Philadelphia, where the American Federation of Teachers had strong local chapters. Teachers struck not only for higher salaries, but to secure representational selections and later to increase organizational security. New York City School Superintendent Calvin Gross warned his colleagues in other cities that they were "babes in the woods" compared to the highly experienced labor experts they would face from the organized teachers.

The early and emergency response to this problem was the hiring by superintendents of highly skilled labor relations counsels, attorneys, or professors who set up the procedures for elections and negotiations. But the hiring of *ad hoc* expertise for crises was not enough. The United Federation of Teachers employed full-time public relations men and other agents who in turn hired sociologists and economists, including former Presidential advisers, to prepare the case for expanding teacher welfare and salary benefits.

The administration response to this "escalation" was the appointment of directors of staff relations, sometimes in addition to directors of personnel who ministered the traditional functions of recruitment, placement, transfer, and promotion. The new offices had to cope with a year-round flow of grievances under the negoti-ated contracts, with the most controversial grievances reaching the central office level. The task of documenting the administrative position on grievances was time-consuming, with four or more steps culminating in the right to secure a final and binding decision from an external arbitrator.

Each of the contract negotiation sessions placed great stress on the central office. First one administrative group, then another, called for representation on the board's bargaining team—first, principals from each level, then supervisors and specialists. In each city the school business officials as well as the personnel officers were required to spend long periods of time first in preparation of background material and then in responding to the many dozens of contract demands.

Many of the sessions brought city school systems to the brink of strike, or over the edge (if mayors and governors considered the strike threat a bluff, or if they failed to help find the money fast enough). Between civil-rights boycotts on the one hand and teacher strike threats on the other, city superintendents saw large chunks of their time and staff time going to emergency planning just to keep the schools in operation. The staff acquired not only a "Cuban crisis" kind of solidarity, but also a "war room" style of operations, complete with maps, special phone listings and calls, and "round-the-clock" staffing for emergencies.

Neither the AFT (American Federation of Teachers) nor the NEA (National Education Association) placed limits either on the scope of negotiations or the tactics their leaders were willing to use. The AFT willingness to use the strike as an instrument to show force and build solidarity eventually provoked the NEA to drop its traditional no-strike policy. In Newark, New Jersey, in 1965, affiliates of both organizations called short strikes during the same year. The NEA field staff found it had no alternative but to support striking affiliates and finally voted for such a policy at its 1967 national convention. Nowhere was the competition between the teacher groups as marked as in the state of Michigan, where teacher strikes of both affiliates were frequent after 1965. But the new militancy of the NEA also became manifest in slashing reports on city school systems, boards, and superintendents (as in the case of Detroit in 1967). City superintendents, so long the backbone of the NEA, began to pull away—as symbolized first by the disbanding of the Educational Policies Commission, a forum that teachers and administrators had co-sponsored for several decades; and later by a withdrawal to "affiliate status" as one step toward a total break.

The responses to teacher critics and to other cries for change included the hiring of public information officers to serve the board and superintendent. Such new jobs could be justified partly by the increasing difficulty of "telling the school story" in the face of newspaper and television stories dramatizing dissatisfaction with the status quo. One large system jettisoned its stodgy report format in favor of a rotogravure publication stressing university projects and dozens of innovations. Another big city superintendent admitted, "We try to have at least one pilot program of every new innovation somewhere in the city, in case someone comes out with a blast in the media."

So the new pressures and protests provoked a strengthening, even a further centralizing, of the top staff surrounding the superintendent. Proposal writers, negotiators, troubleshooters, and public relations men were added—not only to get the job done, but to provide more communications and to strengthen the capacity of the superintendent himself to cope with conflict. They reduced the political vulnerability of the superintendent while enabling the school system either to solve a problem or stall until solutions or funds became available.

Superintendents as Agents of Political Stability

The structural strengthening of the superintendent's office may not explain all of the stability of big-city superintendents. An additional explanation has to do with the personalities of the superintendents themselves, so often men of extraordinary stamina and uncommon sense. Both Herold Hunt and Benjamin Willis thought nothing of devoting 75 hours of work per week on Chicago schools. Others manifest similar staying power, forceful personalities, and skill in dealing with top associates.

Still another explanatory factor is the general style of leadership adopted by many of the most competent men. Superintendents, with rare exceptions:

1. Avoid the appearance of political activity while, in fact, practicing to a high degree the skills of legislative lobbying and "public relations";
2. Control the agendas of boards while allowing the board to take the criticism on most controversial issues (especially the taboo-ridden topics surrounding race, religion, and sex);
3. Mediate or otherwise manage (contain) conflict rather than generate controversial programs.

Educators since the nineteenth century have struggled to wrest educational and personnel decisions away from the "politicians." The slogan most commonly heard is, "Keep education out of politics." This was the recommendation of Joseph Mayer Rice in the 1890's, and urban school reformers since that era continued the fight to curb the politicians' influence(22). Even Fiorello LaGuardia was chastized by the National Education Association for meddling in the affairs of New York City Schools(23).

Nevertheless, H. Thomas James has found that each city school system assigned at least one top administrator to the job of legislative liaison in the state capital. Others report that occasionally a key school business official has taken this assignment. From time to time the head lobbyist eventually becomes superintendent(24). The job is not limited to initiating and promoting new legislation; it also entails the identification and arrest or modification of legislation that would hurt the system as presently constituted. City school systems wish to have a say in virtually all changes in structures or rules affecting them.

On the one hand, superintendents of schools preside over a "sacred" trust, presumably a function far removed from the logrolling atmosphere of a legislature. On the other hand, education, especially finance, has its "secular" side. However, the lobbyist role of city school systems is usually kept as quiet as possible.

Another important function adaptive to the delicate position of a "non-political" political institution is the board-superintendent relationship. Except in Los Angeles, where standing committees are numerous, the use of sub-committees has been reduced so that the board meets as a whole, with the superintendent (and staff) always present. This technique increases the opportunity for a school executive to control not only the flow of information but the chance to monitor school board discussions closely and modify action.

Chicago may provide the best example of a superintendent's tight rein over the meeting agenda. Joseph Pois, a former school board member complained bitterly about the amount of board time spent on business details which allowed more basic educational policy issues to pass by with very limited discussion(25). Eventually even the two major public budget hearings were run by the superintendent. Securing "control over agenda" reduces the surprises to the school staff. In effect, a superintendent tries to reinforce what he views as "desirable" board behavior.

On the other hand, superintendents may wish to put the board out in front on matters of racial, budgetary, and social importance —the latter term covering both sex education proposals and Black teacher recruitment. For example, Robert Crain and others have found that the school board was the critical variable in explaining school system response to requests for racial integration. In fact, they report that civil rights groups registered superintendents' responses as unacceptable, that ". . . the school superintendent, in almost every one of our cases, has found that racial policy was taken from his hands by the school board"(26). Either the school board handled negotiations or used an *ad hoc* committee to secure advice in the eight cities studied. Superintendents in only two of the eight cities appeared to retain influence with the committee on this matter. Crain's verdict on the superintendency is too sweeping:

> It is commonly assumed that school superintendents exert much more influence over the policy of the school system than does the school board. Our data show the precise opposite. The school board sets the tone of the integration decision and the superintendent plays a less important role(27).

The judgment of Joseph Pois may be more accurate, namely that boards allow superintendents more leeway in policy areas when the members have insufficient time for debate—and the time is insufficient mainly because board agendas grow heavy with minor business items. Racial integration was so highly charged an issue that boards were forced to take on the role of buffer and arbitrator. Indicative of the charged nature of the issue and responsive to it is the use by several major universities of test questions on racial problems (even on doctoral admissions forms), the addition of courses on racial policy, and the increased recruitment of nonwhite administrators by both universities and cities. In fact, the hiring of Black administrative assistants or directors in many cities grew directly out of confrontations. Perhaps superintendents may find themselves better prepared to render leadership even on race crises in the next decade, thanks both to the new awareness of their university preparation and to the presence of nonwhite administrators on their staffs.

The Crain study may over-generalize the discovery of "color-blind" superintendents. Roscoe Hill and Malcolm Feeley report strong leadership by integrationist superintendents in Berkeley, New Haven, and Pasadena. Shortly afterward the men in those cities were offered Detroit, Baltimore, and San Francisco superintendencies, and Chicago hired a well-known urban school integrationist(28).

Nevertheless, it is hypothesized that certain issues affecting "taboo" topics or controversy—issues around sex, race, family, and religion—may gravitate away from the superintendent toward the board. In other words, the "sacred" or sensitive social issues require judgments by the citizen elite, whereas the "secular" (rational, professional, e.g., curriculum, buildings, personnel) issues are dominated by the superintendent and his staff.

The third form of adaptation to political life by superintendents is that of service as mediator. Superintendents often receive contradictory sets of signals, to raise expenditure and cut total costs simultaneously, or to change a program and to keep it the same. Given impossible choices, superintendents will often "buy time" by calling for staff study or committee review and perhaps a hearing at some later point in time. In certain areas, superintendents drop the role of "advocate" and instead try to work out some kind of an agreeable compromise—whether in program matters or in personnel. This conciliatory posture annoys ideologues, some of whom call for a forthright stand on issues (as Harold Howe II demanded of superintendents in 1968). Superintendents frequently quit over matters of principle, but they quit still more often over disagreements relating to such an issue as board interference with personnel appointments. Disagreements over issues such as racial integration are less likely to result in a superintendent's resignation. The superintendent serves more often as referee than as policy advocate, more steadily as judge between rival advocates than as initiator of new proposals.

Carl Hansen, formerly superintendent of schools in Washington, D.C. (until he wanted to appeal the Hobson case verdict), certainly advocated particular programs of his own, such as the Amidon Plan and tracking of students. But he admits to helping persuade the board of education to accept a model subsystem with federal money to finance an assistant superintendent, an advisory committee, directors, and aides(29). Although he later decided that using decentralization was a wasteful attempt to raise the level of achievement, he nevertheless went along with it, even reassuring the board that the new organizational form had potential, in hopes that it might help children.

Mark Shedd, Philadelphia superintendent, stopped short of "throwing out the experts" but adapted to community ferment by allowing students and parents to help redefine education. He authorized a substantial number of programs to reach Black students. The system awarded small grants to teachers and schools for innovative project ideas. During an era of high turbulence, Shedd redefined the work of his central office as "a service agency, instead of a controlling agency"(30). This adaptation to demands for community participation accompanied a willingness to decentralize decisions and planning. Shedd, therefore, let others try to veto programs. He viewed his role as one of decreasing the decision-making burden on his office. The movement for community control in more than one city demanded this flexible a response as a prize for allowing the regime to continue.

Conclusion: An Assessment of Urban School Systems

City superintendents may have survived, but their systems lost the innovative edge and reputation for performance. Federal housing and transportation policies drained the cities of the more mobile members of older ethnic groups. National economic trends, including state welfare plans and employment opportunities, lured new racial and ethnic groups to the cities and to their public schools.

One of the most skillful insiders admitted a lack of responsiveness in city school systems themselves. Bernard E. Donovan of New York in 1967 stated that

> . . . fundamentally the public schools have not changed to meet this rapidly changing society. This is particularly true of public school systems in large cities. I say this with full knowledge of the many, many innovative devices, procedures and concepts which have been introduced into the public schools of large cities by forward-looking and dedicated staff members. But I repeat, the general pattern of the public school has not changed to meet a vastly changing society(31).

Only a few savants see the superintendency as the problem; some want to alter the board functioning somehow. For example:

1. The Bundy Plan for Decentralization in New York City retains the superintendency although giving much more power to district boards and "community superintendents"(32).
2. Allen Talbot urges the opening up of the city school superintendency to professionals other than teachers and to businessmen(33). Citing the rapid turnover of superintendents in such cities as New Haven and Baltimore, Talbot urges experimentation with mid-career training opportunities to get

new men into school administrative positions instead of relying so exclusively on the pool of teachers and principals.
3. Luvern Cunningham, Edwin Fensch, and others urge recon-
ceptualization of the superintendency as a "team" rather than
as an individual position(34). A new man must be allowed to
bring in trusted top assistants. The top staff each contribute
specialities and share cabinet-style in certain major decisions
and many minor ones. In each era a few superintendents
manage to bring in allies (Carlson noted that outsiders are
more likely to add staff than are insiders, as did Frank
Spaulding in the first quarter of this century(35). Once again,
the more drastic reforms are of the board itself.

Some would do away with city boards of education, letting the
superintendent report either to the mayor or to the governor or
state education department. Political scientists, especially public
administration experts, have long urged such a step. One of the
more verbally violent epitaphs appeared in a volume on city
management over 30 years ago.

> In general, the urban school board is one of those
> instruments of tortuous propensities which, beaming with an
> unbecoming and reflected wisdom, wanders in a twilight zone
> between civic grandeur and political connivance. Undoubtedly,
> some future public appraisal beyond the board's discernment,
> will snuff it out(36).

Educators only rarely expressed any support for the abolition
of school boards, Charles Judd in the 1930's being one of the few
exceptions(37). A variant would be to combine education with
related "human resources enterprises." Others would strengthen
the board by building its separate research capability. An "evaluation team," presumably with experts in program evaluation and
financial cost effectiveness, would present a board the information
they need.

Of course, such a proposal would draw fire from the superintendent's coterie of assistants, who would see it as an incursion into
their prerogatives. They would ask such questions as: Must there
be an overlap of responsibilities? Would not this undermine confidence in the board's own staff? The reply would be: Not necessarily. Since 1911 city school boards have employed external teams of
evaluators, the most prolific of which emerged under the leadership

of George D. Strayer of Columbia, who led dozens of "school survey teams" in the 1930's and 40's. Such studies often took one or two years to complete and provided major blueprints for action on several fronts—program, reorganization, finance, personnel, etc. In effect, these study teams provided *ad hoc* evaluation and development services which provoked much controversy and some bitterness with city school staffs. The studies also provided useful "mandates for action" to new superintendents, especially the outsiders. In the 1960's the large management consulting firms such as McKinsey Associates and Booz, Allen and Hamilton performed this function, for very few educators would lead more than one big school survey per lifetime (Havighurst of Chicago, Odell of Philadelphia, Passow of the District of Columbia).

The other parallel is the U.S. Bureau of the Budget which checks on the agency staffs of every federal department and autonomous body. No expenditure gets executive approval without B.O.B. scrutiny. In effect, this "watchdog function" resembles on a larger scale the mini-B.O.B.'s that urban school boards need. Such an agency might force a superintendent and staff to justify programs, explain alternatives, and secure board approval on a more rational basis. Of course, no organizational solution alone will suffice; evaluation experts ("evaluation" in a sense much larger than "measurement") are rare, and judgment is a precious commodity.

Lay boards of education may vanish, either because of full state support or a blurring of "community lines," consolidation of functions with other human services, or a combination of these (e.g., mental health and many welfare functions have become state rather than local responsibility). Part of the superintendent's future is linked to that of urban and metropolitan areas generally. The superintendency—despite past durability—may fade rapidly, given a massive shake-up of governmental forms.

The crucible of urban politics in the late 1960's grew unbearably hot for both mayors and superintendents. A few educators and critics began to speak vigorously for proposals to rescue urban education, if not the officials under pressure. Perhaps the time had come, in Hodges' terms, for "some future public appraisal, beyond the board's discernment . . ."(38). The New York State legislature in May of 1969 succumbed to sustained pressures for decentralization by changing the board's form for the second time in a decade and by abolishing the superintendency (a successor would be designated "chancellor"). For a time the state entertained the notion of a small but full-time commission to rule the schools (the commission approach to city management proper early in the century attracted far fewer permanent advocates than the city manager form). But the state decided to retain one chief educational executive for New York City even if the term superintendent would henceforth refer to the leaders of the 30 or more community school districts (none smaller than 20,000 pupils) within the five boroughs.

During the 1950's and 1960's many more cities and counties fought against "metropolitanism" than adopted the idea of a larger unit of school governance. Except in a few Southern states, citizens of suburbs resisted such formal alliances with core cities and their school systems. City school systems were left to fend for themselves.

The prospect of tax-sharing arrangements between federal and state governments may allow the latter to assume all or most of the funding of urban education. In a period of sharply rising teacher and community expectations for higher pay and improved services in the urban crucible, the pressures may otherwise grow unbearable. Youngstown, Ohio, actually experienced in 1969 the closing of schools for lack of funds, and Philadelphia citizens were at least alerted to that possibility. Yet with states generating the financial resources, some of the leverage of city school superintendents over staff and board may diminish. At the same time, parent and community leaders will insist on greater attention to their children's special needs.

Simultaneously, the professionalization of other urban services (from health and housing to transportation and manpower planning) may help to reduce the gap separating education from other "non-political" functions. The need for concerted planning and mutual collaboration among staffs may require the end to the separatism of school leaders so long deplored by public administrators. Judd used this argument to justify the phasing out of school boards in the 1930's. The "new breed" of mayors in the 1960's found it logical to link education to health, medical, housing, and renewal programs. In the future, community leaders, inspired by their poverty councils and model cities planning experiences, may insist upon the fusion of related human services in order to better serve their families and neighborhoods. At that point the superintendent may find himself one of many department heads—paid largely by state or federal funds. Despite the past durability of the office, a massive shakeup of geo-governmental forms could reduce further the vulnerability and visibility of the urban superintendency as a unique and separate entity.

Notes

1. Nathan Glazer and Daniel P. Moynihan, *Beyond the Melting Pot: The Negroes, Puerto Ricans, Jews, Italians and Irish of New York City* (Cambridge, Mass.: MIT Press, 1963), 360 pp.

2. Edward Banfield, *Big City Politics: A Comparative Guide to the Political Systems of Atlanta, Boston, Detroit . . .* (New York: Random House, Inc., 1965), 149 pp.

3. *American School Board Journal*, XI, No. 2, pp. 8f.

4. Raymond E. Callahan, "The Fight to Control Policy," in *Struggle for Power in Education*, ed. Frank Lutz and Joseph Azzarelli (New York: The Center for Applied Research in Education, 1966), pp. 22–30.

5. Ibid., p. 29.

6. Luvern Cunningham, "Community Power: Implications for Education," in *The Politics of Education in the Local Community*, eds. Robert S. Cahill and Stephen P. Hencley (Danville, Ill.: The Interstate Printers and Publishers, Inc., 1964), pp. 47f.

7. See Robert L. Morlan, "Toward City School District Rapprochement," *Public Administration Review*, Vol. 15 (Spring 1958), pp. 113–117.

8. This development in fourteen major cities (some not until the 1920's) is more leisurely described in Joseph M. Cronin, *Big City School Boards* (New York: The Free Press), forthcoming.

9. This is just the opposite task from Callahan's in *Education and the Cult of Efficiency* which stresses the vulnerability of the incumbents. It is true that many fire chiefs and city engineers enjoy more political security, but few top city administrators with boards are paid more homage and money or last longer in the job than urban school superintendents.

10. As of 1966 only 40 percent of the cities with more than 5000 population employed city managers (50 percent of those over 10,000). Only five of the 26 cities of over 50,000 people had city managers (*The Municipal Yearbook* [Chicago: International City Managers Association, 1966], p. 90) The National Municipal League keeps careful tract of "black sheep" or "back sliders" in pamphlets entitled *Manager Plan Abandonments* updated periodically by Arthur W. Bromage.

11. Callahan, in Lutz and Azzarelli, op. cit., pp. 21f.

12. Mark Ash and William Ash, *The Greater New York Charter as Enacted in 1897 and Amended in 1901* (Mount Kisco, N.Y.: Baker, Voorhis & Co., Inc., 1906), pp. 782f.

13. Martin Mayer, "Close to Midnight," *The New York Times,* May 2, 1965, as quoted in the Bundy Report, McGeorge Bundy (Chairman), Alfred A. Giardino, Francis Kepfel, Antonia Pantoja, Mitchell Svindoff, Bennetta B. Washington, *Reconnection for Learning: A Community School System for New York City* (New York: Mayor's Advisory Panel on Decentralization of the New York City Schools, 1967), p. 45.

14. Harry B. Wilson, "Toughest School Job in the Country," *The Saturday Evening Post,* CCXXIII, October 7, 1950, pp. 29ff.

15. Richard O. Carlson, *Executive Succession and Organizational Change: Place-Bound and Career-Bound Superintendents of Schools* (Chicago: Midwest Administration Center, The University of Chicago, 1962). Subsequent studies by Laurence Iannaccone and James Reynolds suggested even more strongly than a mandate for change provokes a search for a new man whom the board expects to propose a larger number of innovations than expected of insiders.

16. Edward Banfield and James Q. Wilson, *City Politics* (Cambridge, Mass.: Harvard University Press and MIT Press, 1963), cf., Chap. 15, pp. 214–15.

17. Those members who seem especially sensitive to the need to reward school employees more adequately might be termed "benefactors," i.e., those who confer benefits. Those who are responsive to claims for community-wide rationality and fiscal responsibility can be labelled "guardians." (From J. M. Cronin, "A Typology of School Board Members," Harvard University, 1966, unpublished manuscript.)

18. This and several other cases will appear in Alan K. Campbell's case book on urban school decision-making (Syracuse, N.Y.: Syracuse University Press), forthcoming.

19. See Michael Usdan and Lee Anderson Case, "The Anatomy of a Compromise," in the Alan K. Campbell case book, op. cit.

20. At least two big city superintendents left office with the clamor of civil rights critics too clear to ignore.

21. During this time in Baltimore, one school superintendent (a reformer) was fired, his successor retired for ill health, and the next man was removed by a reform mayor. Boston had one interim man and then an outsider (1912–1918), its last venture into the hiring of an outside superintendent. In Chicago, Ella Flagg Young was forced to resign, John Schoop died in office, and Charles Chadsey enjoyed only a short regime that was climaxed by his removal which is described vividly by George Counts in *School and Society in Chicago* (New York: Harcourt, Brace and Co., 1928), 367 pp. What's remarkable is the great stability of the era 1920 to 1963, and the relative invulnerability of superintendents as compared to either city managers or mayors.

22. Joseph Mayer Rice, *The Public School System of the United States* (New York: The Century Co., 1893).

23. National Commission for the Defense of Democracy Through Education, *Interference with the Independence of the New York City Board of Education,* Report of an Investigation (Washington, D.C.: The National Education Association, 1944).

24. H. Thomas James et al., *The Determination of Educational Expenditures in Large Cities of the United States* (Stanford, Calif.: School of Education, Stanford University, 1966).

25. Joseph Pois, *School Board Crisis: A Chicago Case Study* (Chicago: Educational Methods, 1964).

26. Robert Crain, *The Politics of School Desegregation* (Chicago: Aldine Publishing Company, 1968), p. 358.

27. Ibid.

28. Roscoe Hill and Malcolm Feeley, *Affirmative School Integration* (Beverly Hills, Calif.: Sage Publications, 1968).

29. Carl F. Hansen, *Danger in Washington* (West Nyack, N.Y.: Parker Publishing Co., 1968), Chap. 8, pp. 127–37.

30. Mark R. Shedd, "Recreating the City Schools," *Pennsylvania School Journal,* October 1968 (reprinted in the Harvard Graduate School of Education Association *Bulletin,* XII, No. 3, Spring 1969, pp. 2–7).

31. Bernard E. Donovan, "The Role of a School System in a Changing Society," conference at the Lincoln Center, New York City, June 15, 1967, p. 1, as reported in the Bundy Report, op. cit., p. 72.

32. Bundy Report, op. cit.

33. Allen R. Talbot, "Needed, a New Breed of School Superintendent," *Harper's Magazine,* No. 232, February 1966, pp. 81f.

34. Edwin A. Fensch and Robert E. Wilson, *The Superintendency Team: Organization and Administration of a School System's Central Staff,* (Columbus, Ohio: Charles E. Merrill Publishing Company, 1964).

35. Frank Spaulding, *School Superintendents in Action in Five Cities* (Rindge, N. H.: Richard R. Smith Co., Inc., 1966), 699 pp. Janowitz complained that "A whole generation of top administrators seems destined to retire or circumvent, rather than re-orient. The successful big-city superintendent is the man who can in advance bargain for the conditions to eliminate the old guard" (Morris Janowitz, "Alternative Models of Change for Inner-City Schools," in *The Quality of Inequality: Urban and Suburban Public Schools,* ed. Charles O. Daly [Chicago: The University of Chicago Center for Policy Study, 1968], p. 148).

36. Henry G. Hodges, *City Management,* (New York: F. S. Crofts and Co., 1939), pp. 680f. The subsequent survival of city school boards is documented in Joseph M. Cronin, "Why City School Boards Change" *Urban Education,* Spring 1966.

37. Charles Judd's proposals appeared while he was director of the Department of Education at the University of Chicago. He spoke out first in several publications read by city managers ("Abolish the School Boards," *Public Management,* Vol. 15 [November 1933] pp. 321ff., and Vol. 16 [January, 1934], pp. 19ff., and "School Boards as an Obstruction to Good Administration," *Nation's Schools,* Vol. 13 [February 1934], pp. 13–15).

One of the most recent articles is by Robert H. Salisbury, "Schools and Politics in the Big City," *Harvard Educational Review,* Vol. 37, No. 3 (1967), pp. 408–424. For earlier comments, see J. M. Cronin, "The Board of Education in the Great Cities, 1890–1964," (Ph.D. diss., Stanford University, 1965).

38. Hodges, op. cit.

10

A Big City Mayor Tries His Hand at School Reform

*David S. Seeley**

Introduction

In the spring of 1967 New York's Mayor John V. Lindsay crossed the Rubicon dividing the world of politics and the world of education and committed himself to a major campaign into school territory—a commitment from which he would not be able to turn back until both he and the school system were badly battered.

Why did he do it? What did he want to achieve? How did he intend to achieve it? And what finally happened? How do we assess this extraordinary attempt of a mayor of a major city to cross the sacred boundary between politics and education and make fundamental changes in the city's public school system?

The Education-Politics Boundary—New York Style

One might have thought that New York City would have been ahead of the rest of the nation in rejecting the sacred boundary between education and politics as a myth. Many things done behind the scenes in other cities are done openly in the raw and brutal politics of New York City. No one in New York expects

* David S. Seeley held the post of Director of Education Liaison in the Lindsay administration between July 1967, and August 1968.

idealism when it comes to politics; however, the prohibition against political interference in education is stronger, if anything, in New York than elsewhere.

The memories of the spoils system and Boss Tweed are still strong in the minds of New Yorkers. New York's Tammany has long been the textbook symbol of nepotism, bribery, and dirty politics. There are dozens of civic groups to remind residents of the corruption they say will flood the city if the dikes of good government are weakened. The merit system has attained a revered status —even more so in the school system where it is felt that defenseless childrens' lives will be violated if politicians are ever allowed to get their hands on school affairs.

Added to the traditional fear of the spoils system, a more recent concern for academic freedom also strengthens the boundary between education and politics. New York likes to think of itself as a liberal city. New Yorkers look with horror upon the right-wing book burners who have won school board elections in some school districts across the nation. The fear is that if politicians are ever allowed to tamper with the city schools they might be like these "marauders." The feeling is that not only must all good New Yorkers fight against encroachments from the mayor and the City Council, they must fight against any kind of political interference with the schools.

As a result, New York mayors have learned not to meddle openly in school affairs. They have not refrained from maneuvers behind the scenes when they could get away with it, but watchdog groups have kept their eye on any encroachment. As recently as the Wagner administration, just before Mayor Lindsay's term, education groups forced the mayor to agree to a lump-sum budget procedure, so that even the city administration's one legal responsibility for schools could be exercised only to decide the total amount of money to be appropriated and not how it should be spent.

Mayor Lindsay's Decision

Why did Mayor Lindsay decide to cross the formidable school-political boundary in New York?

For one thing, it is probable that Mayor Lindsay was not as conscious of the depths of feeling in this area as other mayors might have been because he was not the traditional New York politician. He ran as a congressman from the "silk stocking" distict, where many influential supporters had their children in private schools and tended to look with disdain upon the "civil service mentality." He came from the upper crust of New York society, far removed from the culture of the public school system. Many of his key staff members were equally removed, or they were outsiders who had to get their feel for New York politics secondhand.

Furthermore, Lindsay ran as a reform mayor. He had other political instincts, valid in their own right, which were vindicated at the polls. The Black and Puerto Rican groups, recognizing increasingly that the only hope they had for the future was being blocked by poor schools, were in rebellion. The rebellion had been raging for several years, becoming most dramatic in the integration boycotts of the early 60's. But underlying the integration issue and finally sweeping through and around it was the anger and frusturation that the great bulk of Black and Puerto Rican youngsters simply were not being educated adequately—many not even learning to read effectively by the time they reached adulthood at 17 or 18.

Even the white population was becoming alarmed. Many of those who were seriously dissatisfied with the public school system had their own children enrolled in private schools or had moved to the suburbs. But even these people were concerned that unless something was done to improve public school education, there would be no end to the growth of welfare, crime, and drugs, no end to the resulting rise in their taxes, and no end to the social turmoil building up because of the Black and Puerto Rican rebellion over the schools.

It was becoming evident that integration would not provide the answer. The lower and lower-middle class groups, who were those most likely to be asked to integrate, were shedding the facade of liberalism and making clear their objection to any invasion of their neighborhoods. Even those who retained their liberal principles (who usually were not asked to integrate) began to see that at best no more than a token number of the youngsters in the great ghettoes could have their education improved through integration.

There was then, by the mid-60's, a great frustration in both the Black and white communities over education to which Lindsay was responding as a candidate. The public demanded that something be done about the schools, almost in the same way that a few years later the public would demand that something be done about "law and order." It was not at all clear just what the public demanded be done, but the issue could no longer be avoided. Lindsay as a candidate made it clear that as a reform mayor he would include education along with welfare, housing, unemployment, and all the other urban ills he would tackle if elected.

In the context of 1965 it was almost as if the old fears of political interference in education had been superseded by a widespread recognition that the school crisis was no longer just an educational issue, but a first-class social issue that affected the entire fabric of the city and to which the Mayor was expected to address himself.

Beyond the political instinct that led Lindsay to feel he must address himself to the school crisis—and that indeed in the crisis atmosphere he could get away with violating the traditional school-political boundary—Lindsay was personally convinced in his own mind that something had to be done about the schools. Lindsay's reformism was genuine. He had deep feelings and deep sensitivity for the problems of the poor. The plight of the Black and Puerto Rican youngsters in the city was truly pitiable. Many people (including Blacks and Puerto Ricans) had given up hope that anything could be done about it. But Lindsay would not accept such defeatism. He saw that what was happening to minority youth in the city was a slow death, both for the youth and for the city. Any man of compassion would have to do whatever he could to correct the matter, and Lindsay viewed it as part of his leadership role to arouse the city from its cynicism and reform its long-neglected school system.

New York, therefore, even though it had perhaps as strong a tradition of separation of politics from education of any city in the nation, became the first city in recent times in which a mayor has plunged openly and forcefully into school reform. This was partly because New York was the first city in which the school crisis reached such unbearable proportions, but it was also because a candidate for mayor arrived on the scene who was willing to grasp this difficult political nettle.

The Mayor's Strategy— Or Lack Thereof

Although Lindsay was elected on a platform that included school reform, it was not at all clear what actions he would take when he became Mayor. There were, after all, dozens of other problems that cried out for action in addition to education, and Lindsay was elected Mayor more because people sensed his genuine commitment to face up to these problems than because he presented convincing formulas for finding the solutions.

There were, nevertheless, a number of principles and styles of the Lindsay administration which governed the course he would take in tackling school reform. The most evident of these was his style of activism: Any action is better than no action. He would rather see mistakes made than see inaction. This was the style that appealed to people who had lost confidence in the more cautious politicians of recent years. The feeling didn't carry over once the mistakes started piling up, but it gave a heady and hopeful aura to the beginning of the Lindsay administration.

Closely related to the style of activism, was the Mayor's open emphasis on the problems of the Negro. He had been elected, after all, partly because of people's anxiety about the social revolt in the ghetto. Later, many would turn on him for giving too much to "them" and neglecting the interests of other groups in the city. But in the beginning, it might almost be said he had a mandate from Blacks and whites alike to make the problems of the ghetto a top priority.

The combination of activism and emphasis on the ghetto were also tied in with Mayor Lindsay's much heralded style of personal charisma and courage. His walks through the ghetto showed that he could stand tall while everyone else cringed in doorways. If lesser men had given up hope, he would show that the city's problems could be solved with a combination of compassion, courage, and the will to act. This style gave the Mayor the strength to wade into problems that others consider hopeless, but it also tended to make him overly disdainful of the real problems that often justified the caution of other politicians.

In addition to the Mayor's charisma and courage, there were two other related styles of his administration which strongly affected his actions on the schools. One was his suspicion of the "old bureaucracy" and his preference for bright, "tough-minded" outsiders as his key staff aides. The other was his suspicion of the older style politicians who knew all the old ways of getting things done, but also all the old reasons why many things couldn't be done. As things turned out, Lindsay relied heavily on the hip-pocket advice of his own new group of "back room boys," but he liked to think of his administration in terms of principled, rational solutions, devised by his new "urbanists" or by blue ribbon panels of experts, and applied with vigor and courage, regardless of the political or bureaucratic consequences under the old rules.

Lastly, was the policy of the Lindsay administration which would play such an important role on the issue of decentralization: the preference for local action and responsibility. Not only was Lindsay suspicious of the old bureaucracy he inherited from his predecessors, but of all big central bureaucracies. He was aware that central administration could not be done away with; in fact he set about centralizing it even further in his great "super agencies." But he remained suspicious of it and felt that the real life of the city had to be rebuilt from the bottom up. This preference showed itself in his proposals for "little city halls" and the community corporations in the poverty program, as well as in the decentralization of the school system.

While Lindsay, then, did not have a well-worked out strategy for dealing with school issues, it can be said that he had a style and a set of related principles of operation that to a large degree determined his actions in relation to the various opportunities for educational reform open to the Mayor.

One of the reasons why it was difficult for the Mayor to have an educational strategy was that school reform initiated by a mayor was unknown territory. The mayor in New York had no legal responsibility for the schools, except for providing the budget. The New York Board of Education is an independent body, defined in state law to be an agency of the state government rather than of the city government. Before the new decentralization law, the members of the Board were appointed by the mayor, but only from a list of candidates presented by a statutory blue ribbon panel and for seven years terms, giving a new mayor little opportunity to develop a Board loyal to him.

Mayor Lindsay, therefore, for all his deep concern about the school crisis and his election pledge to do something about it, found himself with little opportunity to take direct action on school reform. The main areas open to him were in the budget process, where he had an official responsibility, and the issues of poverty and decentralization, where history presented him with new opportunities for educational reform. It was in the interplay between the overall style and policies of the Lindsay administration on the one hand, and these three areas of action on the other—budget, poverty, and decentralization—that the Mayor's strategy for school reform took shape.

School Reform
Through the Budget

The fact that in New York the mayor must approve the budget for the Board of Education gives the city administration less power in school affairs than might be expected. "He who controls the purse strings controls the program" tends to be superseded by the tradition of noninterference by the mayor. As reported above, the school system and the educational civic groups had won from Mayor Wagner the right to a "lump sum" budget, and many have maintained that state law in any case protects the right of the school system to spend its money however it wants, without regard to the city's budget categories.

Nevertheless, Mayor Lindsay had some things going for him in tackling the Board of Education budget. During the ten years before he was elected, the school budget had soared from $310,000,000 to over a billion dollars. There was increasing evidence that funds were being wasted through ineffective programs and slipshod management. Certainly the improvements that might have been expected from such an increase in expenditures were not forthcoming, and in many respects the school system was deteriorating. The combination of revolt against skyrocketing taxes and anxiety over mounting unsolved educational problems provided a climate favorable for remedial action.

The new budget director, Fred Hayes, one of the Mayor's ablest assistants, with an impressive record in the federal Budget Bureau, was determined to apply the concept of productivity throughout the city's chaotic budget process, including the budget for the school system.

Progress was made in budget reform up through the early part of 1967. The new policies were still not effectively penetrating the morass of vested interests and inertia that sapped the productivity of the school system, but Hayes' eager staff members were sharpening their tools for screening the multi-million dollar budget requests for bureaus and programs presented by the school system. The Board of Education itself decided to institute a program planning and budgeting system (PPBS) similar to the one Hayes had worked on in Washington and was proposing for the city administration.

It is hard to say what would have come to these new budget policies if they had continued to develop along the lines begun in 1966 and early 1967. But history decreed that this development was to be superseded by a new and more aggressive phase in the Mayor's educational reform campaign.

On Hayes' recommendation, the Mayor announced in the spring of 1967 that the Board of Education could no longer have the lump sum budget that had been won from Mayor Wagner. He argued that the city administration cannot exercise its fiscal responsibilities so long as the school system can ignore the city's budget review and spend its allotted funds any way it wants. What good does it do for the city Budget Bureau to investigate and cut out unproductive programs if the school system is free to put them back in again by shifting funds from approved programs?

The public school forces reacted immediately—and negatively —to the Mayor's action, which hinted at some of the trouble that lay before the Mayor as he moved more boldly into other educational areas. The Public Education Association sounded the alarm with a press release denouncing the Mayor's action as a "dismal climax to a series of moves to downgrade the New York City Board of Education." "This move of the Mayor's," the release went on, "is based on the mistaken assumption that the school system is a department of city government. . . . The Public Education Association urges the Board of Education to resist every attempt to substitute political guesswork for educational judgment in the formulation of policy for the public schools."

At a meeting of civic groups at the Public Education Association in April 1967, the Mayor, who had been generally popular with these groups up to that time, was met with a barrage of angry questions and hostile faces. A *New York Times* editorial condemned the Mayor for his actions.

It was not that the civic groups and the *New York Times* were unaware of the inefficiency in the school system, or the city's inability to support a constantly ballooning school budget with such unpromising results. The problem was that they were terribly fearful of seeing the Mayor—even a reform Mayor—intrude his political power into the educational domain.

The concern over the Mayor's boldness with the education budget came at the time when his educational actions in the poverty program were also beginning to generate a backlash of resentment, and just as he was about to embark upon the even stormier seas of decentralization.

The Poverty Program—
Competition, Coordination,
and Community Action

Unlike the budget process, the poverty program did not give the Mayor an official role in the school system. Federal poverty strategists, however, recognized big city school systems' immunity to reform and had built into the program some tools to effect changes from the outside. The primary strategies were community action and competition, both of which fit in well with the style of the Lindsay administration. They appealed both to the Mayor's preference for local action and to his distrust of the existing bureaucracies.

There were great expectations at the beginning of the Lindsay administration that community programs (e.g., manpower training, early childhood education, after-school study centers, etc.) would soon show up the school system for the inefficient, decaying system that all bright, new "urbanists" knew it was. The Mayor gave these community programs his full backing, and he and his staff hardly tried to conceal their disdain for the officials of the regular school system, who began to resent this competition from the outside. After all, the school system had failed. Furthermore, many of the system's leaders had a discernible lack of empathy for the plight of Black people; how could they be expected to have anything useful to say? The Lindsay administration would build up competing educational programs that would show how the job should be done, and the school system would then have to stop giving excuses and start to shape up. Just in case the school system failed to see the merit of the new programs, the community action agencies would help to organize parents and community leaders to make a more forceful impression on the benighted school officials. Lindsay fully backed these efforts to develop community leadership, even in the face of growing evidence that the cockiness and assertiveness of some of the new leadership was not winning the Mayor political friends among many sections of the city.

The poverty program also gave the Mayor an opportunity to promote the coordination of programs in line with his preference for experts and rational administration. Previous mayors had learned to live with a plethora of confused, overlapping agencies, boards, and commissioners, most of whom were politically appointed and controlled. Lindsay felt that some order had to be brought out of this chaos if the problems of the city were ever to be solved. Certainly this seemed true in such matters as poverty, manpower training, welfare. Lindsay set up a blue ribbon panel of experts, under the Institute of Public Administration and financed by the Ford Foundation, to study the matter and recommend a plan for coordinated action. They came up with the Human Resources Administration (the HRA), which brought together into one "super agency" the Welfare Department, the Youth Board, the manpower programs, and the whole welter of poverty programs that had sprung up under new Federal legislation.

Clearly any rational approach to the problems of human resources had to include education. The planners of the Human Resources Administration were well aware of this. Mitchell Sviridoff, who directed the study and later came to the city to head the new HRA, was brought in from New Haven where he had directed an education-minded poverty program. Mayor Lindsay's own deep concern about the school crisis was based in part on his realization that his plans for the reform of the city could not succeed unless they included thoroughgoing reform of the school system. If the school system had been part of the city administration, it undoubtedly would have been made a part of the Human Resources Administration so that the entire web of education, manpower training, community action, youth activities, adult education, and welfare could be coordinated. As it was, the Board of Education was a separate and independent agency, and the best the planners could do was to recommend the establishment of an "Office of Education Liaison" within the HRA to provide the coordinative link with the Board of Education.

As things turned out, the Office of Education Liaison was not set up until July of 1967, more than a year after the HRA was established and after the various programs within the HRA had already developed their own relationships with the school system —mostly negative relationships based on the competitive strategy of the poverty program. In fact by mid-1967 a backlash was already gathering strength against the "know-it-alls" of the poverty program, and the brash, angry leaders given voice by the community action program.

In the meanwhile, however, the city had locked horns with the Board of Education over decentralization to which the energies of the new Office of Education Liaison were directed almost exclusively. Coordination and smoother relations between the school system and the programs of the HRA had to be postponed until this more fundamental struggle between the city administration and the school system was settled.

Decentralization—
the Mayor Commits Himself

If the poverty program and the Mayor's more aggressive budget policies were beginning to raise the hackles of school and civic groups, these troubles were nothing compared to those he was to face with decentralization. The question naturally arises whether he moved into this most crucial of his school battles by accident or design. It was a little of each.

For all the trouble they were causing him, neither the poverty program nor the new budget procedures gave much promise of making substantial changes in the school system—at least not for many years to come. The poverty program was having its own problems getting organized. Many programs fell far short of expectations, many were visible failures, and even the best programs were doomed to be small, scattered, and outside of the mainstream of education for the million plus school children during their regular school hours. Moreover, the antagonism generated by the poverty program eroded whatever chance the Mayor might have had for positive leadership in persuading the school establishment to initiate changes. Nor did the new budget procedures seem to be able to reach down through the layers of bureaucracy to bring improvement into the performance and attitudes of teachers, which is the only place where school reform counts.

From the way in which it was set up and functioned, the school system seemed impervious to change. No one seemed responsible for anything, and therefore, no one could be held accountable. The whole system was not so much badly managed as not managed at all. Effective school reform, so essential to the Mayor's whole program of reform for the city, obviously was going to require a fundamental approach, going beyond just pressure on the system, since the system, it seemed, could not respond even if it wanted to. It was understandable, therefore, for the Mayor and his advisors to examine the possibilities for changes in the basic structure of the school system. Furthermore, the Mayor's dislike of large bureaucracies—especially old, well-entrenched bureaucracies—and his predisposition for local action led quite naturally to the idea of decentralization once the pretext for such a policy presented itself.

The Lindsay policy on school decentralization, however, did not come about in a logical manner. The initial approach was piecemeal and tentative—more determined by the need to react to a particular crisis than by any grand design. The crisis was the rebellion over the now famous Intermediate School 201. Community leaders had demanded that the proposed site for the new school be moved to an integrated area. The school authorities had originally reacted by promising to rezone the school's attendance area and beef up its program to ensure integration in the original site. When community leaders learned that the school was about to open in the fall of 1966 with an "integration" of 50 percent Black and 50 percent Puerto Rican students, they rebelled. If the school were going to be segregated, they demanded that it be locally controlled. As the first installment of local control, they demanded that the principal appointed by central headquarters be removed in favor of a candidate to be selected by the community.

Between the nationally reported confrontations and boycotts, and the school authorities' waivering between the demands of the community leaders and the demands of the organized professional groups, the whole situation escalated into the very type of racial crisis that the city so feared, and which, in a certain sense, it had elected Mayor Lindsay to deal with. It was one more forceful example that school crises were no longer purely educational matters. The Mayor stepped into the crisis with Human Resources Administrator Mitchell Sviridoff and some of the staff of the Ford Foundation. Given the background of the crisis and their own predilections, they quickly sympathized with the demands of local groups for control over the school, thus starting almost by accident the Lindsay administration's commitment to school decentralization and community control.

I.S. 201 was finally opened for the school year 1966–67 without any resolution of the community control issue. The matter continued to smolder, and the Mayor was determined that something be done to prevent another flare-up. During the winter, city and Ford Foundation staff worked out a plan with the Board of Education for three experimental decentralized districts, an idea with which Mario Fantini of the Ford Foundation, in particular, had had experience in other cities. One of the districts would include I.S. 201 and its feeder elementary schools, thus providing a way of resolving that explosive crisis. A second district would include another area of rebellious dissatisfaction in the Ocean Hill-Brownsville section of Brooklyn. The third would include an area in the Lower East Side called "Two Bridges," where the Ford Foundation was working with several community groups.

The professional staff in the school hierarchy did not like the idea, seeing a threat to their traditional authority and feeling the communities unprepared to run their own schools. The lay Board of Education during this crucial period began to side with this professional attitude, partly because it shared the staff's resentment over the aggressive tactics of community groups, and partly because it resented the intrusion of the Mayor, who was seen as working in alliance with Black and Puerto Rican community groups to wrest power away from the Board of Education.

The Board of Education, however, was vulnerable because it had been unable to resolve the dangerous I.S. 201 crisis that threatened to disrupt the peace of the city. It, therefore, reluctantly agreed to the demonstration district plan in the spring of 1967. Much of the shape of what was to come was determined in the inauspicious origins of decentralization as it developed in these experimental programs worked out to meet the racial crises of 1966–67. The Mayor was committed to a path that was bound to be more of a challenge to the school system and more of a problem for the Mayor than any of his previous school activities.

Before the three demonstration districts could even get underway, however, a new push for decentralization came from an entirely different quarter which was destined to escalate all of the resentments and fears inherent in the demonstration district program. The Mayor had appealed urgently to the State Legislature for more educational funds, and among other things, had argued that if state aid were calculated separately for each of the five boroughs of the city, the lower real estate values in three of the five boroughs would enable the city to receive over $100,000,000 more per year than was being received when aid was calculated for the city as a whole. State legislative leaders were willing to admit the need for more funds for New York City, but felt that the separate borough calculation could be permitted only if the school system were actually split up into five separate districts. Neither the Mayor, nor the Board of Education, nor the State Commissioner of Education liked the five borough system. The Legislature finally agreed, therefore, to provide the extra funds "as if" New York were a five district system, so long as the Mayor proposed a plan to the next session of the Legislature for genuine decentralization of the city system.

This was a turn of events that went far beyond experimenting with decentralization in three small and isolated districts of the school system. Quite unexpectedly there was now the possibility of restructuring the entire city school system, and even more unexpectedly, the *Mayor* had been given the responsibility for drawing up the plan. The Board of Education and education groups protested before the legislation was passed that it was improper for the Mayor to be intruded into this vital educational matter, and they enlisted the State Commissioner in an effort to prevail upon the Legislature to give the responsibility for developing the plan to the Board of Education instead. But the legislative leaders insisted, and apparently the Mayor agreed, that the restructuring of the school system was a *political* matter and should be the responsibility of someone accountable to an electorate.

The Lindsay administration's principle of action made it natural for the Mayor to accept this extraordinarily difficult political responsibility without too many qualms. The school system, after all, did need a fundamental overhauling, and it couldn't be trusted to do the job itself if real change were to take place. The Mayor's propensity for the "new breed" and the outside expert determined how he would carry out his responsibility. Instead of turning to people experienced in the weird and wonderful world of New York educational politics, or trying to put together coalition of all the forces that would have to be involved in educational change, he appointed a blue ribbon panel, chaired by McGeorge Bundy of the Ford Foundation and made up of his Ford-connected HRA Administrator, Mitchell Sviridoff; an outstanding anti-establishment Puerto Rican leader, Antonia Pantoja; an out-of-town Negro, Bennetta B. Washington, who was married to the then Housing Commissioner, Walter Washington, later to be mayor of Washington; the recently-arrived-in-town, ex-U.S. Commissioner of Education, Francis Keppel; and Alfred Giardino, President of the Board of Education, and the only representative of the school system on the panel. The panel, staffed by the Ford Foundation, was charged with the responsibility of studying the entire problem of decentralization and coming up with a recommendation which the Mayor could send to the State Legislature in accordance with the new state aid requirement.

While pressuring the school board to establish the three demonstration districts had committed the Mayor to a tricky and dangerous challenge to the educational establishment, the appointment of the Bundy panel in April of 1967 fully committed him to a major invasion of the sacred preserves of the school system. The nature of the appointments to the panel made it clear that the Mayor intended to respond to the legislative mandate for decentralization with a recommendation for fundamental restructuring of the school system. What he was undertaking was clearly far beyond his efforts at budget reform and his efforts to goad the school system into change through the poverty program. He was now embarked upon a head-on challenge to the power structure of the whole, huge school system of more than one million students and sixty thousand teachers and supervisors. All his other policies for educational reform were swept into the vortex of the battle that ensued for the following two years.

Decentralization—Round One

The result of the Bundy panel was the now famous Bundy Plan for splitting the city into 30 to 60 semi-autonomous districts, governed by local boards. Ominously, Bundy had pointed out from the beginning that his panel could only come up with a recommended plan; the political support for the plan would have to come from the Mayor. The merits of the plan itself are still hotly debated in New York, and presumably will be debated across the country as the decentralization issue reverberates throughout other cities of the nation. But there is almost no debate at all that when it came to political support, the plan was a failure.

History will never be able to settle for sure whether the implacable hostility of the professional staff of the school system was inevitable from the beginning, or whether the very structure and operation of the Bundy panel—as a group of outside "know-it-all's"—made the conflict significantly more bitter than it otherwise would have been. For whatever reason, very early in the development of the plan the teachers' union (UFT) and the Supervisors' Associations postponed their traditional rivalry and began to form an alliance to block what they both could see was going to be a major threat to the power hegemony of the system, which up until then they had shared almost exclusively between them. They felt that city-wide decentralization would just be I.S. 201 and Ocean Hill-Brownsville writ large, with untutored community leaders being given the power not only over educational matters, but even over professional matters such as hiring, firing, promotions, and the awarding of tenure.

The teachers' strike in the fall of 1967 also helped to determine both the hostility of the professional groups to decentralization and the racial overtones of the controversy. The initial union demand in the strike to give teachers more authority to deal with "disruptive pupils" was viewed in the Black community as an act of hostility against Black children. Black community leaders refused to back the strike, and in particular the leaders in the demonstration decentralization districts refused to back it, and looked with a jaundiced eye even upon those union demands purportedly made for the benefit of children, such as the More Effective Schools program for reduced class size, extra staff, etc. The Black community and the professional groups found themselves working further and further into opposite camps.

Just as the lay Board of Education began to side with the professional groups in their negative reactions to the demonstration districts, so did it now begin to join forces with the United Federation of Teachers and the Council of Supervisory Associations (CSA, representing fourteen supervisory groups) to resist the restructuring of the entire system proposed by Bundy and the Mayor. Even before the Bundy panel finished its work, it became clear that the Board's president and sole representative, Alfred Giardino, was going to dissent from the report.

From the moment it was issued, the Bundy Report was in trouble. The Mayor and his political advisors did almost nothing to gain political support for the plan. They counted too heavily on the assumption that most New Yorkers shared their view that the basic structure of the school system was hopeless and required major revisions, such as Bundy proposed. They counted too little on the kind of fight the embattled teachers and supervisors within the system would wage to preserve the existing power structure. And they counted too little also on the growing resentment among significant portions of the population toward the Mayor's emphasis on Negro problems and toward what they viewed as his high-handed and patronizing style. The result was that the professional leaders were able to play effectively upon the resentments of these groups to convince them that the decentralization plan was a scheme to turn the school system over to the Blacks and Black extremists, to the detriment of the middle and blue-collar classes of the city.

Once the alliance of the teachers' union and the supervisors was welded, they had an almost incomparable political campaign machinery to propagate their views through the official school meetings of the parent associations and PTA's located in almost every community throughout the city. In the Black and Puerto Rican sections where there was already such hostility between the school staff and community forces, this mechanism could not be used effectively. But in the white and middle class areas, principals and union officials spoke at literally hundreds of parent meetings throughout the spring of 1968 to spread the word about the dangers of decentralization—how it would destroy educational standards, allow the hiring of incompetent teachers and principals, cost hundreds of millions of dollars in extra administration, "fragment" the city into isolated school districts all with different curricula and, most importantly, how it would give free rein to the Black extremists who lay in wait to seize control of the schools to teach revolution, Black Nationalism, and anti-Semitism.

Just before the end of the legislative session in Albany, the Governing Board of the Ocean Hill-Brownsville Demonstration District provided just the cause the professional groups needed to drive home their case with the already frightened white population. After months of frustration in dealing with the central board and the professional groups in trying to get their experimental district under way, the Ocean Hill-Brownsville Governing Board ordered 19 of their teachers and supervisors, who they felt were trying to sabotage the project, to leave the demonstration district and report to city headquarters for reassignment elsewhere. The leaders of the demonstration district claimed they were asking for nothing more than was routinely done by the school officials for projects or local supervisors they favored. The teachers' union and supervisors groups, however, immediately seized upon these "firings," as they called them, to prove their point that decentralization would mean take-overs by Black extremists who would trample on the hard-won rights of teachers and civil service workers. Rumors already had been spreading during the spring that extremists and anti-Semites were in control of Ocean Hill-Brownsville. The fact that the Mayor seemed unconcerned and took no action either with regard to the rumored extremism or this final act of "firing" the teachers without due process strengthened the position of the professional groups in convincing the white population that the Mayor's plans for restructuring the school system were merely part and parcel of his partiality toward Black militants, and his lack of concern for the rights and interests of the rest of the population.

All through spring, the legislators in Albany received floods of letters, telegrams, telephone calls, and personal visits from teachers and frightened constituents urging the defeat of the decentralization legislation. The Mayor's plan itself was dead before his bill was introduced. No more than a handful of legislators could be found to support it. The only things the cause of decentralization had going for it were, on the one hand, the widespread recognition among legislators that something had to be done with the New York City school system, and on the other, the lack of any alternative proposals from the professional groups, who were successfully lobbying the Mayor's proposal to death. It had been the legislature itself, after all, that had insisted upon a plan to decentralize the system, and many legislators were determined that no more money be poured into the city school system until firm action was taken to straighten out the mess that undermined the productivity of the system and caused such alienation and hostility between the school officials and the communities they were supposed to serve.

Into this vacuum two alternative plans were developed. The State Board of Regents suggested a plan following the basic principles of the Mayor's plan, in calling for the clear shift of authority to local boards, but providing for larger districts (15, instead of 30, with an average of 60,000 pupils instead of 30,000), no mayoral appointments to the local boards (the provision in the Mayor's plan for half the local board members to be appointed by the Mayor had added to the complaints of mayoral political takeover), and the blurring of a number of other controversial points to be left for decision at a later time. The New York City Board of

Education, by this time completely alienated from the Mayor, presented its own alternate plan calling for no clearcut transfer of authority to local boards, but giving the Board of Education the authority to delegate various powers to local boards when, as, and if it thought this would be beneficial.

The Board of Regents, being convinced that decisive action was needed immediately to prevent the further deterioration of the New York City school system and further dangerous racial polarization pressed hard for the enactment of its program. The Mayor very quickly abandoned his own plan as dead and endorsed the Regents' proposal as an acceptable alternative which would accomplish the same basic purpose. Many civic groups also endorsed the Regents' proposal and pleaded with the legislature to decide on the distribution of powers during the 1968 legislative session, fearing that the Black-white polarization would only escalate and make decision the following year still more difficult if the issue were left hanging. Virtually no groups publicly supported the plan of the Board of Education, which would have left the whole authority question undecided, but clearly groups resisting decentralization preferred this to a decision to transfer power to local boards.

The Regents' efforts were to no avail. The fear campaign was such that few legislators could bring themselves to vote for a plan which shifted real authority to local boards. Most legislators admitted that the fears were primarily racial. The white population of the city had been successfully convinced that its only protection against Black extremism lay in leaving power in the hands of the central board, even if this meant in effect leaving it in the hands of the central professional bureaucracy and the teachers' union. Whites could at least identify with these groups, and whatever their faults and limitations, they were viewed as a better lot than the unruly Black mobs and militant extremists who they feared would take over the schools if local boards were given authority. The upstate legislators, virtually all white and mostly conservative, could also identify with these fears, especially after the Ocean Hill-Brownsville controversy at the end of the session dramatized the "Black menace" for many days running on the front pages of the newspapers.

In the end, the legislation that was passed in May of 1968 was worked out by State Senator John Marchi, a conservative Republican from Staten Island, who was little known then, but who had worked closely on legislation with the teachers' union and other civil service groups, and was the following year to wrest the Republican mayoral nomination from Mayor Lindsay.

The so-called "Marchi Act" followed the program advocated by the then New York City Board of Education, namely making no decision whatever in the legislation as to the distribution of power between the central and local boards, and leaving it up to the city Board of Education to decide what to delegate to local boards. The act also gave the Mayor authority to appoint four additional members to the city Board of Education, and called upon it, rather than the Mayor, to come back the following year with another decentralization plan. In other words, the whole power issue was left undecided, and the stage was set for the chaos and bitterness that was to follow in the coming school year.

The Mayor had been badly bruised. His own plan had been defeated virtually without a battle, and the alternate Regents' plan had lost in the final legislative struggle in the face of a successful campaign waged by the teachers' union, the supervisors, and the then existing Board of Education. The city also had been bruised by the polarization that had developed and by anger, fear, and suspicion growing on all sides. But the fight was not yet over. The Mayor had learned some lessons and would be much more cautious the following year. But what he had set in motion could not be stopped, and the final outcome of the struggle, as well as the full measure of damage to the combatants, was yet to be revealed.

Decentralization—Round Two

Although the Marchi Act gave the Mayor power to appoint only four additional members to add to the old nine-man central Board of Education, a series of retirements and resignations from the Board, and the adherence of one of the old members to the Mayor's policies, gave him within a short time a majority of eight or nine of the thirteen-man Board who favored his approach to decentralization. The most outspoken member of the new majority was the Reverend Milton Galamison, who had led the famous school boycotts in favor of integration five years before, and who was now a strong advocate of decentralization and community control. The Board became known as the "Lindsay Board," and became thoroughly despised by those who defended the existing school system and by those who feared a Black takeover.

Even by the middle of the summer of 1968 it became clear that the majority of the expanded Board would develop a "strong" decentralization plan to present to the next session of the legislature, and, in the meantime, would use its power of delegation to transfer significant powers to the 30 existing local school boards and the three demonstration districts. If the professional groups were to succeed in keeping the power where it was they would have to fight hard, and that is what they did. The legislature had left the power issue "up for grabs," and in New York City anything up for grabs will not lack for takers.

The Ocean Hill-Brownsville controversy over the 19 "fired" teachers was left smoldering over the summer. The members in the district who had gone out on strike in the last weeks of the spring term to protest the "firings" stayed out through the end of the term. Negotiations between the expanded "Lindsay Board," the Ocean Hill-Brownsville Governing Board, and the UFT failed to bring a resolution. During the summer the Ocean Hill Board sent a notice to the striking teachers asking which of them planned to return to Ocean Hill in the fall. Upon receiving either notice of non-return or more characteristically no notice at all, the local board proceeded, with the approval of the central school officials, to hire replacements so that school could open in the fall.

When school was ready to open in September there was the inevitable show-down: The UFT insisted that the teachers who had been out on strike, plus the original 19 who had been "fired" without due process, be returned to teaching duties in the district. The Ocean Hill Board, on the other hand, insisted that the transfer of the 19 was no different from the transfers, routinely, if unofficially, made by the school system in problem situations, and that the hiring of replacements for the striking teachers was the only thing that a board responsible for the education of children could do in face of the known transfer of many of the teachers and no indication from the others as to whether they planned to return to Ocean Hill in the fall.

With no resolution of this stalemate at the opening of school, the UFT struck the entire city to enforce its demands for the return of the teachers to Ocean Hill.

From the start it was clear that the issue in the strike went far beyond what might or what might not have been settled in the immediate Ocean Hill-Brownsville controversy. The strike became the vehicle through which the professional groups would attempt to finish off once and for all any further efforts to transfer authority to local boards. The campaign of local parents' meetings through-out the white areas of the city was intensified. Newspaper ads paid for by the UFT and the CSA appealed to the populace to support the cause of the teachers as the only barrier against Black extrem-ism, etc. (ads in Staten Island, for instance, to which many whites had fled from the "Black tide" in Brooklyn, reminded readers that "Ocean Hill-Brownsville is Only a Bridge Away" and the the opening of the schools in defiance of the strike was like the "Ocean Hill-Brownsville takeover"). The most notorious tactic, that in the end turned many supporters away from the teachers, was the union's distribution in Jewish neighborhoods of tens of thousands of copies of falsified propaganda sheets linking Ocean Hill with vicious anti-Semitic hate statements. Jewish community relations organizations later called the union to task for thus irresponsibly escalating the Black-Jewish polarization, since inves-tigation showed that the Ocean Hill officials were not responsible for the hate statements. But the damage was already done. Many in the Jewish community were in a state of panic over what might happen to them if local boards were given power.

The fact that nearly a million school children were out of school during the strike greatly intensified emotions on all sides. The UFT successfully called the largest City Hall demonstration in the city's history. Over 40,000 angry white parents, teachers, and supporters marched on City Hall, demanding that the Ocean Hill-Brownsville district be abolished so that the teachers and pupils could go back to school. They carried placards demanding the impeachment of Mayor Lindsay for his refusal to enforce "due process." "Shanker for Mayor," "Whites Have Rights Too," etc. expressed the substance of the demonstrators' feelings, while the anger and hostility on their faces expressed the degree of their emotions. After going out for the second of the three successive strikes that lasted over a period of 11 weeks, Albert Shanker, the president of the UFT, promised the frightened teachers and the angry white parents that he would not call off the city-wide strike until the Ocean Hill experimental district was abolished—a kind of symbol that this dangerous tinkering with local control would have to end if people were ever again to see peace return to the school system. The hearts and minds of a mighty army of people were successfully molded by the strike into a potent force against the transfer of power to local boards.

Emotions on the other side, however, were equally heightened by the strike. Many in the Black community and a number of religious and civic groups became convinced that the UFT had created what amounted to a lynch mob to wipe out one of the few experiments where Black people for once could try their own hand at ending the educational disaster that afflicted their children in the schools. They saw the union tactics as directed against any attempt by citizens, especially Black citizens, to challenge the exclusive power of the white controlled school hierarchy. Although many were union people themselves, defense of Ocean Hill-Brownsville and defeat of the strike became a civil rights crusade. Just before the end of the strike (and probably contributing significantly to its termination) an impressive group of Black union leaders, from some of the largest unions in the city, met with officials of the Central Labor Council to warn them that further prolongation of the strike would so embitter Black union members as to endanger the unity of the labor movement.

Schools in most of the ghetto areas and in a few of the white areas were kept open during the strike. This was often done without incident in most of the Black and Puerto Rican areas, where community feeling ran so high that the UFT feared even to picket the schools. But in other areas the schools were kept open only in the face of bitter exchanges with union pickets, principals, and district superintendents. Supervisors openly defied the official Board of Education policy of keeping the schools open. For the first time in history the Council of Supervisory Associations publicly supported the UFT strike, and its members often cooperated with the striking teachers, custodians, and even sympathetic police and firemen, to harass the teachers and parents who tried to keep their schools open. Schools opened by the official orders of the

Board of Education were relocked in the dead of night with new padlocks; cement was poured into locks; crucial pieces of school furnaces were removed; fire inspectors paraded through the schools during the day to disrupt the classes of the "scab" teachers and students who came to school during the strike.

Never in living memory had an issue caused such bitterness, polarization, and hostility in the city. And in the end, after 11 weeks of disruption in which the city hung on the edge of an abyss of racial warfare and chaos, the strike ended in a stalemate. The Ocean Hill district was put into trusteeship under the State Commissioner of Education and money was found to hire both the teachers who had been on strike the previous year in Ocean Hill and those who had been hired to replace them (a solution which had been accepted by the Ocean Hill officials for all but the original 19 transferees even before the first strike).

An uneasy calm returned to the city school system. Issues continued to rumble out of Ocean Hill-Brownsville under the State trusteeship, as alternately the UFT threatened to go out on strike and the Black community threatened to rebel, and three successive State trustees wore themselves out wavering back and forth between the conflicting claims of the two sides.

Much bitterness still remained throughout the city and would remain for many months to come between Blacks and whites, between striking and non-striking teachers, and between liberals who still supported the UFT and those who had split with the old liberal-labor coalition in the conviction that the UFT had taken a reactionary and racist position. But with the children back in schools across the city and the growing awareness of the harm that would come from further strife, the warring sides tried to avoid open conflict.

Seemingly nothing was decided by the strike. The power struggle was still "up for grabs," and there would continue to be a good deal of fight from both sides until the legislature resolved the issue. But the strike did result in changes in the dynamics of the struggle that would be significant for later developments. Community groups and their liberal supporters became more aware of the depths of feeling regarding teachers' rights and the extent of the real fear on the part of the white community toward Black extremism. Not only was it necessary to take these factors into account as political realities, but the underlying justice of some of the concerns had to be accepted. Proponents of decentralization and community control in the future would generally be more careful to point out that they were in no sense opposed to the protection of legitimate teachers' rights.

Likewise on the other side, the strike brought a growing recognition that an adjustment in the power relationships would have to be made. The tenacity with which the Ocean Hill people held on, the fact that they got widespread support in the Black community and the strong support of many liberal and even labor groups formerly aligned with the teachers' union, the fact that both the Board of Education and the State Board of Regents made it clear that they would not tolerate the stamping out of the Ocean Hill experiment in a lynch mob atmosphere—all made it clear that continued resistance to change along the lines that had developed could only lead to total racial polarization and irreversible alienation between the school staffs and a large part of the communities they would have to serve. Just as the UFT had shown its mettle and the strength of its determination to protect its interests as it saw them, so did the Black and Puerto Rican forces show that they were ready to fight to the limit to protect what they viewed to be their interests.

The movement for the shift of real authority to local boards could no longer be ignored, and probably could not be stopped. The groups that had been fighting against the transfer of powers to local boards began more and more to emphasize that they were not opposed to a change in structure but were only interested in protecting the rights of teachers and staff—not against decentralization even, but only against "community control," which they equated with extremist control and community leaders directly administering the schools without regard to state laws and due processes.

The changes brought about by the strike by no means meant that the battle was over. It was more that each side had greater appreciation of the other's strength and determination. Such appreciation is sometimes more important to ultimate peace than soothing words; at least one must hope so, since there were few soothing words to be found in the immediate aftermath of the strike.

Another change that came about as a result of the strike was a change in the role of the Mayor. The UFT campaign turned the anxious parents' anger directly on the Mayor, demanding that he could end the strike if he would use the power of his office to bring the rebellious Ocean Hill district to heel. Participants in one of the mass UFT rallys had chanted "Ho, Ho, Ho, Lindsay Must Go!" The placards they carried made it clear that the Mayor was their target. Such powerful pressure was brought to bear that the Mayor found himself shifting from the role of an advocate for decentralization and for the Ocean Hill experiment into more of a mediator, seeing what could be worked out between the Ocean Hill Board, the Board of Education, and the UFT so that the terrible strike could end. In the process, his support for the "Lindsay Board" began to wane. By the time the strike was over, the Mayor, to a large extent, had withdrawn from the remaining battle over decentralization. The official sponsorship of decentralization shifted from the Mayor to the expanded Board of Education, headed by John Doar, who had been appointed by Lindsay but was now quite isolated from mayoral support. The other chief forces in the struggle were the professional groups on the one hand, still trying to limit the change as much as possible, and on the other side, the Black and Puerto Rican groups and a number of civic groups convinced by now that the change was necessary to the further progress, if not the survival, of the public school system.

In December the Board of Education published its proposed "Community School District System Plan," closely tracking the basic principles of the Mayor's and Regents' plans of the previous school year, but spelling out more clearly the protections for school personnel. Whether because people were simply weary of fighting, or because of the psychological readjustments growing out of the strike, as mentioned here, the plan did not meet with the same shrill cries of anguish that had reverberated throughout the city ever since the Bundy Plan had been announced the year before.

The Board held hearings on its proposals throughout the city and, after making a few changes, sent its final plan to the State Board of Regents on February 1, as required by the Marchi Act. The Regents suggested a few additional changes of their own, and transmitted the bill to the State Legislature on March 1, again as prescribed by the Marchi Act. There was by this time a certain sense of inevitability that the legislature could no longer postpone action and would have to make significant readjustments in the power relationships within the school system.

The professional group's main aim from this point on was not to prevent a change, but to limit the powers of the local boards as much as possible and build up the maximum protection for the interests of the school staff. In addition, the UFT pushed especially hard to ensure that the legislation would eliminate the hated "Lindsay Board" and replace it with an elected central board, although the UFT had historically opposed the idea of an elected board of education. The legislature was, if anything, in a more reactionary mood than in the previous session. The prevailing backlash atmosphere and newspaper publicity continued to stimulate a strong emotional resistence to decentralization. It was still viewed by many as "giving in to Black extremists," and the professional spokesmen did their best to play upon this psychology.

The resulting clash between the forces for change, led by the Black and Puerto Rican legislators and a small group of Reform Democrats and backed by a sense of inevitability that a change had to be made, and the forces for the status quo, backed by a diffuse but potent backlash sentiment, produced a stalemate the likes of which the legislature had not seen in many years. Compromises were tried and fell apart. The leaders used their muscle, but a solution eluded them. It became evident that it was difficult indeed to shift the basic responsibility for education to local boards, as seemed to be required, and at the same time leave the basic power and authority with the central authorities, where the professional groups could have reasonable assurance of controlling them and protecting their interests against "extremists."

Finally, the Governor had to step in and keep the legislature in more or less continuous session, with legislative leaders meeting around-the-clock, until some kind of compromise was hammered out. What resulted is what might be expected—a badly botched mess. The basic structure of local boards with responsibility and the basic authority for elementary and intermediate schools was conceded. But then the powers of the local boards were so hedged about with powers of intervention by the central board and special promotion privileges for existing personnel, that it will take an army of lawyers and probably much confusion and community turmoil to straighten out just exactly how the new system is to operate.

In return for giving up on the basic restructuring of the system, the professional groups were given their way in abolishing the "Lindsay Board" and replacing it with a mostly elected central board: one member is to be elected from each of the five boroughs, and two are to be appointed by the Mayor. Just to give the final twist, Mayor Lindsay was excluded from the appointment of two mayoral appointees to serve on the Interim Board until the new board is to take over on July 1, 1970. The Interim Board was established with only five members, one appointed by each of the Borough Presidents.

In fact, ironically, with the passage of the decentralization bill, representing the final legislative outcome of the Mayor's boldest intervention into school affairs, the Mayor was excluded from any significant role in the new system. But in a certain sense this was only a further step in the withdrawal of the Mayor that had been evident since the great cataclysm and strike at the beginning of the school year.

Conclusion: Assessment of the Mayor's Role in School Reform

Politically, Mayor Lindsay's invasion of the educational world was disastrous. There were many factors which contributed to his loss of the Republican primary in June of 1969, but discontent with his educational efforts was certainly one of them. Furthermore, the racial polarization that grew out of the school crisis created an atmosphere much less favorable to Lindsay's type of leadership and much more favorable to reactionary and backlash sentiments. Lindsay even lost ground with many liberals as a result of his efforts in education, since many of them, although agreeing with his basic policies, felt that his handling of school affairs had been less than satisfactory. But then Mayor Lindsay did not enter upon his educational crusade to gain political credit. He did it in spite of politics, and against all the accumulated political wisdom of decades that had kept politically oriented mayors clear of overt involvement with school affairs. Lindsay went in because he felt that a job had to be done, and had to be done by him. The city simply could not grow and prosper—indeed it could probably not even survive—unless there were fundamental changes and improvements in the school system. These changes were going to have to come from outside the established system. They would have to come either from the State Legislature or from the Mayor, and since the legislature was unlikely to take the lead, the Mayor would have to.

How do we assess the results? First of all we must recognize the enormous difficulty of bringing about change in any large and well-entrenched institution such as a big city school system. No large city school system in the country has as yet been able to respond to the needs for change emerging since World War II. Even Lindsay's strategies with the poverty program and the budget, although bolder than the policies of most other mayors, were not likely to have made much of a dent in the huge educational system. Unless something as bold and fundamental as decentralization had been tried it is virtually certain that the school system would still be drifting ever more dangerously into mediocrity, alienation, and chaos.

One may say that, if a mayor with different political skills than Lindsay had undertaken the fundamental restructuring of the school system, it might have been done with less trauma. But then it is probable that a mayor with different skills would not have tried it at all, recognizing as he would that he could only lose politically by taking on the prickly problems of education, which the State Legislature had been kind enough to leave in the lap of a separate Board of Education. A politically motivated mayor has too many other tough problems he can't dodge to be willing to take on this one too.

Because Lindsay was willing to wade into the school business, and wade in on a fundamental level, the people of New York City now have a chance to rebuild public education into a system that can function effectively in the 1970's and 80's. It is not certain that the opportunity will be well used. No one ever promised that decentralization would work as a panacea to cure the manifold ills of urban education by itself. All it does is provide a framework within which people and forces within the city, previously excluded from a constructive role in education, can assume responsibility and begin the process of reconstruction and improvement.

The question of whether people will actually begin to assume these responsibilities remains to be seen. It may prove too difficult for people to change their old habits of unawareness of responsibility to education. There is also still much bitterness left from the decentralization struggle, and it may be that those people most interested in education and most capable of leadership will find themselves emotionally and politically trapped into playing out old hostilities instead of seizing the new opportunities that now lie open. And the school staff, still resentful of the rough treatment they received from those who invaded their protected preserve, and still only half aware of the changes that. are now demanded of them, may continue to fight a rear guard action and keep the coals of old fires burning. But there is at least a chance now for the city —a way in which people can begin to work constructively together to build a new system.

Because of the way the politics of educational change developed in New York, it will be unlikely for the Mayor to play a major role for some time to come. Mayoral intervention has spent itself for the time being. But it has left a legacy of opportunity as well as bitterness. It will be up to the people of the city to see to it that the opportunity is seized upon constructively and used to carry forth the reform of the city school system until it is a system of true excellence for every child in the city.

11

The Politics of
Educational Reform

Paul E. Peterson

Introduction*

Demands for change in educational practices in American cities have been made in the past decade with increasing frequency. The massive study conducted by the Office of Education under the direction of James Coleman concluded that educational systems have not yet found ways of reaching children whose family backgrounds have not already prepared them for school life(1). This was but one contribution to a much broader discussion condemning educational practices which under-represent Negroes in curricular materials; permit the migration of better-qualified, more experienced teachers to the fringe areas of the city; assign and advise students according to intelligence tests which are alleged to be biased in favor of the middle-class, white child; and allocate resources among schools without taking into account the greater problems involved in educating the disadvantaged child(2). Yet the energy devoted to documenting educational deficiencies has produced little alteration in school practices, particularly those affecting class and race relations. Schools seem unwilling or unable to adapt their practices in scarcely any of the directions suggested by their critics.

In order to foster desired educational reforms, at least three

* This chapter is based upon material from a paper presented at the 1967 convention of the American Orthopsychiatric Association. The research was made possible through grants from the Russell Sage and Woodrow Wilson Foundations.

major political strategies have been advocated: 1) rely on the liberal orientation of the President's national constituency to stimulate nationwide change; 2) enlarge the constituency of the local school system by involving it in a coordinating committee that includes important local elites and institutions; and 3) develop a new constituency by organizing low-income and minority groups to influence educational decision-making. Even though these strategies were relevant not only for education but also for policies in such areas as welfare, health, and employment, this in no way reduces their significance for understanding the politics of *educational* reform. Since all these strategies were advocated within the Johnson Administration during the development of the "War on Poverty," we shall illuminate the strengths and limitations of each strategy by considering recent research on the experiences of poverty and related programs.

Reliance on the Presidential Constituency

A strategy for reform proposed by members of the staff of the President's Committee on Juvenile Delinquency and Youth Crime and the staff of the Public Affairs Department of the Ford Foundation was to rely on the liberal orientation of the President's national constituency. These individuals, who participated in developing poverty program legislation, favored the creation of a poverty "czar" with responsibilities affecting major operating agencies of the federal government, including the Departments of Labor; Interior; Commerce; Agriculture; and Health, Education and Welfare. Their position was based on a belief that "an effective antipoverty effort would require a coordinated approach not feasible under existing single-purpose federal programs"(3). Under this plan the poverty "czar" would have had no operating responsibilities himself, but would have administered a sizeable sum— more than a billion dollars—to stimulate new programs and orientations among the operating departments of the government. Backed by the power of the President and supported by a high-quality staff, the "czar" would have coordinated "Great Society" programs.

This strategy for reform conformed to the ideology of what ironically may now be called the "old left" in that its solutions to the problems of the poor called for further centralization of power. The "old left" was a product of the Socialist movement in Europe, which had transformed the "liberal" view of the relation between man and state. Rather than seeking to free the individual from the bonds imposed by the old feudal state, as was the goal of pre-Socialist nineteenth century Liberalism, the "old left" in the twentieth century has sought to ameliorate the plight of the poor by transforming the state to serve the needs of the lower and working classes. Although the United States has been impervious to a Socialist Party and to their demands for the nationalization of industry, "old left" liberals in numbers sufficient to be politically significant demanded that the government should "redress the balance of private actions by compensating public actions"(4). The civil rights movement of the 1950's was clearly within the tradition of the "old left." Negro leaders felt that only through the intervention of the federal government could they improve race relations by changing practices in education, public accommodations, housing, and employment. Proposals for a poverty "czar" acting as a spokesman for the President were also formulated within this tradition.

This strategy of reform has in the past achieved noteworthy accomplishments by virtue of its resting on a reasonably accurate assessment of the realities of power relations in America. The broad constituency of the President has freed him, at least to some extent, from the constraints that entrenched interests in society are able to place on political leaders accountable to more narrow constituencies. Grant McConnell points out that instead the Presidency is beholden to ". . . all the people. The prestige of its occupant is so great that when his power is husbanded and skillfully used he can make innovations of policy in the interest of those who are outside the pluralist scheme of rule"(5). This has been particularly evident since the restructuring of the political order by Presidential candidates Al Smith and Franklin Roosevelt, who ushered in a two-party system that, to an extent far surpassing previous patterns, articulated the political demands of conflicting class interests in an industrial society(6). National political divisions have approximated class divisions, facilitating the expression of the interests of depressed class and ethnic groups(7). The generally more liberal orientation of the national government, and particularly the Presidency, is further accentuated by the peculiarities of the electoral college, which has made Presidential candidates especially dependent upon the minority vote in the urban metropolises.

Those who advocated for the poverty program director a coordinating role in the shadow of the President were thus acting within the well-established "old left" tradition that was based on political forces providing some realistic hope for social change. But their strategy for reform had its limitations as well, for they were overly optimistic in their assessment of the President's political strength. Although the President is the single most potent individual in American politics, the breadth of his concerns limits his actions in any one area. A decentralized party system, moreover, weakens a President's capacity to control the activities of his own departments, to say nothing of altering traditional practices at the local level. Had the director of the poverty program adopted the coordinating role of the "czar," he would have had the arduous task of breaking through the "whirlpools of government" which decide much of domestic policy(8). These whirlpools, which include governmental bureaus, organized interest groups with narrow constituencies, and Congressional committees have, in the past, been unusually successful in resisting intervention on the part of the President.

In fact, these whirlpools of governmental power resisted coordination even before the "czar proposal" emerged from the secrecy of the executive branch. According to Sar Levitan, the Department of Health, Education and Welfare (HEW) sought for itself "the responsibility for the antipoverty program," a move which was opposed by those who argued that the "department's 'old line' bureaucracy would oppose the new approaches envisioned in the antipoverty program"(9). The Labor Department, too, felt that a single department should administer this program; if it could not be Labor, then it should be HEW. Labor evidently felt that there would be less interference in its affairs by another governmental department than by a "czar" operating out of the Executive Office of the President.

As these debates were continuing in early 1964 at the highest levels of the Johnson Administration, the President appointed Sargent Shriver, who had gained widespread and favorable publicity for his supervision of the Peace Corps, as the director of the forthcoming poverty program. Shriver, sensing immediately the difficulties that would inevitably accompany efforts to work through established governmental agencies, rejected the coordination role in favor of establishing an operating agency under his direction(10). To be sure, lip service was still given to coordination within the federal establishment. The Economic Opportunity Act provided for an Economic Opportunity Council, which was authorized to "consult with and advise the Director in carrying out his functions, including the coordination of antipoverty efforts by all segments of the Federal Government"(11). But the legislation gave Shriver no formal authority to enforce any such coordinated approach among federal agencies. He had alienated too many other officials in his drive to maximize the number of poverty programs under the control of his own agency, the Office of Economic Opportunity (OEO). HEW conceded to Shriver direction of the community action program, and Labor was forced to give up administration of the Job Corps. The *quid pro quo* which the departments received, was little, if any, supervision by Shriver over the programs which had been left within their jurisdiction. The strategy of reform through coordination and centralization of power within the Executive Office of the President collapsed even before a legislative package was presented to Congress in 1964.

Expanding the School System's Constituency

School systems, it has frequently been alleged, have developed such autonomous political structures and have so isolated themselves from other institutions, political elites, and community interests that they have been impervious to calls for change in their operations. As Marilyn Gittell has put it, "Any effort to change the school system . . . must face the concentration of power in the professional bureaucracy and the resistance by the bureaucracy to any plan that would erode its power"(12). The difficulties that prestigious foundations and federal agencies have faced when seeking to induce educational changes exemplify the bureaucracies' powers of resistance. When the Ford Foundation initially became interested in urban problems, it sought to work through the superintendents of big city school systems. But the Foundation's educational experiments, when put into practice by the resistant bureaucracies, lacked the coherence and imagination of their original design and became, as Peter Marris and Martin Rein have said, "fragmentary and diffuse"(13). Moreover, in keeping with school systems' abhorrence for independent measures of their performance, "the value of the experiments was . . . seldom thoroughly examined"(14).

Later, the federal government sought to infiltrate school systems with reform-minded teachers and administrators through the Teacher Corps program. Bernard Watson demonstrates, however, that educationists first used their power to weaken federal authority *vis a vis* local school systems and then subdued and co-opted the program through the practice of hiring "insiders" as administrators for it(15). Consequently, the enthusiastic, reformist thrust of the program was largely diffused.

Perhaps even more significant, the Office of Education by the end of 1967 had been unable to use the leverage provided by the Civil Rights Act of 1964 and the Elementary and Secondary Education Act of 1965 (ESEA) to increase efforts for integration within northern school systems. Even though the Office doubled and tripled the percentage of Negroes going to school with whites in the South, virtually no action was taken in the North. The only time the Office applied the procedures used in the South to northern school systems, it suffered a blistering defeat. In 1965, Office of Education officials attempted to withhold funds from the Chicago school system until charges of de facto segregation had been investigated. But the decentralization of America's political party system gave the local school system leverage to resist such federal intervention. Chicago's Mayor Richard Daley, who can depend on the loyal support of a unified Congressional delegation, forced the office to reverse its decision almost immediately(16). The conflict dramatically revealed the limited power of the Presidency and his subordinate agencies and the obstacles that must be surmounted in order to persuade autonomous educational bureaucracies to alter their traditional patterns of operation.

A second strategy for educational reform was developed to reduce this school system autonomy by enticing school leaders to join coordinating committees consisting of representatives of the local political and economic elite, other institutions affecting the welfare of minority groups, and eventually even representatives of the poor. Once superintendents and their administrative staffs were sitting together with other community leaders, they would join, so it was believed, in a common endeavor to find imaginative new ways of serving the needs of the disadvantaged child. The justification for this strategy was again similar to that of the "old left," but the political reasoning for this second strategy was far more tenuous. The strategy also rested on the assumption that by enlarging an agency's constituency, by enlarging the numbers and kinds of individuals and groups with whom the agency must come into contact, it would be possible to open the agency to innovative practices. Thus, the political justification for coordinated activity was not the efficiency that accompanies such cooperation but the broader, more liberal outlook which was believed to accompany a larger constituency. The mere inclusion of representatives of school systems on citywide coordinating committees, however, does not *by itself* change the constituency to which the school system is responsive. Coordination is likely to have only marginal effect on a system's policies unless it is accompanied by more significant changes in power relations.

Support for these observations can be found in a proliferating number of studies of the Ford Foundation's "grey areas" program, the program of the President's Committee on Juvenile Delinquency and Youth Development and the OEO's community action program. All three of these programs emphasized coordination at the local level that had been impossible to achieve at the national. None of them, however, was particularly successful at using this device as a means for generating educational reform. After examining the coordinating committees for the "grey areas" and juvenile delinquency programs in 15 major cities, Marris and Rein concluded that since such committees

> had usually little power to enforce any solution, [they] brought the conflict within [their] own organization, and often stultified in indecision, unworkable compromises and endless

disputes. [They] lacked authority to integrate [such] jurisdictions [as school systems], and by pressing them to innovate and cooperate, only made each more anxiously self-protective(17).

The ineffectiveness of the citywide coordinating committees for the juvenile delinquency and "grey areas" programs in many American cities did not prevent their national directors from recommending to the OEO that such committees be the mechanism for reform through the community action program. Representative Edith Green of Oregon, the staunch and powerful defender of public school autonomy on the House Committee on Labor and Education, succeeded in eliminating from the Economic Opportunity Act any legal requirement that such committees be formed. Her familiarity with the juvenile delinquency program had convinced her that these committees had the potential for intruding on the independence of school systems. But even though Green was able to keep the Act from requiring coordinating committees, she was not able to prevent their formation, and OEO administrators, convinced that this was a viable mechanism for reform, encouraged their establishment in virtually every major city in the country. The coordinating committees for the community action agencies became not only the entities through which OEO funds to the local community were channeled, but they were also given authority by the ESEA to cooperate with local school systems in developing educational programs funded under Title I.

In general, the local community action agencies seem to have been hardly more successful in changing traditional practices through coordination than were the committees for the "grey areas" and juvenile delinquency programs. After examining the impact of the community action program on schools in six large cities throughout the country, Nicholas Masters et al., conclude:

> Local community action agencies have not in and of themselves been the major innovators or primary agents of change in decision-making with regard to educational problems and needs of the poor within the public school systems examined(18).

Later the authors observe that "community action agencies" have not been involved "to any meaningful extent in the formulation and execution of educational policy" as a result of ESEA legislation(19). In another study of three smaller cities, Michael Usdan and Ray Nystrand found that the relationships between the community action agencies and the school systems were affected not by the coordinating committee but by the experts involved. In two of the three cities these experts consisted solely of school district administrators(20). In still another study of nine cities, Kirschner Associates report that:

> Initially, it was envisaged that a . . . community action program, in cooperation with concerned agencies, [would] design a community-wide educational program fully responsive to the needs of the poor. After this step . . . the program would be turned over to one or more delegate agencies [usually, the public schools] for implementation. One of the basic difficulties of this approach has been that the implementation of the programs has been carried out independently by each delegate agency and . . . has required operating decisions fundamentally affecting the goals, character and operations of the component. . . . The influence of the community action program was dissipated by not being involved with actual operations(21).

It is significant that these three studies, written from different perspectives by different observers in different cities, reach such similar conclusions. If these cases are at all representative, the dominant pattern seems to be a relatively low level of change in educational policy through attempts to broaden the constituency of school systems by including them on coordinating committees.

Organizing a New Constituency

In addition to these rather feeble attempts at coordination at both the national and local levels, OEO pursued a third strategy of reform as well: develop a new constituency for school systems by organizing low-income and minority groups. Relying on the now-celebrated phrase that community action programs be "developed, conducted, and administered with the maximum feasible participation of residents of the areas and members of the groups served," OEO sought to increase the political power of the Negroes, Puerto Ricans, and other disadvantaged citizens(22). According to the

OEO's Community Action Workbook, for example, a "promising method" of implementing maximum feasible participation was "to assist the poor in developing autonomous and self-managed organizations which are competent to exert political influence on behalf of their own self-interest"(23).

This strategy of organizing a new constituency closely resembles the political strategy vociferously advocated by what has recently been called the "new left." Whereas the "old left" had fought entrenched economic interests and Republican refusals to use state power for humanitarian goals, the "new left," the young radicals usually associated with the Students for Democratic Society and the Student Non-Violent Coordinating Committee, "regard the welfare state . . . as the incarnation of the status quo"(24). As one frank spokesman for this new reform movement phrased it:

> The special powerlessness of the poor derives from the same welfare state that was intended to remedy the excesses of unbridled capitalism. While the poor have been kept alive, they have been subjected to a new set of institutions that extort elementary freedoms as the price of sustenance(25).

Having lost hope in social reform via federal intervention, they instead revived the anti-state, individualist theories of nineteenth century Liberalism to the extent of proposing "new political institutions . . . to localize and distribute as much power as possible"(26). The techniques by which they proposed that this be done included ". . . organizing strong independent movements of the poor through protests, community centers and cooperatives, union organizing among low-income workers, and insurgent political campaigns"(27).

This strategy, too, takes into account critical factors in American politics. The poor and minority groups, in fact, have been peripheral participants in the political process. They continue to be known for low voter turnout where parties are weak and for the ease with which their vote can be "controlled" by strong party organizations. Most important of all, the poor have had few autonomous organizations which articulate their collective demands and maximize their electoral influence—requisites for becoming more than a "potential group" in urban politics(28). A strategy which succeeded in mobilizing this latent political force could alter power relations in both urban areas and in the nation as a whole.

Other political considerations seriously limited this strategy, however. The OEO, for the most part, attempted to disperse power to the poor solely through the rather formalistic requirement that representatives of the poor—chosen "whenever feasible" in accord with "traditional democratic approaches and techniques"—comprise approximately one-third of the policy-making body for local community action agencies(29). These representatives of the poor tended in most cities to be rather ineffective articulators of demands that could generate educational reform. In the six cities studied by Masters et al., representation of the poor did not *"substantially"* affect "policies or priorities with regard to education. . . . Representatives of the poor [did] not raise issues with sufficient force to push the entire board to intrude on the educational system"(30). Usdan and Nystrand observed that in their cities "representatives of the poor were ineffectual Community Action committee members"(31). And Kirshner Associates argued that "the poor, by themselves, are not generally able to design educational components to satisfy their own needs and they are not able to represent their needs effectively to other agencies"(32).

In our own research in Chicago and Philadelphia, we found that the representatives of the poor were co-opted by more powerful interests in the city rather than becoming the spokesmen for institutional reform(33). Thus, formal representation of the poor, by and large, scarcely altered community action proposals, to say nothing of general educational practices. Inasmuch as OEO was left with few weapons to obtain more substantive representation of the poor in the policy-making process, its policies were again frustrated by a decentralized political system.

New York City, however, proved an exception to this general pattern, permitting further investigation of the consequences for educational reform of attempts to form politically active neighborhood organizations. In particular, one New York City community —East Harlem—was mobilized with the aid of poverty funds to focus its attention on educational reform. McConnell provides an analytical framework that illuminates the political behavior of East Harlem activists; he finds a relationship among an organization's constituency, its ideology, its tactics, and the goals it seeks. An organization having a small, narrow constituency, according to McConnell, is likely to hold to an ideology of democratic participation, adopt a "tactic of economic action such as collective bargaining, a boycott, or a cooperative," and, finally, pursue ends which "will be narrow, specific, concrete, and usually material in character"(34). This contrasts with an organization having a broad constituency which will find an ideology of direct participation incompatible with the size and heterogeneity of its membership and which uses political tactics to seek broad, general, and rather diffuse ends.

The constituency of the East Harlem organization, as is the case with most, if not all, neighborhood groups, was a comparatively narrow one. East Harlem had long had active community leadership which had attempted to improve governmental, particularly educational, services to the neighborhood. In the early 1960's the East Harlem Project, formed under the auspices of two settlement houses, had stimulated community support for the increased number of schools needed to service the community, whose density had increased with the massive building of highrise public housing. But with the improvement of school facilities, the activated community became interested in school operations, and turned from a friendly ally to a hostile critic of the local school administration.

The poverty program clearly hastened this process. With the announcement of the War on Poverty, community leaders embarked to Washington, demanding that this new program pay attention to their problems. A high-ranking official in the OEO visited East Harlem the following week; after addressing a crowded school auditorium, he told local leaders to form an organization that could tackle the problems of their neighborhood. In the ensuing months, the community leadership, supported by strong private welfare institutions, formed Massive Economic Neighborhood Development (MEND).

In keeping with a narrow constituency confined to one neighborhood, the newly incorporated organization adopted an ideology which explicitly favored the maximum of direct participation in the democratic processes. In its proposal, MEND sought funds:

> . . . to enable "legitimate locals" to assume some responsibility for guiding the destiny of East Harlem.

> . . . to engage individuals, groups and organizations—grass
> roots and others, public or private, in a *joint and concerted* effort
> to identify those needs for which there is available energy—
> public or private—which can be called into service in order to
> meet them(35).

After a lengthy struggle, MEND finally won the approval of city
officials for this proposal. The community leadership, strengthened
by federal funds available to them, turned their attention to the
recently completed junior high school, Intermediate School 201.

In the ensuing dispute, the tactics of the neighborhood groups,
as McConnell's thesis would lead one to expect, were those of
direct action, boycott, and demonstrations. The threat of a boycott
prevented the school system from opening I.S. 201 in the spring of
1966 when the building was completed. Nor was the building used
for summer programs for fear that disturbances would occur. As
the dispute came to a head in September, 1966, school officials
temporarily utilized a condemned school instead of I.S. 201 to
forestall a boycott. In the meantime, the parents negotiated with
the school administrators and representatives of Mayor John Lindsay. For a day, it seemed that the parents had won most of their
demands, but their temporary victory sparked a boycott by the
teachers at I.S. 201. Pressure from the teachers union and the
school bureaucracy forced the school board to withdraw its conces-
sions, which led to a boycott on the part of the parents. They were
now joined by militant civil rights and Black nationalist groups,
rallying support with the cry of "Black power." Picketing parents
and civil rights militants attempted to block the white principal
from entering his school. Eventually, the public agitation died
down, only to flare up again several months later when neighborhood groups from Harlem and East Harlem broke up a school
board meeting and staged a prolonged sit-in in the board room.

Although the parents were willing to negotiate and try to reach
a compromise, their small constituency and their emphasis on participation easily led them to choose the tactics of boycott and sit-in
rather than utilizing more traditional political channels. But of
greatest importance, the goals that the neighborhood groups
tended to advocate were narrow and specific to their needs. Originally they requested the Board of Education to facilitate integra-

tion by building the school closer to the edge of the ghetto, but the board instead built the school well in the middle of the Negro and Puerto Rican community. Next, community activists, upon completion of the school in the spring of 1966, insisted that it be integrated by bussing students to I.S. 201. The school board, opposed to "compulsory bussing," i.e., bussing white children to schools in Negro and Puerto Rican areas, rejected the proposal. The third alternative proposed by the East Harlem parents was:

> . . . a school-community committee, with power to screen and select a principal and top staff, run after-school and adult programs, oversee curriculum, and take part in what was happening in Harlem—fish fries or protest actions—beyond the regular schooling process(36).

As intensity of feeling rose during the ensuing negotiations, the conflict became personalized, and parents demanded a Negro or Puerto Rican principal for the school instead of the white principal who had been appointed.

After still another rejection of the parent's demands, Dr. Kenneth Clark, the Negro educational leader who had recently been appointed to the State Board of Regents, acted as a broker between the parents and the board. During the ensuing negotiations, East Harlem activists significantly moderated their demands. They proposed this time that a committee providing one-third representation each for the school administration, East Harlem parents, and university personnel govern I.S. 201 and its feeder schools. In this "Operation Demonstration Project Excellence," the schools could improve their quality by drawing upon university resources. Again the school board rejected the parents, countering with a proposal that would have given such a committee advisory powers only. They claimed that the Board of Education could not properly abdicate the responsibilities specifically laid upon it by law. But the board finally was forced to abdicate what it felt to be its responsibilities, and an experimental school district was established in East Harlem. The experimental district was designed to give considerable opportunities for participation to parent and neighborhood groups.

It is crucial to understand that the demands of the East Harlem activists tended to be narrow and neighborhood-oriented rather than to be for broad and significant changes in the educational system as a whole. The East Harlem leaders sought neighborhood control; but neighborhood control, if applied equally throughout the city, would scarcely increase school integration. The East Harlem leaders sought a Negro or Puerto Rican principal for their school rather than insisting on changes in the general recruitment pattern for administrative positions that had effectively excluded minority groups. Even the compromise proposal sought quality improvements through a special arrangement with a university for a few East Harlem schools rather than a far-reaching program to improve quality of education in low-income areas throughout the city. The narrow constituency of the neighborhood organization made it an unsatisfactory vehicle for the articulation of broad demands necessary for major educational reform.

In trying to achieve reform by developing a new constituency, the OEO adopted a policy that conformed to the strategy proposed by the "new left" which had accurately assessed the need in low-income communities for political mobilization. The OEO, however, was constrained in pursuing such a goal by the decentralized party system in the United States, which enabled urban political leadership to thwart OEO's goals by co-opting the representatives of the poor. But even where the OEO achieved considerable success, as in East Harlem, the organizations newly organized had such narrow constituencies that their demands were usually narrow and neighborhood-oriented rather than calls for broad reform which would improve education for all those in their class or ethnic group.

Merging the Strategies for Reform

The national strategy of the "old left," which involved reliance on the constituency of the Presidency, failed to recognize that the decentralized party system handicapped the President, to say nothing of a "czar" operating within his shadow, in any attempts at centralizing power for reformist ends. The strategy of the "old left" at the local level, which involved expanding the constituency of the school system through coordination, confused changes in formal relationships with changes in power relations in a community. The strategy of the "new left," which involved the formation of a new, organized constituency among low-income groups, floundered not only on the limitations on federal power to achieve this objective, but also on the narrow interests of such neighborhood groups once they become politically active.

Yet some amalgamation of these three strategies may provide the political conditions for educational reform. Beginning with the third strategy, the formation of neighborhood groups at least facilitates public recognition of educational needs in disadvantaged areas. Edward Banfield and James Wilson have noted that issues in city politics commonly "arise in response to the maintenance and enhancement needs of large formal organizations"(37). The very lack of such organizations in low-income communities often means that their problems are not satisfactorily considered by public bureaucracies simply because no mechanisms are available for translating these problems into public issues. Politically oriented neighborhood groups, however, depend for their existence on identifying problems that can be translated into spectacular controversies that will involve neighborhood residents in the activities of the organization. Although the organizations may not phrase their demands for resolving these problems in broad enough terms to bring about citywide reform, they do tend to identify areas of concern that may lead others to political action.

On the other hand, neighborhood organizations in minority-group communities do not have the political resources to transform their demands into reform policies. They have neither the numbers, the money, the prestige, the expertise, nor the leadership skills to mobilize by themselves major changes in educational policy. Just as representatives of the poor on coordinating committees are either co-opted or ignored by more powerful interests, organizations of the poor tend to have the capacity to raise issues but not to change educational policies. In Robert Crain's study of school desegregation in eight northern cities, he found that the responsiveness of the school board to civil rights demands was not related in any apparent way to the visible political strength of the civil rights movement(38). That other factors determined the outcome only demonstrates more clearly that such groups do not have the necessary resources to alter public policies through their actions alone.

Yet, once they have publicly dramatized the need for educational reform, neighborhood organizations under certain circumstances are able to generate support for their position on the part of more powerful allies. These allies at the local level are usually members of the business and professional communities who begin to take an interest in ameliorating the plight of Negroes and other minority group citizens. Viewing the community as a functioning whole whose parts are intertwined and interdependent, the ideology of these allies focuses on the community's common needs. The inefficient use of human resources among the lowest stratum of their community is regarded by such leaders as a weakness that reduces the productivity of the community as a whole. Moreover, such conditions generate civil strife and potentially could damage the image of the community throughout the country.

Although these individuals have much in common, it is possible to discern two groups, each having a separate social base and a somewhat distinct ideology. Following Robert Agger, Daniel Goldrich, and Bert Swanson, we shall call these two groups the Progressive Conservatives and the Community Conservationists(39). The Progressive Conservatives are businessmen who believe the community can best prosper if it is guided by men who have sound business sense. They do not believe that business should govern in their own narrowly defined interests but should pursue wise policies that redound to the benefit of the community as a whole. In the area of education they stress not so much economy as the need for rationalization of the educational enterprise so that the "output" of the educational system can be measureably improved. Community Conservationists are upper-middle-class professionals and political leaders who also resist identifying their policies as favoring any particular group. Like the Progressive Conservatives, they too are concerned with rationality and efficiency, but the Community Conservationists are equally concerned with participation by all the people in the common life of the city. They do not agree with the Progressive Conservatives that businessmen are the only ones who can develop sound public policies; in fact, they prefer government by men trained for public service. But though these differences between Community Conservationists and Progressive Conservatives are significant, their mutual concern for common public problems and the similarity of their social status facilitates their coalescing together.

Progressive Conservatives, Community Conservationists, or

some coalition of the two groups have from time to time developed the political strength to achieve significant reform in education. Of the six cities studied by Masters et al., only Trenton, N.J., seemed to be using community action funds effectively to make dramatic changes in educational programming. An apparently crucial change in power relations that preceded this development was the rapidly growing strength of Progressive Conservatives. When Trenton was attacked in a national magazine as a decaying city, business leaders were galvanized to action in order "to repair the city image"(40). After investigating six large cities, Marilyn Gittell et al. report the most extensive educational reforms in the 1960's have occurred in Philadelphia. Reform developments again could be directly traced to changing power relations in the community; the Progressive Conservative–Community Conservationist coalition that had made considerable efforts to reform city government in the 1950's turned its attention to the public school system in the sixties(41). Gittell also reports that Detroit, which made steady but more gradual reforms in the fifties and sixties, also made the most significant reforms when a citywide coalition of Progressive Conservatives and Community Conservationists became interested in school policy(42). Moreover, Crain found school boards most acquiescent to civil rights demands when they were dominated by cohesive groups of Progressive Conservatives(43). Finally, in New York City the pressures for school decentralization are forcing changes in school policy not only because neighborhood groups have made community control an issue but also because a Community Conservationist mayor with the support of leaders in the business and professional community is backing their demands.

The activation of Progressive Conservatives and Community Conservationists in urban school politics thus functions as the coordinating committees were expected to do. This coalition broadens the base for educational reform and forces previously autonomous school officials to listen to a wider public. Whereas the formation of a citywide coordinating committee gives the appearance of changing formal relationships and communication patterns, a citywide reform effort on the part of the business and/or professional community changes power relationships and influence patterns. Such political action has provided a more effective political base for reform than the formal changes promoted by the OEO.

Thirdly, the effectiveness of such a reform effort is greatly enhanced by the availability of federal funds that encourage innovative programming. Mass opposition to school reform is usually limited to defenses of the neighborhood school and resistance to voting higher taxes. Federal contributions to local schools can seriously weaken the tax opposition to reform. Both in Trenton and Philadelphia the reformers relied heavily on poverty program and ESEA funds to finance their innovative policies(44). Thus, even though the decentralized political system makes it impossible for the federal government to change local educational policy directly through centralizing power in the hands of a Presidential "czar," the federal government can assist local reformers by weakening the resistance of a tax-conscious opposition.

National and Local Reform Forces

Throughout such a political process a strange irony is apparent. The allies of Negroes and other minority groups change at different levels of government. A class alliance between the Black and white components of the working and lower classes provides the political base for federal assistance to reform efforts. Since Roosevelt assisted the labor movement in the 1930's, labor unions have become in many ways the organizational arm of the Democratic party, perpetuating in organized form the realignment of the two-party system along class lines. With the working class as its social base and unions as its organizational arm, the northern Democratic party has consistently defended the interests of consumers, urbanites, minority groups, and the poor. The juvenile delinquency program, the Economic Opportunity Act, and the Elementary and Secondary Education Act were all programs sponsored by Democratic Presidents and overwhelmingly supported by northern Democratic Congressmen. Consequently, minority groups find the national Democratic party with a working-class base a crucial political asset.

Thus, the "new left" might well consider organizing the deprived for political action which will strengthen the Democratic party as the expression of the interests of the working and lower classes. It would then add a dynamic component to the strategy of the "old left." The "old left," content with the power relations produced by the realignment of the parties in the thirties, has failed to remember that its own strength in American political life was related to the extension of the political community to include unskilled workers. If the "new left" recognizes the validity of the "old left's" emphasis on federal action, it may then orient the constituency it seeks to develop toward the broad class coalition of forces necessary to support liberal uses of Presidential power. This would provide the dynamic component necessary to strengthen Presidential power so that federal assistance to educational reform continues to expand.

At the local level, on the other hand, class alliances apparently do not provide the political base for educational reform in the interest of minority groups. Instead, the most consistent allies of Negroes in the past few years have been middle-class professionals and prominent businessmen. These groups, to be sure, have not supported the most militant demands of the Black community, even as the national Democratic party has made only modest commitments to solving urban problems. Nonetheless, the cleavage at the local level has been more a conflict between "public-regarding" versus "private-regarding" groups than that of class conflict. The "public-regarding" faction, as Banfield and Wilson have described it, consists of Negroes and upper-middle-class, Protestant and Jewish businessmen and professionals—the Progressive Conservatives and Community Conservationists(45). This faction has in common a concern for increasing the scope of government to resolve the mutual problems faced by the community. The "private-regarding" faction, consisting of working- and lower-middle-class immigrant groups of Eastern and Southern European descent, are more concerned with maintaining low taxes and protecting their own neighborhood than with resolving citywide problems through increased government intervention.

This disjunction between national and local politics is easier to recognize and characterize than it is to explain. The reasons for upper- and middle-class support for conservative policies nationally and reform policies locally and for working- and lower-middle-class support for liberal policies nationally and status quo policies locally are not readily apparent. But an explanation may begin to emerge from the following observations.

National and local tax structures are noticeably different. The preponderance of national sources of revenue come from taxes on the incomes of individuals and corporations. This is not only the most progressive tax in the country, but the withholding feature also makes it relatively invisible. The primary local sources of revenue for educational systems is the property tax, which falls particularly noticeably and heavily on the lower-middle- and working-class homeowner. The price for educational improvements paid out of local revenue appears to be, and actually is, much greater for this working-class population than is federal assistance. Secondly, the working class attachment to the Democratic party has been more an attachment to a long-standing supporter of working class interests dating back to a dark and bitter depression experience than it is the attachment of individuals who have well-organized ideologies which dictate certain policy preferences. Thus, working-class citizens may support a party even though they do not overtly agree with every program the party develops. Leaders within the Democratic party and the trade union movement, however, have a much more highly organized ideology which constrains them to act in a more consistently liberal direction than they would if their constituency's preferences more directly controlled their behavior(46).

On the other hand, the business community finds itself willing to support government expansion to meet community problems locally even though it supports Republican opposition to such policies nationally. The latter can be partly explained by the long-standing and close relationship between the business community and the Republican party in national politics. The former may be due to the greater personal and business identification businessmen have with the fate of the local community. Whereas working class citizens oppose reform locally because of the visibility of the cost of reform, business supports reform locally because of the visibility of the benefits. Personally familiar with the directors of the educational enterprise, they can take pride in knowing that their investment has been well spent. The competition among communities generates concern that their city not be overtaken by spectacular performances elsewhere. They also desire that their city gets its fair share of the federal dollar, which may explain the familiar but peculiar finding that businessmen, opposed as they are to federal control, invariably accept federal aid for a wide array of educational programs.

Conclusion

There are undoubtedly many variations to the politics of educational reform that we have not taken into account here. Yet the basic tendencies that have been identified lead to the rather pessimistic conclusion that such reform is not likely to proliferate rapidly across the country. Major educational reform seems to depend on the joint coincidence of organized demands for change in minority group communities, the rise of a Progressive Conservative–Community Conservationist movement in local school politics, and the availability of substantial federal funds. Newspaper publicity to the contrary, organized Negro militancy (as distinct from anomic outbursts of protest) is an ephemeral phenomenon; reform movements, as George Washington Plunkitt observed, are only "mornin' glories" that wither away in the heat of political infighting; and federal aid to education increases only slowly, subject always to the vagaries of both international and national partisan conflict. The confluence of these factors has only begun to occur with some degree of regularity, which may help to explain the low repute into which urban education has fallen. Only a bold optimist would claim that a secular trend in favor of educational reform will steadily and surely develop in most American cities in the next decade. The political obstacles to such reform are too entrenched a part of the American political system to be swept away without further turmoil and conflict.

Notes

1. James S. Coleman et al., *Equality of Educational Opportunity* (Washington: U.S. Government Printing Office, 1966), p. 325.

2. A critical look at Harlem schools can be found in the planning document for a New York poverty program written under the direction of Kenneth Clark, *Youth in the Ghetto* (New York: Harlem Youth Opportunities, Unlimited, 1964). The disproportionate spending on schools in higher

income communities rather than lower income communities in Detroit in the mid-fifties is documented in Patricia Sexton, *Education and Income* (New York: Viking Press, 1962).

3. Sar A. Levitan, "Planning the Anti-Poverty Strategy," *Poverty and Human Resources Abstracts,* II (January 1967), 10.

4. This phrase by Walter Lippmann is quoted in Arthur Schlesinger, Jr., *The Politics of Upheavel* (Boston: Houghton Mifflin Company, 1960), p. 399.

5. Grant McConnell, *Private Power and American Democracy* (New York: Alfred A. Knopf, Inc., 1966), p. 351.

6. For analyses of the changing social compositions of the two parties during this period, see V. O. Key, "A Theory of Critical Elections," *Journal of Politics,* XXVII (1955), 3–18; and Angus Campbell et al., *The American Voter* (New York: John Wiley & Sons, Inc., 1960), pp. 149–67.

7. When class divisions are confused by the electoral process, such as in one-party states in the South and in non-partisan politics in many communities, the electoral system facilitates the dominance of the economic and social elite. V. O. Key, *Southern Politics* (New York: Random House, Inc., 1949). Also see Oliver Williams and Charles Adrian, "The Insulation of Local Politics under the Nonpartisan Ballot," *American Political Science Review,* LII (1958), 1059–61.

8. Ernest Griffith, *The American System of Government* (New York: Frederick A. Praeger, Inc., 1960), p. 93.

9. Levitan, op. cit., pp. 13–14.

10. Sar A. Levitan, "Planning the Anti-Poverty Strategy, Part II," *Poverty and Human Resources Abstracts,* II (March 1967), 9.

11. U.S. Congress, *An Act to Mobilize the Human and Financial Resources of the Nation to Combat Poverty in the United States,* Public Law 88–452, 88th Cong., 2d sess. (Washington, D.C.: Government Printing Office, 1964), p. 24.

12. Marilyn Gittell, *Participants and Participation* (New York: Center for Urban Education, 1967), p. 57.

13. Peter Marris and Martin Rein, *Dilemmas of Social Reform* (New York: Atherton Press, 1967), p. 17.

14. Ibid.

15. Bernard C. Watson, "The National Teachers Corps: A Tale of Three Cities," *Administrator's Notebook,* XVI (January 1968), No. 5.

16. Gary Orfield, "The Reconstruction of Southern Education" (Ph.D. diss., Department of Political Science, University of Chicago, 1965).

17. Marris and Rein, op. cit., p. 229.

18. Nicholas A. Masters et al., "Politics, Poverty and Education: An Analysis of Decision-making Structures," Report submitted to the Office of Economic Opportunity by the Institute of Public Administration (University Park, Pa.: Pennsylvania State University, February 1968), p. 366.

19. Ibid., p. 382.

20. Michael Usdan and Raphael Nystrand, "Towards Participative Decision-making: The Impact of Community Action Programs," *Teachers College Record,* LXVIII (November 1966), 101.

21. Kirschner Associates, Inc., "A Description and Evaluation of Selected Educational Components of Community Action Programs," Report submitted to the Office of Economic Opportunity, I (Albuquerque, New Mexico, May 1967), 69–70.

22. U.S. Congress, *An Act to Mobilize the Human and Financial Resources of the Nation to Combat Poverty,* op. cit., p. 9.

23. Office of Economic Opportunity, *Community Action Workbook,* I (Washington, D.C., 1965), 18.

24. Michael Harrington, "The Mystical Militants," *New Republic,* CLIV, No. 8 (1966), 21–22.

25. T. Gitlin, "Power and the Myth of Progress," *New Republic,* CLIII, No. 26 (1965), 20–21.

26. Ibid.

27. Tom Hayden, "The Ability to Face Whatever Comes," *New Republic,* CLIV, No. 3 (1966), 17.

28. The concept is taken from David Truman, *The Governmental Process* (New York: Alfred A. Knopf, Inc., 1955).

29. Office of Economic Opportunity, *Community Action Program Guide,* I (Washington, D.C., 1965), 18.

30. Masters et al., p. 381, their italics.

31. Usdan and Nystrand, op. cit., p. 102.

32. Kirschner Associates, op. cit., p. 70.

33. Paul E. Peterson, "City Politics and Community Action," (Ph.D. diss., Department of Political Science, University of Chicago, 1967), Ch. 3 and 4.

34. McConnell, op. cit., pp. 113, 345.

35. Massive Economic Neighborhood Development, "A Proposal for Community Action in East Harlem" (Proposal submitted to the Office of Economic Opportunity, 1965), mimeographed.

36. Andrew Kopkind, "Down the Down Staircase," *New Republic,* CLV, No. 17 (1966), 12.

37. Edward Banfield and James Wilson, *City Politics* (Cambridge, Mass.: Harvard University Press, 1963), p. 28.

38. Robert Crain, "Desegregation in the North," Report 110-A of the National Opinion Research Center (Chicago, Ill.: University of Chicago, April 1966), Ch. 10–11.

39. Robert Agger, Daniel Goldrich, and Bert Swanson, *The Rulers and the Ruled* (New York: John Wiley & Sons, Inc., 1964), *passim.*

40. Masters et al., op. cit., p. 375.

41. Marilyn Gittell, T. Edward Hollander, and William S. Vincent, "Investigation of Fiscally Independent and Dependent City School Districts," Cooperative Research Project of the Office of Education No. 3237 (New York, 1967), Part II, Ch. 3.

42. Ibid., pp. 145–55.

43. Crain, op. cit., Ch. 12–13.

44. Masters et al., op. cit., pp. 284–363; Gittell, Hollander, and Vincent, op. cit., Part II, Ch. 3.

45. Banfield and Wilson, op. cit., pp. 234–40.

46. The greater organization of belief systems among political elites than among the mass population is elaborated in Philip E. Converse, "The Nature of Belief Systems in Mass Publics," in *Ideology and Discontent,* ed. David E. Apter (New York: Free Press, 1964), pp. 206–61.

12

Norms Governing Urban-State Politics of Education

Laurence Iannaccone

Introduction

The problems of urban education are not usually viewed from the standpoint of the state politics of education. Yet, it is increasingly important to be realistically aware of the general relationships which exist between the schools of urban centers and their state governments. This awareness is necessary because the constitutional view of the relationship between the states and their urban centers suggests that paramount power over the city's educational system is lodged in the state. The hope consequently exists that, however discouraging the immediate urban educational scene, whatever the presently insoluble problems of the city schools, and despite the apparent immutableness of their governments, things eventually will be improved.

The question this chapter seeks to answer is: how realistic is this hope? Any attempt to answer the question must take into account the political realities which characterize the relationships between states and their largest school districts. Such an assessment must include the major norms governing the state politics of education and those governing urban-state educational politics. From the standpoint of key decision-makers, these provide the frames of reference for their behavior in the decision-making process. The norms involved are also interdependent with the social structures that contain and channel the decision-making processes for educational issues in the urban-state relationship. Finally, the significance of the major norms, the characteristic behavior of the actors, and the social structures in which they operate will be examined under a condition of stress. The New York City reorganization struggle at Albany will provide a vehicle for this.

A realistic examination indicates that educational issues are taken up by the state board, legislature, and governor only when the urban educational government cannot deal with the problems it faces. This inability may result from the urban school district's lack of legal power. State legislative action is often needed to modify elements in the body of special legislation applicable to one or a few large cities in the state. In general, when the organized professionals and lay interest groups involved in education are largely agreed, the political consequences of this agreement reinforce the status quo. No extensive power struggle is likely to ensue in the city. The city's major political figures will probably ignore these matters. The central bodies of state government tend to ratify routinely those agreements coming from the urban center. Most of the state legislation about urban education is processed this way. The vast bulk of such legislation is concerned with regulation of the profession itself and day-to-day operations of the school.

The Initiative Norm

The first norm of urban educational state politics is *the initiative norm*. It dictates that: *State governments take up urban educational problems only on request from the urban educational authorities and interest groups.*

The stress placed upon the political systems by requests for special financial aid for urban schools sometimes appears to violate this norm. In fact, the flow of events subsequent to such requests is governed by the initiative norm in conjunction with other major norms discussed later in this chapter. When the urban educational government's incapacity to deal with its problems stems from a lack of financial resources instead, more important political consequences exist for the city. These matters are also more serious for the participants to decisions in the central state bodies and offices when requests come from the city for special financial aid. Then the legislators and governor are faced with the problem of reallocating state funds, to the advantage of the city, at least to some extent, and at the expense of the rest of the state. This becomes a matter of concern for legislators, other officials, and their constituencies outside of the city. Struggles between state and city political machines may be expected around the legislative bodies and the governor's office. Consequences of these more or less serious struggles will be felt in the city's political structure. A reallocation of state monies to provide relief for urban schools will at least engage the attention and require time from the city's political machinery and may threaten the urban educational government with interference from the city government.

Most often the city school district's success at obtaining special financial aid from the state requires the support and active services of the mayor and the city's political bosses. Thus the mayor of Chicago may have to by-pass the School Problems Commission in Illinois and deal directly with the governor's office and the party leaders of the legislative houses. The customary political bargaining characterizing city-state politics will then take place. Frequently the bargaining and political struggles seen in such instances engage the political party structures. Partisan politics become especially visible when the dominant party in state legislatures or in control of the governor's office is different from the dominant party in the city. The activities in these instances are more usefully viewed as party politics and the politics of conflict between the city and its state parties than as peculiarly the politics of education. Given a condition of stress, state governmental leaders and legislators generally treat urban educational matters primarily as urban affairs rather than firstly as educational issues.

Norm of Political Stress

The second major norm can be seen providing the frame of reference for the actors, *the norm of political stress. Educational issues involving urban educational, municipal and state governmental structures and actors will be viewed by legislator and the governor's office as urban politics rather than as educational politics.*

The State Politics of Education

The state pattern of educational politics is a major element indeed; it forms part of the framework for the urban-state politics surrounding educational issues, and needs to be understood as supporting both the initiative and stress norms.

The dominant two-party system of American politics has been customarily avoided by the politics of education. Nicholas A. Masters et al., found politicians, at least at the state level, had concluded there is no political coinage in education(1). This results from the broad American commitment to education and belief that education is operating in the public interest. The public school lobby in most states thus finds ready access to the key decision-makers in state government: education and finance committee leaders in the legislative houses, majority and minority party leaders in each house, state school board members, the state's chief school officer, and of course, the governor. Education's demands for state governmental action are articulated in each state by a pyramid of power organized in statewide associations of professional educators, e.g., elementary principals, superintendents, and classroom teachers, and their lay allies such as the White House Conference group in Missouri. Thus, acting directly upon state offices inside and outside of the legislature, instead of through the parties, the lobby plays a dominant role in developing state educational policies. This conforms to and supports the initiative norm.

The survival of the monolithic statewide pattern of educational politics rests upon the continuance of uncritical public support of the present educational system. It does not require the automatic support of every feature of public education or each element of the curriculum but the unquestioned support of the basic system of public education as it has developed in America. This has to date been a development largely in conformity to sacred community values. These specifically maximize the values of social integration and conservative maintenance of the social status quo.

Given the direct involvement of the professional associational leadership in state educational legislation and the sacred community values represented by schools not to mention the organized schoolmen, it is understandable that low-pressure politics characterizes the state politics of education. The characteristic behavioral style of schoolmen engaged in the state politics of education is one of avoidance of confrontation and political conflict. The mythology that education and politics are and should remain separate reinforce this low-pressure style and the political power of schoolmen associations. The commitment to sacred values, also, means that the profession's associational leadership will be slow to adjust to needed innovation and be suspicious of the larger and secular urban areas.

The natural leadership of the state educational associations tends to insure further that conservative sacred community values will be expressed by the educational lobby. The continued existence through this century of such associations and the iron law of oligarchy to which such associations are subject tend to produce a conservative, rurally oriented, low-pressure, and consensus-rather-than-conflict type of politician. These politicians work especially through the legislative committees of education and finance, which are chaired most often by rural legislators. They seldom understand nor can they feel deeply the urban educational plight.

Finally, while the typical schoolman's pyramid is described as statewide in its organizational form, the large city tends not to be included in it. This is true of Detroit in Michigan, Los Angeles in California, New York City in New York, and St. Louis in Missouri —to cite four instances. Nor is this the result of recent teacher union growth in such cities. Instead, it is more fundamentally a cultural reflection of the politics preferred by pedagogues, and the result of the historic reorganization of the National Education Association, designed to destroy the influence of the urban teachers(2). The brutal fact is that the city's organized educators, such as New York City's Council of Supervisory Associations, simply have no role in the traditional educationist lobby found in the prevailing pattern of state educationist politics.

It was stated earlier that the legislator's view under stress of urban educational issues as urban politics rather than educational was supported by the most commonly found pattern of state educational politics. The absence of the city's professionals from the schoolman's lobby plays a large part here. The sacred rural orientation and suspicion of the city is shared by the leaders of the lobby and legislative committees. Then, too, the secular values and political style of the city's spokesmen stand in contrast to those prevailing among the state educational association careerists. There is little in the prevailing pattern of educational politics, as experienced by the state legislator, which would make him view urban educational issues as primarily matters of schooling.

Two other patterns of state educational politics exist. These are found less often than the prevailing pattern described earlier. In states where the power of localism outweighs the statewide influence of the educational associations and interest groups, the state educational pyramids lack the power to initiate legislative policy successfully. Their victories are many fewer and legislators tend to rely on local schoolmen rather than the state association careerists for advice. These states tend, also, to give less fiscal support to education. The ready access to legislative leaders through the educationist pyramids, found in the more common pattern, is missing here.

However, the attitudes of schoolmen and legislators are no less suspicious of the urbanities and the city's problems than is found in the prevailing pattern. If anything, in the states where localism prevails, the school is even more expected to support socially integrative values and help maintain the status quo. The political style reflects the rural community values, and low-pressure politics prevail. The largest school district in such a state and its educational needs are likely to be treated as primarily local affairs and not as a general state concern. In these states, too, it can be seen, the initiative and stress norms govern the politics of urban educational and state political affairs.

An additional pattern of educational politics at the state level has been studied(3). It appears to be one of the least common and has been described as *statewide fragmented*.

The associational networks of school people are found fragmented and in conflict in this pattern. Intense political struggles occur at times, breaking into the open even in the legislative process. Secular values tend to be held in these legislatures. Emphasis is placed upon the school as an agency of change. The urban center is viewed more favorably than in any of the other patterns. Nevertheless, the traditional educational lobby of these states also operate without the inclusion of large-city educators. The larger city school districts may obtain a better hearing in these legislatures than in most; nevertheless, the city's affairs, even those of its schools, are treated as local matters here because of the fragmentation.

It may be seen that in each of these patterns the propensity of state officials to view the problems of the city's schools as primarily urban issues is reinforced by the state's characteristic educational interest group pattern. In the most common pattern, the rural bias and the omission of the city school professionals from the educationist lobby hardly challenges that viewpoint. In states where localism dominates the legislative minds generally and educational policies specifically there is even less chance that urban education matters will be seen as generally significant to the entire state. The fragmented pattern of state educational politics, by its very nature, better opens the way to state officials for the city's spokesmen and representatives. Still, the fragmented condition of the educational interest groups makes it virtually impossible to develop a general concern for urban educational problems. Thus, despite the variations in the patterns of state educational politics, the initiative and stress norms are the same in all. They decrease the probability that state governmental action will solve the knotty problems faced by urban education.

One myth in the politics of urban-state political relations is that the state legislative blocs, for example the "outstate" representatives in Missouri or "upstate" legislators in New York, combine systematically against the big city and its interests. The myth is not supported by the facts at the capitols. Were the myth a true representation of legislative voting behavior, the practical political possibility might exist of intervention by the state to solve the city's educational problems where the city's schools and their establishment failed. But the chief norms governing state legislative involvement in urban education would be violated by such action.

Additional Political Reasons
Supporting the Norms

Almost always the initiative for state action on urban educational problems lies exclusively in the hands of the local urban educational authorities. As was pointed out at the beginning of this chapter, most of the city school district's requests will be honored by the legislature as long as the city's educational interest groups are united in support of such requests. This also assumes that the requests are not at the expense of the rest of the state. Where limited resources are needed, political conflict is more likely to result. Still a third situation exists when requests come from the city schools for state action—particularly legislative—without agreement among the city's appropriate interest groups. Then political conflict will be highly visible both within the city and at the state capitol. Not infrequently, requests for special funds and internecine conflict among the city's educational interests groups are significantly related.

The unusual event of a request for a special financial aid for the city schools is now becoming more frequent. It is triggered by any one of a variety of causes and often a combination of several. The city schools may have developed an overgrown bureaucracy which absorbs too much of its funds in specialized or administrative services. Its civil service maintenance operations may cost much more than the services are worth. The influx of new population into the city may require more specialized help than can be provided within the traditional budget. Teacher organizations with militant leadership may use the strike effectively to absorb all new funds arising through the normal means of funding the city schools. The shift of wealth to the suburbs and the increase in the city poor with larger families may place great stress on the schools. But whatever the trigger, major internal political conflict is likely to result. The request for special state financial aid is very likely to be the one issue on which the city's population and the educational interest groups are agreed. In other words, there is probably a high correlation between urban requests for special state aid and the breakdown of urban consensus around educational policy. This also suggests that a serious gap exists between the educational authorities and the clients of the urban schools. Such gaps are usually the product of relatively closed and isolated political systems in education(4).

The largest urban school districts will, in most states at least, have developed increasingly isolated from the rest of the state. Gradually the body of special legislation governing city school employees, for example, has expanded, making them different in training, recruitment, selection, and general outlook from the rest of the state's people. It is predictable that urban school people will more and more attribute these differences to the uniqueness of the city's educational problems. They will "sweep under the rug" the extent to which that "uniqueness" is artificially produced by the cumulative effects of a half-century or more or special legislation and local governmental isolation.

It may be noted in passing that city employees, including teachers, have profited to no small extent from this local governmental isolation. Except for requests from the state for more dollars, urban educational organizations will almost always be found mounting a thrust for greater isolation and insulation from other governments. The most common state legislative activities on behalf of the city schools have acceded to this thrust for the control of personnel, procedural regulation of the system's daily affairs, and its internal governmental operations. Often such special legislation further solidifies the rigidity and peculiar parochialism displayed by the civil service operators of the most cosmopolitan cities. Requests for state action in the usual course of business hardly ever get to the state capitol until prior agreement is achieved among the urban educational interest groups. These can afford to wait for agreement because the matters that chiefly engage them tend to be the timeless concern of professions for autonomy and control of their service area rather than the anxiety displayed by the liberal establishment over decaying school systems and the intellectual death of children. The issues involved seldom command the serious attention of any other appreciable bloc of voters in the city. Almost no one else in the state is even aware of them. But the urban educational lobby has its allies at the capitol.

The urban politics of education focuses on the special privileges and privileged sanctuaries produced by special legislation. Its political conflicts occur mainly in its own governmental arenas and those of the city, e.g., mayor and council, city board of estimates. Its local political activities are likely to involve other public service areas and employee groups; sometimes education is in conflict with some of these and sometimes in alliances with them in struggles over the city's scarce resources. Such services areas and their organized interest groups, especially employee groups, are likely to display a solidarity of city labor forces in confrontations with state legislatures and state offices.

The city coalitions tend to operate within a tradition reflecting their local urban political norms. At the center of this tradition is the understanding that each public service and public employee group will control its own world. Thus while teachers and administrators fight over control of school employees the firemen, policemen, and sanitation workers will often stay out of the struggle. It is a family fight. Similarly, struggles between the organized patrolmen and the top brass of the city police force are not supposed to be interferred with by teachers. When the political struggle involves tapping the public till, the municipal employee groups tend to stay out of each other's way at least.

Thus it is consistent with these norms that at the state capitol each municipal service area is allowed to initiate its own proposals for its service area. Indeed, the norm calls for neutrality at least, if not support, from the rest of the city's municipal lobbies. It may readily be seen that only extreme circumstances would produce a situation in which the legislature itself initiated remedial legislation concerning city schools. To do otherwise would subject it to the intense pressure of the combined lobbies of organized municipal management, municipal employee groups, and their urban labor allies with all of the urban political machinery this alliance normally influences! Why would any sane legislative leadership group or governor undertake this struggle?

Thus, the urban norms for public-service groups reinforce and refine the state legislative norms for dealing with urban educational problems. Proposals to solve the city's problems must come from the city, and the vested interests in the public service areas play by the rule of "live and let live." Consequently, the norm is that the state government responds to the initiatives of the urban educational authorities.

The results of the norms found at state and local levels are to increase the isolation and political closedness of the urban educational authorities and employee associations. In turn, this produces a more and more rigid set of policies and practices in the urban school system. If, as has been increasingly the case since World War II, the social makeup of the city undergoes change, the educational policies and practices of the schools will become increasingly irrelevant to the social groups the schools are supposed to serve. The growing gap between the societal demands on the schools and the policies of the urban educational government will result in political conflict(5). The political conflict beginning in the city will eventually challenge the norms governing the relationship between urban educational politics and state government. Whether such challenges are likely to be successful is another question.

The Local Unity Norm

It is the combination of an urban request for special financial aid and internal urban political conflict which results in a challenge to the norm of leaving the initiative for urban educational decisions in the city. Nevertheless, the norm is preserved as much as possible even under these circumstances. Thus the need for special financial aid for the New York City schools in the early 1960's led to demands by the legislature for studies of the schools' problems and changes in the board and central administration. These may have been mere sops to appease the legislative conscience. But the efforts by Mayor John V. Lindsay to obtain special funds in 1967 and the subsequent political struggles over reorganization, decentralization, and community control serve to illustrate how the combination of a request for special funds and urban political conflict in education may challenge the norm concerning the source of urban educational legislation. These events severely tested the third great norm governing the state politics of urban education, *the local unity norm*.

The local unity norm calls for legislators to support local representatives when they are united in requesting legislation affecting only their locality. This norm is the basis for most special legislation. The norm is essentially conservative because, if the local representatives are not united, the other legislators will not approve requests for change. Thus proposals for change affecting a given local area, including local educational proposals, must enlist the near-unanimous support of local legislators for passage. The process is heavily weighted against change. It is also heavily weighted in favor of local political establishments and against challengers of old-guard establishments. Nor can it be used by a single innovative local legislator as a means to blackmail the rest of the local delegation into action. For the norm of local unity is not used mechanically or blindly. The definition of local agreement is flexible in most circumstances, so it is a workable norm. It neither requires complete unanimity nor bipartisan agreement but does require substantial agreement in the local delegation, and particularly respected or powerful leaders of local legislative delegations must be together for them to win. Thus united local interests win on educational issues involving their area; but divided, they lose.

It follows that rural interests are not correctly described as intransigently united in opposition to urban interests. Further, the local unity norm and the norm of state dependence upon the initiative of the urban area reinforce each other. The myth that the rural and suburban legislators block efforts at solving urban educational problems is useful to the large-city establishments which wish to avoid change. Together the three norms, in effect, place the initiative for urban educational policy change in the hands of the urban school district's authorities, even under extreme stress. When people look to the state legislature for relief from these, they encounter a norm which says the initiative for change must come from these same local urban educational authorities.

Even if some local legislators or interest group can be talked into trying to lead the way toward innovation or reform of the urban educational system, they would encounter the local unity norm requiring substantial agreement among the area's representatives. But if such a political consensus for change existed in the urban school district, it would not need to look to the state capitol to solve its problems. The request of the local educational establishment would be honored by the legislature, given the agreement of the local state representatives. This condition may be one of the chief reasons that a request for special financial aid often touches off a demand for urban school district reform at the state capitol. When such a demand converges with the urban conflicts generated by the widened gap between the urban school's clientele and the policies of its educational authorities, major political struggles may shake the state legislative leadership itself. It is the stress that such events place upon the state machinery of government and its relationships to the urban educational government which engages the latent social structures and more fully reveals their significance. The stress norm is brought into play and the matters at issue become defined as urban politics—not education. In this process the public interest in education constitutionally retained in the state becomes effectively redefined as the special private interest of the profession delegated to the city.

Cause of Stress

The fundamental cause producing major stress in the urban-state politics of education lies in the development of a major discrepancy between the policies of educational authorities and the demands of their clients. The discrepancy is produced by the fully-developed isolation and closed nature of the urban school district's political system when the city's population has recently undergone major change in social composition. Stated another way, the gap produced by a changing social composition of the city, while its educational government continues to reflect the city's former social composition, is the proximate cause of major political stress pushing educational issues to the state capitol.

The necessary but not sufficient conditions for this stress include the local unity norm and the norm of leaving the initiative on urban educational affairs to the local educational authorities. In addition, the urban norm which makes the city's educational issues the exclusive affair of the educational authorities and of the organized education employees is necessary. Further, one should not ignore the role played by ignorance. The changed social composition of the city almost certainly implies the influx of new citizens largely unsophisticated in the political ways of city bureaucracies. Much energy and time is spent by them in going through formal channels and being baffled by public hearings. The knowledgeable insiders of the bureaucracy will bypass such channels and meetings or, where necessary, go through proper motions in these but still use the many semi-formal by-paths developed by all large, complex, and security-bound civil service bureaus. The explosiveness of urban educational politics, when these surface in the legislature, is partly to be attributed to the frustration and lack of mutual understanding produced by ignorance of the system on the part of the city's new populations in contrast to the cleverness of the bureaucrats and public employees associations. Because of that ignorance, political stress develops slowly upon the central agencies of state government.

Governmental decision-making bodies, the urban school board for example, display a habit of repetitive behavior. Old bureaucracies, urban educational ones no less than any other, develop rigidity and repeatedly provide their clients with whatever services their regulations call for regardless of the clients' needs. This conservative and rule-bound behavior is precisely the opposite of what is needed by the new urban dwellers. Conflict follows and increases.

It is rigid policies in the areas of the curriculum and teaching behavior which first become the target of the new city's population. The failure to achieve serious curriculum change or the continued and growing hostility between their children and teachers forces the new population to turn to the replacement of teachers for ones more understanding and sympathetic to their children. The conflict produced illuminates further how the bureaucratic rigidity at the lower levels of the urban school finds its counterpart in the rigidity of central office and school board. These defend and continue to promulgate outmoded personnel policies. To illustrate: Most urban school districts continue to use local examinations and exclusive licensure patterns to select teachers. This, first of all, ignores the fact that such local selection systems were developed in response to a form of political corruption which requires a shortage of teaching jobs for its proper function. Today there is instead a shortage of teachers, particularly in the largest school districts. Secondly, these local selection systems were developed at a time when the states' systems of certifying teachers was qualitative. The relative quality requirements of state certification versus city licensure has been reversed by the history of the last 30 years. Thirdly, the chief sources of political patronage in the city schools have changed from the teaching roles to the safer custodial and maintenance jobs or contracts. Despite this, the vested interests developed by organized teacher groups and headquarter's staffs in running their own licensure system perpetuates the outmoded patterns and policies in the personnel area.

However dysfunctional the outmoded personnel policies and systems may be viewed from the perspective of the new urban dwellers' needs, there are good reasons for their persistence from the viewpoint of the civil servants involved. The belief that the particular urban schools are unique and therefore should be the subject of special legislation is supported by these personnel policies and systems. They help support the defensive behavior of the urban teachers, their organizations, and the city schools' management groups. Most important, the local personnel system's isolation from the rest of the state protects the insiders from outside competition for up-the-line professional positions, such as administrative, supervisory, and central office ones. With the increasingly closed nature of these systems comes protection for the older urban dwellers against the competition that the new urban dwellers might offer, too. It is the chief means by which the vested interests of the older civil servants, including teachers, can protect their advantages in spite of the changed social composition of the large city. Naturally, the longer they manage to hang on to their perquisites the greater the gap between their performance and the needs of the new urban populations. The gap grows even greater when older residents of the city move out, especially when these live in the suburb but work in the city. Conflict between the new urban dwellers and the city school personnel becomes sharpest when the latter move out of the city but cling to authority positions within the urban schools. These are developments which more and more characterize the political structures of urban education in the United States.

The failure of new urban residents to modify educational programs and replace personnel, even custodial employees, in time calls into question the legitimacy of the governing group itself. The new urban residents challenge the membership of the school board and, if this coincides with requests to the state government for special funds, it is likely to produce some political conflict at the state capitol between elected representatives of the changing urban neighborhoods and those representing the more stable ones. Not infrequently, state-initiated investigations of the urban schools are undertaken. Often the membership of the urban school board is changed. This in part reflects the challengers' lack of sophistication concerning the internal politics of city bureaus, including the educational one. Merely changing the composition of the school board does little to break the hold that the headquarters staff and municipal employee groups have over educational operations. It does, after a time, indicate their real power over school board decisions. That power rests largely upon the control of board agendas, a monopoly of the information flow from the schools to the board, the organized strength of the employee groups over their members, their political alliances to other municipal employees, and the city political machines from their grassroots to the bosses.

If these repeated failures do not drive the politically-deprived residents of the city into apathy, learning takes place. As this occurs, the focus of the challenge to the city's educational establishment shifts by successive approximations closer to the heart of the resistance to change. This is the structure of governance of the urban school itself. With the failure to accomplish meaningful reform of the schools through changing the membership of the board there comes the demand to reform the governmental structure of the school district itself. This demand must be made of the state's legislature and of the governor to be effective. Often the constitutional arrangement determines this. But given the political realities, regardless of the constitutional latitude a city's school system may have to change its structure of governance, the effort must be made at the state capitol. Otherwise we should see a system which, having successfully beaten off the reformer's challengers, turns around at its moment of success and reforms itself!

A Case of Stress

The importance of financial failure in the city can be clearly seen here. Triggered by whatever combination of factors, the request for special funds made at the state capitol at least forces some questioning of the norms governing urban-state political relations in education. The legislature must at least symbolically indicate to the city, but especially to its other constituencies, that such special requests will not be treated as automatic. Some effort must be made by the legislature to protect itself from the charge that it supports the city's corruption or fiscal irresponsibility. The apologies for giving special financial aid to the city at the expense of the rest of the state often take the form of investigation of the city's educational operation to insure prudent use of future monies and to prevent the special request from becoming a biennial affair. This opens the legislative door to reformers. Thus, for example, the request by Mayor Lindsay for special funds for the New York City schools in 1967 gave a mayor more sympathetic to the plight of the Black and Puerto Rican neighborhoods an opportunity to restructure the New York City school government. The legislature in voting special funds requested of the Mayor a plan for reorganizing the city's schools so as to make it more responsive to the city's inhabitants.

Seldom in recent years has any issue, other than the state budget, stalled the process of a legislature as much as the proposed reorganization of the governing structure of the New York City schools. During the course of two legislative sessions—with a presidential election year intervening—the governor, leaders of both houses, the state board, and the state's chief school officer were repeatedly and frustratingly sucked into the vortex of political conflict over this situation. So were the Mayor of New York, the legislators of New York City, and its school board. The activity of the city lobbies could be felt repeatedly in Albany.

The sequence of events in the legislative process is instructive. They began with a request by Mayor Lindsay for fiscal aid to the New York City schools. In order to avoid tampering with the state-aid formula and still give the city schools financial relief, it was suggested that each of the city's five boroughs be treated as a different district. In addition, the Mayor was asked to provide a plan for decentralization of the city's schools. The evidence indicates the legislature's leaders did not anticipate serious political stress to come from this. It did, however, provide the reformers in the city with a launching pad for their work. During the following legislative year, when the Mayor presented his proposals, the majority leader in the lower house, which normally would have led the way in any action concerning the city's finances, was ready to institutionalize the new mode of computing state aid for the city schools without further action. Thus the city might have obtained a regular increase in state aid by means of a *pro forma* compliance with the request for a plan of decentralization.

Matters did not go so smoothly. Political pressures mounted

for the reform of the urban school's system of governance. The Mayor's proposals, and subsequent bills for this purpose, were not sent to the education committee of either house. They were handled by the New York City Committee in each case. Despite the colorful details of the political tactics of each side of the struggle, despite the repeated failures of legislative leadership to effect a compromise, despite the emotional response to the murder of Martin Luther King, despite the rare initiative of the New York State Board of Regents, and despite the involvement of the commissioner, the governor, and a variety of national, state, and local figures, most of what took place followed predictions based upon the norms described earlier.

The newspaper accounts and observations at Albany agreed that the legislative leadership and the governor could have mustered enough votes for or against a genuine decentralization in either legislative session, if one condition had existed. That condition was substantial agreement among New York City legislators. In the absence of this, the basic decision in each of two legislative sessions was to modify the composition of the board and its mode of selection but to return the responsibility for reorganization back to the city.

Thus, under conditions of massive political stress, the basic norms governing the urban-state politics of education remained. The occasion for serious state-level political bargaining around urban educational issues, specifically a request for special funds, existed. The Office of the Mayor was called upon for this and hence the traditional isolation of the city schools' government from the municipal government was modified, at least for a time. The initial state action was designed to avoid tampering with the public school state-aid formula. From this point on, the traditional state politics of education was excluded from future developments. In fact, the New York State Educational Conference Board and the state education lobby were remarkable for their absence from these conflicts through two years. The state education lobby treats education issues of the large city as urban rather education matters. As pointed out earlier, the prevailing pattern in the state politics of education reinforces the legislators' view that city school issues are primarily urban rather than educational. The referral of the decentralization bills to the city committees and to the education committees of the legislature further pays tribute to this frame of reference.

The initiative normally found in the city for all urban educational matters taken up by the state was modified by these events only a little. The stress generated by the request for special aid provoked a demand for action by the state. This time there was a proposal for decentralization which was consistent with the clever solution of counting each borough separately for state financing. But one should not be misled. The legislative leaders repeatedly stated afterward that they did not anticipate the political storm which followed. They were going through the motions as, indeed, they had less than a decade earlier. Probably they hoped something would come of it, but they did not anticipate much. The legislative leaders did not expect to produce much of a change in the city schools. More important while they initiated to the Mayor they also gave him the future initiative of presenting them with a plan for decentralization. The old balance of forces normally would have been restored easily, and the initiative norm would have been supported by state action to ratify special legislation from the city.

It must be remembered that the local unity norm is central to the urban-state politics of education. The referral of proposals to the city committees of each legislative house provides an easy vehicle for the operation of this norm. Usually the failure of the city to agree will be reflected on such committees, and they will be unable to report a bill out. The legislative leadership and other legislators need not to be too concerned with the operations of such committees. But the convergence of the special-aid request and a reform challenge from the city upset the usual process. Partly through its own fault, the New York State Legislature was caught in going beyond the customary observance of the norms and *pro forma* demand for studies from the urban schools. It had asked the Mayor for a plan of action. The inability of the city delegation to find a basis for accommodation, even through two years of negotiation, is virtually unprecedented and indicates just how far the gap between the establishment and the new city population had grown. The customary observance of the local unity norm would imply that the legislature should take no action on these matters. The power of the reform groups, the prominence of the issues in the national press and the persistent need for the additional funds made this usual solution impossible.

In the face of these events, the power of the local unity norm is noteworthy. The first legislative decision in May, 1968, effectively added representatives of the newer urban population selected by the Mayor to the urban school board and gave the board the mandate to prepare a reorganization. Thus the decision was delayed a year and conformity to the initiative norm was maintained. Further, the way was opened for agreement at the local level on a board with representatives from both the major camps in the city. It was precisely because the proposals from the board, via the city committees of the legislature, could not command substantial agreement from the city delegations (primarily Democratic) that the leaders of the legislature (Republican in 1968–69) were forced to try once again to find a compromise. Again and again in these events, the legislative leaders appealed to the local unity norm to explain their behavior. Final legislation once more modified the urban board's membership and handed to it the task of reorganization.

The reformers have for now lost the bulk of their program. The legislature reaffirmed the civil service power of the municipal employees, explicitly emasculating the power over personnel of most of the city's future reorganized districts. In the process, the local unity norm and the initiative norm were supported. The behavior of the legislature, even faced with the need to supply substantial special aid annually to the city, belies the myth that rural or up-state delegations of conservative representatives lacking sympathy for the city blocked the road to the solution. Quite the reverse: In the New York State case it was a division between liberals and labor in the city delegations which blocked action.

Finally, the stress norm can be seen governing the urban-state political relations surrounding educational issues. From start to finish in the New York State case, the bulk of the political actors involved, and educational authorities and teacher lobbyists as well, viewed these events as urban politics, not with an educationist frame of reference. The generalization is equally implicit in the reports of the Masters et al. team as they discuss the application of the local unity norm. Their research was done in Missouri, Michigan, and Illinois(6).

Conclusion

At the beginning of this chapter it was asserted that the constitutional status of urban education appeared to offer hope that the remedy for the problems of the urban school might be found in the state. The political realities give the lie to this constitutional-law picture. The New York State case is instructive not because that particular story is likely to be repeated, although it would be reckless indeed to bet against such a repetition. But the norms which govern so much of the New York State story are common to most of the other states as well. These say that an appeal against the local urban educational authorities may be heard and the board members may even be replaced. However, if the governmental structure of the urban educational system is to be modified, then proposals for this should come from the urban educational authorities. They must be agreed upon by the local delegation in the legislature. Such proposals will be urban politics, not education, as viewed by legislators. There is no help to be found in the state educational interest groups because they share the belief that urban education is firstly urban politics. The message is clear: the new city dweller, Black for the most part in our day, must look to himself, his own power blocs, and the alliances he can make using whatever he has to offer for these. From the educational establishments he can expect hostility if they are old urban ones or neutrality if they are statewide in nature.

Notes

1. Nicholas A. Masters et al., *State Politics and the Public Schools* (New York: Alfred A. Knopf, Inc., 1964), p. 275.

2. Laurence Iannaccone, *Politics in Education* (New York: The Center for Applied Research in Education, Inc., 1967), pp. 19–25.

3. Ibid., pp. 37–81.

4. Ibid., pp. 14–18.

5. The theory briefly touched here is discussed more extensively in Iannaccone's book cited above.

6. Masters et al., op. cit., pp. 26–36.

13

Financing
Urban Education

Walter I. Garms
James A. Kelly

255

Introduction

If it is a cliché to say that city schools are in trouble, it is also a cliché to say that they are in financial trouble. Basic to a solution of the multifarious problems besetting urban schools is financing adequate to the purpose. The level of resources being allocated to urban schools by local, state, and national governments is inadequate when compared to requirements for expensive educational services, and below levels of suburbs. City schools actually face bankruptcy with increasing frequency, and there are cases where operating funds are inadequate to keep schools open for the entire school year. Detroit, New York, Chicago, and Youngstown are examples of cities where this condition existed in 1969.

But the seemingly simple problem of resources turns out, on closer examination, to be a combination of numerous overlapping and sometimes contradictory factors deeply imbedded in the intergovernmental relations of the federal system, and in shifts in the makeup of urban populations. In this chapter, attention will be turned first to the changing socioeconomic characteristics of urban populations; next to some local, state, and federal fiscal arrangements influencing urban public schools; and finally to a suggested approach to revision of state school finance plans which might result in greater equity for urban areas.

Changing Face of the City

The rise of the large city in the United States has been a phenomenon of the last century, and particularly of the last half-century. At first, the city was a remarkable thing: a center of culture and of industry, it contained among its citizens the rich and powerful and the emerging middle class, as well as the poor and the new immigrant. This concentration of industry and commerce, and the well-to-do citizens residing in it, gave the city a vitality and the necessary monetary resources to provide well for itself, and it usually did. Thus, it was cities which were best able to provide an adequate education for their children. In 1905 Ellwood Cubberly said

> In two-thirds of the states of the Union no adequate provision is made for the maintenance of the smaller schools of the state, and usually these are maintained in a most unsatisfactory manner and at a sacrifice entirely out of proportion to the local benefits received. On the other hand, the cities with their aggregations of people and wealth are able to maintain excellent school systems on a relatively small expenditure(1).

The response to pleas by Cubberly and others was the state foundation program, which favored the rural areas over the cities, and in most cases still does.

But the cities have changed. The realization came slowly, partially because the change itself was evolutionary, but also because adequate and comparable data are gathered only at the time of the U.S. Census. In most cases, the city is no longer the center of wealth and excellence, but has become the "sick giant." The implications of this change for financing urban education are large and urgent.

There has been a great difference in the growth rates of central cities and suburbs. In 1950, approximately 60 percent of the population of the Standard Metropolitan Statistical Areas (SMSA's) of the United States was in the central cities. By 1962, the distribution between inside and outside central city was about 50 percent for each. By 1975, assuming that present trends continue, about 60 percent of the population of the SMSA's will live outside the central cities(2). In 1960, of the 21 cities with more than 500,000 population, 13 actually lost population during the preceding decade. The only cities showing substantial gains in population were those which pursued aggressive annexation policies(3).

New and improved highways and federal encouragement of construction of single-family houses have hastened the exodus from the city of those financially able to leave. If there had been no annexations by central cities from 1950 to 1960, the percentage increase in population of central cities during that period would have been 1.5 percent, and that of the portion outside central cities would have been 61.7 percent. Roughly these same percentages apply regardless of the size of the SMSA. However, with annexations, the increase for SMSA's of 3,000,000 or more population was 1.0 percent in central cities and 71.3 percent outside central cities, while in the smallest SMSA's (under 100,000) it was 29.2 percent in central cities and 10.9 percent outside central cities. The smaller cities have been able to retain their more affluent citizens simply by annexing the suburbs. It is particularly the larger, older cities of the East and Midwest that have found themselves unable to expand because they are surrounded by other, smaller incorporated communities.

Compounding the problem of the middle-class flight to the suburbs has been the rapid influx into the central cities of persons less able to make an economic contribution to the city, but who have needs calling for higher government expeditures. Negroes constitute one of these groups. For all SMSA's the white population in the central cities rose only 4.7 percent between 1950 and 1960 while the Negro population grew 50 percent. In the five largest SMSA's, white population declined almost 7 percent; Negro population rose by 56 percent. For all SMSA's in 1960, 16.7 percent of the population of central cities was Negro, while 4.5 percent of the population outside central cities was Negro. Some SMSA's show a much more one-sided distribution, as is shown in Table 1. Aside from other problems, this puts a heavy numerical load on the central city because a higher percentage of the Negro population is of school age. About 36 percent of the Negro population is under 15 years of age, while only about 27 percent of the

Table 1   Negro Populations in Selected Standard
Metropolitan Statistical Areas, 1960

| | Percentage of Population Negro | |
SMSA	Central Cities	Outside Central Cities
Washington, D.C.	53.9	6.1
Chicago, Illinois	22.9	2.9
Indianapolis, Indiana	20.6	0.8
Cleveland, Ohio	28.6	0.7
Newark, New Jersey	34.1	6.7

white population is under 15. In addition, a higher percentage of Negroes than whites attend public schools.

The cities also have a higher proportion of aged than have the suburbs. In 1960, 14.3 percent of the population was over the age of 60 in central cities, whereas only 10.6 percent of the population of SMSA's outside central cities was over 60.

Table 2   Public-Assistance Impact in Selected Cities, 1966

| | City's Share of State Total | | |
City	Population	Public Assistance Recipients	Aid for Dependent Children Recipients
New York City	44%	70%	72%
Philadelphia	18%	30%	33%
Baltimore	29%	66%	71%
Boston	14%	32%	38%
St. Louis	16%	26%	37%

One result of the changes in the population mix of central cities has been a high public-assistance case load, as is shown in Table 2. Arrangements for local sharing of the tax burden of public-assistance payments vary from state to state, but in cities where a large proportion of this aid must be raised through local taxes a heavy load is thus added on an already overburdened tax structure.

The difference in population mix between central city and suburb is also reflected in patterns of income and educational attainment. In 1959, the median family income for central cities in all SMSA's was $5,940, while outside the central cities it was $6,707, a difference in favor of the suburbs of $767. In 1964, the figures were $6,697 for central cities and $7,772 for suburbs, a difference of $1,075. The disparity grew by $308 in only five years. The discrepancy would be even greater if it were possible to consider only the suburbs, rather than including a sizeable number of rural families, as the smaller SMSA's do. In fact, if a correction is made for the fact that rural incomes are on the whole much lower than the suburbs, and are even lower than incomes in the central city, the discrepancy in income is evident for central cities of all SMSA's. "For many Southern and Western metropolitan areas, this rural adjustment has a highly significant 'turn-around' effect—instead of the income differential favoring the central city it now clearly favors suburbia"(4). This turn-around effect is seen in Los Angeles, San Diego, Tampa, Atlanta, Portland, Dallas, Houston, and Seattle.

Other indicators reinforce this picture of urban problems. Only 19.8 percent of central-city housing had been built during the fifties (as reported by the 1960 census), whereas 41.5 percent of the housing outside the central cities had been built during this decade. The 1960 census classified 20.4 percent of housing in central cities as unsound, and 15.6 percent of housing outside central cities. It is probably safe to assume, although data are unavailable, that most of the unsound housing outside central cities was rural, rather than suburban. Median years of schooling of the adult population in 1960 was 10.7 years in central cities, but 11.8 years outside the central cities. Unemployment presents a similar picture. For all SMSA's in 1960, 5.5 percent of central-city residents were unemployed, compared with 4.1 percent of residents outside central cities. In only two of the 38 largest SMSA's (St. Petersburg, Florida, and San Bernardino-Riverside-Ontario, California) was the central-city unemployment rate lower than that outside the central city.

Not surprisingly, crime rates are also higher in the central city, as is shown for some cities in Table 3. There is no doubt that the crime rate has always been higher in cities. But it is also true that the discrepancy has been increasing. The additional burden upon police departments constitutes a part of the "municipal overbur-

Table 3   Crime Rates per 100,000 Population in Selected Metropolitan Statistical Areas, 1965

Area	Central City	Metropolitan Areas Including Central City
Chicago	421	244
Newark	380	109
Washington	359	153
Miami	341	164
Los Angeles	293	189
Cleveland	213	101
Houston	135	96
Dayton	130	55

den," and the higher cost of insurance helps to increase the cost of living in the city.

Fiscal Problems:
Local, State, and Federal

Some may argue that, while shifting populations have created the need for extraordinarily high levels of public service, the city has an overwhelming share of the commerce and industry of an area and thus can collect locally the revenues that are necessary to finance the services it needs. But the cities are not retaining their traditional lead in nonresidential tax base. The increasing ease of transportation has made it feasible for not only factories but many wholesale and retail businesses to relocate outside the central cities. And there are very attractive advantages to so doing. Land cost is lower, tax rates are lower, parking is no problem, and employees can live in pleasant communities with good schools.

The exodus of business from the cities began in the late 1930's, and is now in full swing. In the 37 largest SMSA's, for the five-year period of 1958 to 1963, retail sales in central cities increased 4.8 percent, whereas retail sales outside these central cities increased 45.5 percent. In general, retail activity moved to the suburbs at a much faster rate than did population. Industrial employment shows a similar trend. Manufacturing employment in central cities declined 6 percent from 1958 to 1963, but rose 15.6

percent outside those cities. This flight of industry from the city has made it increasingly difficult for the disadvantaged citizens who are forced to remain in the cities to find employment.

Increasingly, our cities are being inhabited by citizens whose needs for public services are greater, and whose ability to help finance those services is less. At the same time, the commerce and industry that were the traditional underpinning of the city's economy are deserting the city. All of these forces have contributed to bringing about a financial crisis that most cities cannot solve locally. One reaction to the crisis has been to favor noneducational expenditures, where the immediate returns are higher, over educational expenditures, which give diffuse and long-term results. In the 36 largest SMSA's in 1964–65, central cities spent an average of $232 per capita for noneducational expenditures, whereas outside those cities local governments spent only $132 per capita. On the other hand, central cities spent only $82 per capita for education in that year, while $113 per capita was spent outside central cities. It is true that more children attend private school in the city, so that the per-capita burden for public education would be smaller, but it should be noted that the *per-pupil* expenditures for public schools that year were $449 in central cities and $573 outside those cities. Actually, in the period 1957 to 1964–65, the percentage of total population attending public schools in cities has increased from 16.1 to 17.4 percent, while that outside these cities has decreased slightly from 20.8 to 20.4 percent. This change probably reflects partially a flight to the suburbs of families who formerly sent their children to parochial schools, and partially the higher birth rate of the Negro families who have replaced them.

The trend in educational expenditures per pupil is unmistakable, as Table 4 shows. One of the ways in which central city

Table 4   Educational Expenditures Per Pupil in All
Standard Metropolitan Statistical Areas

Year	Central Cities	Outside Central Cities	Difference
1957	$310	$300	$ 10
1962	$375	$430	−$ 55
1965	$450	$575	−$125

schools have been able to keep some kind of a reasonable program going is to defer replacement of school buildings. In 1965, for 15 of the largest central cities, the most important source of local revenues, especially for school purposes was real property. Some examples of the increase in real property assessed valuations for certain large cities and their environs are given in Table 5.

Table 5   Increases in Assessed Valuations of Real Property in Selected Standard Metropolitan Statistical Areas, 1961–1966

Central City		Outside Central City	
City	% Increase	Surrounding Area	% Increase
Denver	5.1	Jefferson County	49.1
Washington, D.C.	29.3	Montgomery, Prince Georges, and Arlington Counties	78.2
Chicago	7.2	Remainder of Cook County	22.2
Baltimore City	4.1	Baltimore County	30.6
Boston	2.7	Rest of Suffolk County	40.5
Detroit	4.5	Rest of Wayne County	53.0
New York City	18.7	Nassau and Westchester Counties	11.1
Cleveland	− 2.3	Rest of Cuyahoga County	21.6
Pittsburgh	2.2	Rest of Allegheny County	15.3
Seattle	19.9	Rest of King County	79.8

It can be seen from Table 5 that for most of these large cities the assessed value of real property contributes to the same discouraging urban-suburban disparity as observed for expenditure data. And the picture is even more bleak for cities when it is taken into account that they have allowed their property assessment ratios to decline steadily over the past 40 years, in effect shielding more and more existing property from taxation for school or municipal services. City schools thus find themselves in a bind so serious that the problems exceed the capacity of local structures and resources to solve them.

State Aid

Unfortunately, fiscal problems of cities are more often compounded than alleviated by state action. City schools are often hamstrung by state limitations on their taxing power and state-aid formulas which favor rural and suburban districts. State school-aid and formulas do not take into account that the central-city tax base must be used in a much heavier proportion for noneducation purposes than is true in suburbia. The result is that with few exceptions state aid, measured on a per-student basis, is higher to suburban districts than it is to city districts.

State and federal aid can be an important equalizing influence to combat inequalities in taxing ability. But, on the average, it has not been. In 1957, per capita state and federal aid was $44 in the 37 largest central cities and $48 outside them. In 1964–65, it was $88 in these cities and $80 outside them. This shows some improvement, but the amount has been too small to be of much help. In 1964–65, federal and state aid represented 27 percent of central-city expenditures, 29 percent of outside central-city expenditures, and 37 percent of local expenditures in the rest of the nation. Looked at another way, federal and state aid is 44 percent as large as local taxes in central cities, 53 percent as large outside those cities, and 74 percent as large in the rest of the country. Central cities clearly must carry a greater share of the expenditure burden locally.

These overall figures conceal disparities in aid to education. Per-capita federal and state aid to education was $16.12 in central cities in 1957, and $28.43 outside those cities. By 1962, per-capita aid was $20.73 in the cities, but had risen to $37.66 outside. Even on a per-pupil basis, the central cities received less aid than the outside central-city areas, primarily reflecting the suburban and rural bias of many state "equalization" formulas. These data do not include the effect of the Elementary and Secondary Education Act of 1965, which funnels aid more heavily to the cities than to the areas outside them, but the effect of this money is probably insufficient to reverse the general situation described.

It is difficult to look into the future with confidence. However, a projection may help to outline the urgency of the fiscal problem faced by the cities. For the central-city areas of the 36 largest central cities, local tax collections in 1965 were $7.2 billion. If the future pattern of expenditures and revenue requires local tax collections to continue to expand at the same rate as from 1957 to 1965, these same central cities in 1975 will collect $12.6 billion in local taxes. If the property tax base of these cities expands at the same rate as it did from 1957 to 1965, $2.5 billion of the increase in taxes by 1975 would be provided by this expansion of the base without increasing the 1965 tax rate. This would leave $2.8 billion of the increase to come from increased property tax rates or additional nonproperty taxes. A weighted average of property tax rate increases for these 36 cities from 1957 to 1965 is 24 percent. The imputed rate of increase in the property tax rate from the projections given is approximately 30 percent from 1965 to 1975, or about 3 percent per year.

Federal Aid

Then, there are problems flowing from the nature of federal aid to public schools. This aid is for the most part small in volume, fragmented in structure, and uncoordinated in administration.

One problem relevant to federal aid is that even if the present resource differences between city and suburban schools were filled (temporarily) by federal money (a most unlikely occurrence), suburban-oriented state legislatures might well match federal aid to cities with additional state aid to suburbs as a way of maintaining the favorable position of suburbs vis-a-vis cities. Further, the form of federal aid is important, because general-aid dollars usually allow local officials the *de facto* choices of spending the dollars for increased services, reducing local tax effort (either directly or by juggling the local property assessment ratio), or having the funds substantially absorbed by pay increases for school personnel. These questions of how federal dollars can stimulate and guide local and state fiscal policy along constructive lines are particularly important in public education where 93 percent of all dollars are local and state dollars and where the allocation of those non-federal dollars is a critical component of the problems of urban education.

Federal education programs should feature fiscal arrangements which require and/or stimulate state governments to reform their own state school finance programs. Specifically, federal aid could be designed to encourage state governments to build state-aid plans which not only measure differences in local property values per pupil, but also take into account the total fiscal effort of the locality, and measures reflecting differences in pupil characteristics which correlate closely with low achievement. Use of these two sets of factors would almost surely increase the state aid flowing to urban districts, and would tend to decrease the possibility that states might balance any federal increase in urban aid by increases in state aid to suburbs.

A second part of this same problem is the difficulty of assuring that increases in federal aid are not completely absorbed through salary increases for school personnel, or for tax relief. The former can be partially handled through procedures requiring some sort of proposal from the local district which specifies the educational services to be provided with the federal money. (Title I of the Elementary and Secondary Education Act is an example of such an arrangement.) The tax relief problem can partially be handled by Congressional provision that state and local appropriations shall not be reduced. However, this is difficult to administer or enforce and does not provide protection against action by local tax assessors, who, perceiving new resources available to the schools, may lower assessments or fail to raise them in accordance with growth of market values, thereby reducing the actual taxing power of many urban and some other boards of education which operate under fixed maximum rates.

It seems unlikely that the federal government in the foreseeable future will assert any direct control over either state or local assessment decisions. However, the Census of Governments is providing each five years some reasonably good estimates of assessment ratios down to the smallest subdivision of government. It would seem desirable for the results of the five-year studies to be given wider publicity than they now have and for support to be given to scholars, to voluntary associations, and to state governments to study the wide variations in property assessment practices. In the long run such publicity might encourage more states to take firmer control of property assessment and taxation, and to set better standards and guidelines for its administration.

In the meantime, new federal legislation could grant the U.S. Commissioner of Education authority to review cases of flagrant tax substitution, either due to reduced appropriations or manipulations in assessment, and to withhold funds where the facts indicate that the result of increased federal aid was an unlawful decrease in local appropriations.

The matter of fragmentation of federal policy is symptomatic of a more serious problem. One of the key fiscal statistics upon which federal policy should be built is the aggregate federal aid to each local educational agency, including all federal programs aiding public schools. Such data would be extremely useful in identifying the extent to which a particular national priority—say, urban education—is receiving support at the present time. In other words, it would disclose what federal policy now is. In the absence of such data, the federal government does not have a systematic way of assessing its own resource allocation priorities in education.

Unfortunately, these data are now available only in crude and incomplete form. Fragmentary 1968 data (shown in Table 6) for nine key federal programs and 14 large cities reveal that most federal programs do not provide cities with the same share of federal dollars the cities would receive if allocations were simply made on a per-pupil basis.

The data in Table 6 show that ten of 12 cities for which data were available received a smaller share of their states' vocational education funds than if the money were distributed on a per-pupil basis. Ten of 11 cities for which data were available were below this enrollment standard in the school lunch program; eight of 13 below in P.L. 874; ten of 11 below for N.D.E.A. Title V-A; and nine of 12 below for N.D.E.A. Title III. Federal aid itself is thus indirectly contributing to unfortunate urban/non-urban disparities in education, and nothing in present distribution patterns of federal aid to education, except Title I of E.S.E.A., even suggests that the nation has an urban problem.

When such data are available for a more complete sample of cities, it will be possible to focus attention for the first time on the aggregate impact of federal aid on a particular type of local district, say, urban districts. Lack of aggregate data today underscores the fragmented pattern of thinking about federal aid to education, and suggests that the best measure of federal policy toward a local school district is the relative distribution of federal dollars among local districts.

Table 6 Percentage of Federal Education Aid Received by Certain States As Allocated to Certain Large City School Districts, 1968[a]

City	Average Daily Membership[b]	ESEA Title I[c]	ESEA Title II	ESEA Title III	NDEA Title III	NDEA Title V-A	P.L. 874	Vocational Education	School Lunch
Atlanta, Georgia	10.5%	7.5%	9.3%	5.6%	6.9%	N.A.	3.5%	10.2%	13.4%
Baltimore, Maryland	22.2	44.7	14.4	2.0	N.A.	11.3%	5.4	16.3	11.3
Cleveland, Ohio	6.4	13.2	5.1	44.2	5.2	3.0	1.8	2.7	4.8
Denver, Colorado	18.8	17.4	24.5	14.7	11.8	7.0	11.5	N.A.	10.7
Detroit, Michigan	14.6	25.6	15.2	1.2	0.6	12.8	17.0	33.2	8.9
Hartford, Connecticut	4.5	16.5	5.7	10.4	2.0	4.1	2.8	3.0	N.A.
Indianapolis, Indiana	8.3	10.4	9.9	N.A.	7.2	21.9	36.6	10.4	4.0
Memphis, Tennessee	14.1	8.8	15.3	0.1	23.4	10.8	16.0	9.3	6.8
Milwaukee, Wisconsin	13.5	13.5	2.0	2.7	8.0	12.5	17.9	4.0	3.7
Philadelphia, Pennsylvania	12.3	37.1	9.4	12.5	N.A.	N.A.	N.A.	1.2	N.A.
Pittsburgh, Pennsylvania	3.3	1.4	0.9	8.8	7.1	3.2	39.1	4.5	N.A.
Providence, Rhode Island	15.7	38.7	0.7	64.4	3.7	0.5	8.1	N.A.	0.8
Seattle, Washington	12.2	12.2	3.1	11.3	13.3	N.A.	4.7	4.0	9.4
St. Louis, Missouri	11.2	16.8	10.0	21.7	3.4	6.9	7.4	7.1	3.4

[a] Data are drawn from U.S. Office of Education data and were developed through the assistance of the Urban Coalition.

[b] Figures represent the percentage of state average daily membership found in the city.

[c] Figures represent the percentage of the state's ESEA Title I funds received by the city. The rest of the columns have a similar meaning.

We urge that the Secretary of Health, Education, and Welfare and the Commissioner of Education annually collect, prepare, and publish data on the flow of federal funds to the central-city school districts in each of the 212 Standard Metropolitan Statistical Areas. Other districts could of course be included, but we feel it is essential that these data concerning cities be published regularly. The rationale for this effort has been presented earlier; it is simply that actual federal policy toward a particular type of local school district is inseparable from the flow of federal funds to that district, and no one knows precisely what is the aggregate flow of federal funds to city school districts. An attempt was made to make a preliminary study for the purposes of this report, but the federal government should be doing this annually and on its own accord.

A Suggested Revision of State School Finance Plans

The authors, in a study sponsored by the New York State Educational Conference Board(5), have proposed a way of helping to relieve part of the financial problems of city schools. That way is to base state aid not only on the fiscal ability of the school district, but also on its "educational need." We have stated that educational need exists wherever persistent average differences in educational achievement exist. In other words, we do not deny that individual differences in educational achievement should exist, but where the average achievement of a group of students with the same socioeconomic characteristics is consistently below that of a group with different characteristics, we believe that educational need exists and that government resources should be applied in an attempt to decrease or erase it.

The current New York state-aid formula is similar to that of many states in that it attempts to equalize resources by providing more state aid to poorer districts. The basic formula looks like this:

State Aid = WADA × Current Expenditures per WADA (up to $760) × Aid Ratio where WADA is the Weighted Average Daily Attendance of the district and the aid ratio of the district is dependent upon the ratio of the full property value per WADA of the district to the average full property value per WADA for the state. The amount of state aid, then, depends upon the number of pupils in the district and the relative financial resources of the district. There is no accounting for differences in the kinds of students districts have and the costs of bringing them up to some uniform standard of achievement.

Our proposal is based upon the results of a number of studies that have shown a close connection between socioeconomic characteristics and school achievement(6). We propose to predict the average achievement of students in a school through knowledge of the socioeconomic characteristics of the students in that school. The school would be provided extra state money to the extent that it had in it students whose socioeconomic characteristics predict that they would achieve poorly under the present educational system. We chose the school as the unit for several reasons: the individual student is too small a unit because differences in innate ability make for wide variations in achievement; the school district is too large a unit because averaging all schools in the district hides large variations among schools; school district consolidation or decentralization would be unlikely to affect individual schools. In short, we feel that the individual school is the unit where innovative programs based upon the needs of that school's pupils are most likely to be implemented.

To predict achievement on the basis of socioeconomic characteristics, it was necessary to find socioeconomic measures on which data could reasonably be collected by local school personnel, and which were highly predictive of school achievement. We asked school personnel in a representative sample of New York schools to collect data and subjected the results to a multiple regression statistical analysis. *Using data on four variables we can predict 71 percent of the variation in average school achievement, even though we know nothing about the instructional program in the individual schools.* These variables are percentage of Negroes and Puerto Ricans in the school, percentage of children from broken homes (homes where one or both of the parents is missing), average number of schools attended by the pupils during the last three years, and average years of schooling of the students' parents.

We have proposed that data on these variables be gathered by every public school in New York, and the results be used to define, for each school, an "NWADA" (Need Weighted Average Daily Attendance). The NWADA would be a prediction, based upon the socioeconomic characteristics of the children in the school, of the number of pupils who would be below an acceptable level in reading and arithmetic achievement. Based on this NWADA, a supplementary amount of state aid would be given to each district. It would be stipulated that this supplementary amount must be spent in the individual schools of the district in proportion to their contribution to the NWADA of the district. Finally, we recommend that after a school has had a chance to use this money in whatever way seems best, a comparison be made between the actual achievement of the students and the achievement level that is predicted by their socioeconomic characteristics. Those schools in which actual achievement is better than predicted (or has significantly improved while receiving NWADA aid) would be rewarded in some tangible way, perhaps through increased subventions for the school or through special payments to the teachers and principal. For those in which actual achievement is worse than predicted (or fails to improve with increased state aid spent through local discretion), state-controlled mandatory outside assistance would be provided. This should be a powerful stimulus to effective innovation, rather than to innovation for the sake of doing something different.

Conclusion

This proposal offers one method for distributing additional state and federal dollars to local schools, but of course the basic problem is not one of technical distribution methods. If the nation wanted to "attack" its urban cancers, it could do so through a variety of means. Perhaps it lacks the will. We have set forth the problems as we see them, and suggested some directions for change which would help city schools.

Notes

1. Ellwood P. Cubberly, *School Funds and Their Apportionment* (New York: New York Teachers College, 1905), p. 5.

2. Advisory Commission on Intergovernmental Relations, *Fiscal Balance in the American Federal System, Vol. 2: Metropolitan Fiscal Disparities* (Washington, D.C.: U.S. Government Printing Office, 1967), p. 30. This portion of this chapter draws heavily on this source. Figures cited, unless otherwise footnoted, are from this publication.

3. These cities were Los Angeles, San Diego, Dallas, Houston, and San Antonio.

4. A.C.I.R., op. cit., p. 44.

5. The final report of this study was issued by the New York State Educational Conference Board in Albany in August, 1969. The report is co-authored by Walter I. Garms (who directed the study) and Mark C. Smith.

6. For an excellent review of these studies, see Hendrik D. Gideonse, "The Relative Impact of Instructional Variables," *The Teachers College Record,* 69, No. 7 (April 1968), 625–40.

14.

City Schools
in a Federal Vise

*James W. Guthrie**

Introduction

At the time of its founding, the United States was characterized neither by cities nor by a particular concern for schools. The population was for the most part rural and the economy rested principally upon agriculture and a few skilled crafts. Literacy was of consequence in order to understand the Bible, but only the children of a wealthy few pursued an extensive formal education. What concern there was for public education held that such schooling was a matter to be determined locally. These social and economic conditions were reflected in the arrangements made for a national government. As a consequence, it is difficult today to make that government responsive to the needs of a post-industrial and increasingly urban society. This is particularly the case when an attempt is made to extend federal support for educational services in urban areas; this endeavor appears to rub heavily against the grain of the rural forces which formed our federal machinery.

Nevertheless, the situation is not devoid of hope. For a variety of reasons the executive branch of the federal government has grown increasingly sensitive to the needs of cities and has been able to formulate and gain legislative enactment of several programs aimed at solving urban problems. Furthermore, though

---

* The author is indebted to Charles E. Hansen, Rey A. Carr, and Stephen B. Lawton for their substantial assistance in the research for this chapter.

painfully slow, there are signs that the legislative branch may in time soften its prejudices against urban areas. The question remains, however, as to whether or not the political processes which have operated in the past to render our national government sensitive to social change will begin to make themselves felt more strongly before the torment which grips our cities becomes so pervasive as to defy effective solution.

It is the intention in this chapter to describe the political factors which presently inhibit the federal government in its efforts to provide assistance to urban schools and to trace the evolution of other forces which have the potential to overcome those inhibitors. Some of the existing federal programs aimed at alleviating urban education problems will be described and suggestions will be offered for their improvement and extension.

Congress: Its Rural Bias

Congress, like our broader social system, is engaged in a tug of war between the forces identified with the rural, agrarian ideology of an earlier day and values more representative of contemporary urban life. The problem, at least for proponents of an expanded federal role in urban education, is that the rural forces are yet able to exert the greater pull. This appears to be due to at least two factors: 1) the processes by which congressmen are recruited and elected, and 2) somewhat more importantly, the processes by which Congress conducts its business.

Selection Procedures

The Constitution stipulates that a census shall be conducted every ten years and that the allocation of seats in the House of Representatives shall be reapportioned among the states accordingly. These provisions have enabled House membership to shift in keeping with the flow and growth of population state by state, but they have not guaranteed that the House be representative of the increased urban populations within states. Census results are used only to determine the proportion of the 435 total House seats to which a particular state is entitled; they are not necessarily used to determine the manner in which seats will be distributed within a particular state. The Constitution grants Congress the right to establish criteria respecting its membership, but it gives individual congressmen nothing to say formally regarding the makeup of their constituencies at a time of reapportionment. Rather, the drawing of congressional district boundaries is a power reserved to state legislatures.

There is reason to believe that the situation may slowly be changing, but, at least up until very recent times, state legislatures have themselves been under the rather overwhelming domination of rural interests. Consequently, almost without regard for the political party in power, state legislators have drawn the boundaries of congressional districts in ways which favored rural areas. One means was by creating pie-shaped districts. The point of the pie would dip into the heart of the city with the broad end of the slab extending out into the countryside. This procedure tended to emasculate the power of urban voters by concentrating them at the apex and diluting their numbers with a majority of non-urban voters at the periphery of the wedge. Another tactic was simply to create a small number of very concentrated districts encompassing vast numbers of urban voters and many rural districts, each containing smaller numbers of persons. Yet a third means was by not reapportioning congressional districts in accord with census findings but, rather, running candidates at large when population growth warranted a state's having one or more additional representatives. Illinois provides an excellent example of this subterfuge. No redistricting took place between 1901 and 1948 and, as a consequence, Chicago, with more than half the state's population, elected only 10 representatives while the remainder of the state elected 15(1). Neither the Constitution nor federal statutes contain provisions sufficient to curtail such practices.

The selection of individual Senators no longer suffers so greatly from a rural bias. With ratification in 1913 of the 17th Amendment, the election of Senators was removed from the purview of state legislatures and placed in the hands of a state's citizens. The direct election of Senators, based on the number of popular votes received, gives each urban voter an equal voice with his rural peer. An injustice, at least in a rural-versus-urban sense, remains, however. Under the Constitutional provision which allows but two Senators per state, regardless of population size and degree of urbanization, heavily populated states—which are the ones which tend to contain the large urban concentrations—receive no more representation than do sparsely populated states—which are the ones which tend to be more rural in their makeup. Thus, at the extremes, the voters of urban states such as New York, California, and Pennsylvania have less of a voice in the Senate than do voters in rural states such as Alaska, the Dakotas, and Montana. In fact, the votes of the Senators from the nine least populous states, containing less than three percent of the nation's citizens, can cancel the Senate votes of the nine most populous states, containing in excess of 51 percent of the U.S. population. The number of Senators due each state is fixed by the Constitution and is not likely to be altered. Thus, it is somewhat fortunate that a number of other factors render the Senate slightly more "liberal," or responsive to urban problems, than is the House of Representatives(2). This is by no means to imply, however, that the Senate has amassed a legislative record of solid support for urban concerns; on the contrary, the upper house still remains unbalanced in favor of rural interests.

The *Baker v. Carr* Supreme Court decision in 1962(3) and the *Wesberry v. Sanders* verdict in 1964(4) touched off a series of judicial rulings regarding legislative reapportionments which in time should affect significantly the rural bias of the House of Representatives. The first-mentioned case was decided in favor of the plaintiffs and sustained their view that Tennessee's refusal to redistrict since 1901 had diluted their vote. The *Wesberry* case reinforced the *Baker* verdict, and subsequent court decisions have repeatedly ruled that congressional districts within any particular state may have only the most "minimal" numerical deviations in population. "Minimal" has not been defined precisely, but a recent Supreme Court action (*Branegan v. Grills et al.*) permitted a variation from the ideal of only 1.58 percent(5). These judgments do not absolutely prohibit the gerrymandering of districts to dilute the urban vote; they do, however, curtail the ability of state legislatures to create a few clusters of highly concentrated urban districts while allowing for many more and more thinly populated rural ones.

However, even though judicial actions may in time cause some weakening of the rural bias in Congress, it is not immediately obvious that urban interests will gain proportionate influence. Preliminary examination of the characteristics of congressional district constituencies before and after reapportionment suggests that many of the new districts being created are weighted in favor of the voters who ring the cities rather than those who live in them. This change may dilute rural interests, but it does not necessarily bolster urban power.

In addition to suffering at the hands of rural interests by the manner in which congressional districts are established, urban areas are also underrepresented in another way. The Constitution requires that a Representative be only 25 years of age and a Senator 30 at the time they assume office; however, the practicalities of amassing a political base and financing a campaign are such as to preclude many young men from running. It is more typical that candidates for Congress are in their forties or fifties. It is true that the tendency toward urban expansion was initiated 40 or 50 years ago, but the largest migrations from the country to the city began more like 20 to 30 years ago with the industrial explosion accompanying World War II. Thus it is that many present incumbents of Congress, even many of those representing urban areas, are not the boyhood product of a city. The probability is great that they were born and had their early views shaped in a rural environment. An examination of the backgrounds of the 535 men holding office in the House and the Senate in the second session of the 90th Congress revealed that only 119 listed a city of over 250,000 inhabitants as their birthplace. Thirty or forty years ago a smaller percentage of our population lived in the large cities in the U.S. This would seem to make the point all the stronger. I do not wish to appear to undermine the virtues of a rural upbringing. However, I do feel the likelihood is greater that those who have experienced the problems of urban centers may have more sensitivity and sympathy for the pulse of a throbbing metropolis than does the person who spent his youth in pastoral environs.

Congressional Procedures

Somewhat more to the detriment of urban interests are the means by which Congress conducts its own business. The root cause here can be summed up in the term "seniority system." Regardless of which party organizes Congress, the positions controlling the most power and influence are awarded members who have the most years of continuous congressional service. Committee chairmen are selected on the basis of being ranking members of the majority party, in terms of continuous years of service on the committee involved. Moreover, particularly in the House, simple assignment to any specific committee is in large measure based upon seniority. Membership on the most prestigious committees —for example, Ways and Means, Appropriations, and Rules—is reserved for the most senior and regular members of each party. Thus, not only are powerful committee chairmen selected because of their tenure of service, but also the committees which control the legislative heartland are populated by "old timers"(6).

The significance here is that the seniority system favors the rural areas and discriminates against urban interests. It happens like this: Congressional districts in rural areas tend to be less competitive politically and are more likely to be dominated by a single political party. By contrast, congressional seats in urban areas tend to turn over more rapidly and generally are subject to greater interparty competition. Consequently, rural representatives have a better chance of repeatedly returning to their seats and amassing the all-important seniority. This condition is particularly favorable to Southern Democrats and, when their party is in power, Midwestern Republicans. These tend to be the two geographic areas of the nation where interparty competition has historically been the lowest; thus, they are sections from which an incumbent can expect the least serious electoral competition. They also are the sections which are the least urbanized or, conversely, the most rural. Tables 1 and 2 depict the rural nature of the chairmanships of important House and Senate committees in the second session of the 90th Congress. Of the 20 House standing committees, only seven are led by Representatives from urban areas. More significant, however, is the fact that these (with the exception of the Judiciary Committee) tend to be among the least

Table 1   House Committee Chairmen
(Second Session, 90th Congress)

Committee	Chairman	District & State	City of 250,000+ in District
Agriculture	H. R. Poage	Texas-11	No
Appropriations	George H. Mahon	Texas-19	No
Armed Services	L. Mendel Rivers	S. Carolina-1	No
Banking & Currency	Wright Patman	Texas-1	No
District of Columbia	John McMillan	S. Carolina-6	No
Education & Labor	Carl D. Perkins	Kentucky-7	No
Foreign Affairs	Thomas Morgan	Pa.-26	No
Govt. Operations	William L. Dawson	Illinois-1	Yes-Chicago
House Administration	Omar Burleson	Texas-17	No
Interior & Insular Affairs	Wayne Aspinall	Colorado-4	No
Interstate & Foreign Commerce	Harley Staggers	W. Va.-2	No
Judiciary	Emanuel Celler	N.Y.-10	Yes-New York City
Merchant Marine & Fisheries	Edward Garmatz	Maryland-3	Yes-Baltimore
Post Office & Civil Service	Thaddeus Dulski	N.Y.-41	Yes-Buffalo
Public Works	George H. Fallon	Maryland-4	Yes-Baltimore
Rules	William Colmer	Mississippi-5	No
Science & Astronautics	George P. Miller	Calif.-8	Yes-Oakland
Un-American Activities	Edwin Willis	Louisiana-3	No
Veterans' Affairs	Olin E. Teaque	Texas-6	Yes-Dallas
Ways & Means	Wilbur D. Mills	Arkansas-2	No

significant committees. In the Senate there are 16 standing committees of which only two are chaired by Senators from states which could in any way be pictured as urban (Warren Magnusen and Henry Jackson from Washington).

Rural Bias of the House

Congressional discrimination against urban concerns operates in dozens of subtle and devious ways. Congress does not place a great many of its actions on display for public scrutiny. The decision of a rurally biased committee chairman not to hold hear-

Table 2   Senate Committee Chairmen
(Second Session, 90th Congress)

Committee	Chairman	State
Aeronautics & Space	Clinton P. Anderson	New Mexico
Agriculture & Forestry	Allen J. Ellender	Louisiana
Appropriations	Carl Hayden	Arizona
Armed Services	Richard Russell	Georgia
Banking & Currency	John J. Sparkman	Alabama
Commerce	Warren G. Magnusen	Washington
District of Columbia	Alan Bible	Nevada
Finance	Russell B. Long	Louisiana
Foreign Relations	J. W. Fulbright	Arkansas
Government Operations	John L. McClellan	Arkansas
Interior & Insular Affairs	Henry M. Jackson	Washington
Judiciary	James O. Eastland	Mississippi
Labor & Public Welfare	Lister Hill	Alabama
Post Office & Civil Service	Mike Monroney	Oklahoma
Public Works	Jennings Randolph	West Virginia
Rules & Administration	B. Everett Jordan	North Carolina

ings on an urban-oriented piece of legislation is seldom publicized in the mass media. Or, if hearings are held and committee action is favorable, the risk is substantial that the rurally weighted but not widely publicized Rules Committee will attempt to prevent the measure from reaching the floor for consideration by the whole House. Or, in the rare probability that the bill should be enacted, the rurally dominated Appropriations Committee may decide in executive session (closed to the press and the public) to allocate but a minimum of funds. This mantle of secrecy makes it difficult to pin a rural rap on Congress.

One of the exceptions to such subterranean congressional action is the floor vote on a piece of legislation. Even here, of course, there exist procedures which enable non-recorded votes to be taken, but in some conscience-stricken cases, or more likely when one party feels it can gain political mileage and embarrass the opposition, a recorded or "roll call" vote is taken and the results are available for analysis. It is such votes, specifically on education legislation, that will be used in an attempt to display empirically the antipathy of rural-oriented Representatives toward urban programs.

Legislative Roll Call Analysis   A key step in this analysis
was the creation of two scales of favorability toward education
legislation(7).

There were, in addition, other variables which helped to explain the voting of congressmen on education legislation. Although
the scales were necessarily rather crude measures of the Representatives' positions, a step-wise multiple regression analysis for the
88th Congress, with *voting rank* as the dependent variable, produced a significant multiple correlation of .536 explaining almost
30 percent of the variance in voting behavior. This multiple correlation was obtained by using 30 variables; of this number, six
proved to be by far the most potent predictors of a congressman's
voting behavior. They are: percent of constituency living on rural
farms, the Representative's seniority as a congressman, percent of
a constituency born in foreign countries, constituency population
density per square mile, and the amount of geographic mobility
among constituents.

Finally, the opposition to greater federal involvement in the
support of education came from the more senior members of the
House. This variable, combined with the *percent rural farm* ex-
plains almost two-thirds of the variance in voting explained by all
30 variables utilized in the study.

Who Benefits From the Aid Which Exists?

Despite the reluctance of many rurally oriented congressmen
to support federal school aid legislation, a few such bills do pass.
One might rightfully ask how this is so. What is it that enables
some education measures to work their way past numerous procedural hazards, reach the floor for consideration, and be approved?
The political magic which leads to passage undoubtedly differs in
some respect for each piece of legislation. It is not wise to general-
ize regarding the reasons for passage of each existing education
act. It is suggested, however, that the degree of benefit a particular
measure holds out for rural areas is in some substantial way
associated with its success.

Evidence in support of the preceding proposition comes from
the following analysis. The total number of federal education

dollars flowing to each state was divided by the number of public elementary and secondary school students enrolled in the state. The range is wide: $260.04 per pupil in Alaska to $23.55 in Wyoming. The mean for all states is $56.55. Next, a comparison was made between the degree of a state's urbanization, as measured by *percent urban,* and the number of federal dollars it received per pupil. The correlation is a highly significant −.320, in the direction anticipated. That is, the more rural a state, the greater the contribution to its per-pupil expenditures from federal funds.

Such a measure, though correct, is not as precise as one might desire. More precise confirmation comes from the figures in Table 3. Here for the 24 largest cities in the United States are listed the percent of a state's students residing in that city, the percent of a state's poor children (from families with annual incomes of $2,000 or below) residing in the city, and the percent of the state's federal funds from five statutory authorities which flow to the city. From these figures, it can be seen that the typical pattern is for a city to receive a lower proportion of federal funds than it has of its state's poor pupils. The exception to this pattern, as would be expected, is Title I of the Elementary and Secondary Education Act—which has a distribution formula based directly upon poverty-impacted students.

The Executive Branch: Its Urban Bias

While Congress leans toward America's rural agrarian ideology, the Presidency tends to be the primary national government agent favoring the concerns of our cities and their emerging ethnic groups. Some of the same processes, namely election arrangements, which serve to orient Congress to rural interests, operate in an almost antithetical fashion in the case of the Presidency.

A primary mechanism accounting for the potential urban bias of the Presidency is the electoral college. By Constitutional provision, each state is entitled to electoral votes equal to the total number of its Representatives and Senators. By virtue of custom, and to a lesser degree, state statutes, a state's electoral votes do not

Table 3   Federal Funds to Urban Areas as a Percent of State Total[a]

State and City		1 Percent of State's Enrollment	2 Percent of State's Poverty Impacted Pupils[b]	Voc. Ed.	NDEA III	ESEA I	ESEA II	ESEA III
California:	Los Angeles	14.59%	20.60%	14.35%	.21%	20.03%	7.58%	5.67%
	San Francisco	2.49	4.53	3.53	.84	4.38	1.87	3.17
	San Diego	2.78	3.09	2.70	2.44	3.03	.82	2.55
Colorado:	Denver	19.38	29.10	12.74	7.81	26.02	17.02	28.65
Georgia:	Atlanta	10.53	6.92	5.88	12.10	5.74	22.84	7.95
Illinois:	Chicago	26.51	50.89	24.24	29.89	53.87	32.99	17.50
Louisiana:	New Orleans	13.02	11.65	9.46	12.53	15.01	20.78	23.38
Maryland:	Baltimore	24.31	50.81	7.90	19.62	49.67	10.51	2.65
Massachusetts:	Boston	8.68	26.10	3.93	6.17	24.63	6.42	0
Michigan:	Detroit	14.79	33.25	25.24	28.47	34.97	14.56	.50
Minnesota:	Minneapolis	8.52	12.61	8.63	15.19	13.43	9.33	8.05
Missouri:	St. Louis	13.94	18.90	9.35	3.69	19.44	18.43	21.06
New York:	New York	33.31	63.80	10.74	34.30	61.39	29.58	28.18
	Buffalo	2.26	4.46	3.18	1.62	4.34	2.56	5.02
Ohio:	Cleveland	8.21	14.31	11.52	4.72	14.70	6.47	5.07
	Cincinnati	3.84	8.48	1.46	3.67	8.60	3.09	13.00
Pennsylvania:	Philadelphia	12.65	25.37	10.88	17.79	24.60	8.51	17.28
	Pittsburgh	7.58	6.93	22.83	7.04	6.62	1.84	11.31
Tennessee:	Memphis	14.74	9.33	0	0	9.25	13.94	1.16
Texas:	Houston	10.93	5.23	4.04	5.20	5.13	8.24	12.20
	Dallas	5.93	3.76	3.31	4.08	3.69	5.42	.84
	San Antonio	5.27	4.39	3.77	1.60	4.30	3.29	7.06
Washington:	Seattle	18.46	15.67	18.99	12.55	14.79	12.09	44.36
Wisconsin:	Milwaukee	13.34	18.37	10.09	11.92	17.84	10.26	15.70
Mean		19.6	28.6	15.6	15.7	31.9	16.9	17.5

[a] Information obtained from the U.S. Office of Education.
[b] Actually based on number of poverty-impacted pupils in the county in which the central city involved is located.

go to Presidential candidates in proportion to the popular vote; rather, they are cast *en masse* for the candidate receiving the most votes. Thus a candidate can come out ahead in a state by the slimmest of popular vote margins—at the extreme, one vote—and still reap the benefit of that state's entire electoral-vote package. This is known as the "unit rule," and it is a kind of winner-take-all, loser-get-nothing situation. At a national scale, the operation is well illustrated by the results of the 1960 election. John F. Kennedy captured 119,000 more votes than Richard M. Nixon; this is but sixteen hundredths of one percent (.16%) of all votes cast, yet our indirect system awarded Kennedy 303 electoral votes to his opponent's 219(8). An earlier example, from a time when our nation was less populous, is provided by the 1880 election. Garfield received 48.32 percent of the vote and Hancock 48.21 percent, a difference of eleven-hundredths of one percent. The machinations of the electoral college, however, awarded Garfield 214 votes and his opponent only 155, a difference of 16 percent.

One of the consequences of this lopsided procedure is that a Presidential candidate, with limited time and scarce financial resources, is best advised to concentrate his campaign efforts in states with the largest number of electoral votes—that is, the most urban states. Thus, at one extreme a candidate can capture an electoral majority if he is successful in winning a popular majority in just 13 states. The total electoral votes of the 13 most populated states equal 281; the remaining 37 states and the District of Columbia account for 257 electoral votes. Thus, it is to the heavily populated, heavily urban states that a Presidential candidate must turn most of his attention. The farms and suburbs may elect Congressmen, but the big cities elect Presidents(9). This situation serves not only to orient a candidate to the needs of the cities, but also it keeps the attention of a Presidential incumbent focused on urban populations.

Within individual states, urban areas are also of disproportionate electoral significance. Voters are of course concentrated in urban areas, and if one keeps in mind that only a simple majority of popular votes is needed to capture all of a state's electoral votes, then it is understandable why candidates spend a major portion of their time campaigning in urban areas and on urban issues. It is here that the most voters can be reached in the shortest time.

Moreover, it is sometimes the cities' ethnic groups which control the balance of power. For example, in 1960 the election results were so close that shifts in just a small percentage of the popular vote of urban ethnic groups might have awarded the election to Nixon. We do not wish to push this point too far because in such a close election any minority component could claim that its votes made the critical difference. To illustrate the possibility, however, we turn to the following description from Nelson Polsby and Aaron Wildavsky:

> Illinois and Texas together account for 51 electoral votes. Out of the approximately 4.7 million votes cast in Illinois, Kennedy's margin of victory was 8,858. Where a shift of 4,500 votes by any group would have been enough to spell the difference, it would not be difficult to find any number of groups which could be considered necessary for the victory. Gallup reports that on a national basis the votes of Jews increased from 75 percent to 81 percent Democratic over 1956 and the votes of Negroes from 61 percent to 68 percent. Evidently Kennedy needed the additional votes from the Jews and the Negroes who live in Illinois in order to have won there. In Texas, Kennedy's margin was 46,233 out of 2.3 million votes cast. There could easily have been a shift by as many as 25,000 Texas Negro voters toward Kennedy(10).

Not all Jews and not all Negroes live in cities by any means, but the majority of them do in Illinois and many thousands, possibly a majority, do in Texas.

Certainly no candidate can count on being victorious in enough urban states, and thus he must also make campaign forays to rural states. In a nation threatened by "cold war," nuclear destruction, and balance of payments problems, no candidate can restrict himself to urban issues. And, no candidate, even in highly urban states, can bank on obtaining all the urban votes; thus, he must also make a suburban and a rural appeal. The contention here is simply that the electoral arrangements surrounding the Presidency are such as to bias the process in favor of the urban voter. The situation is by no means black and white, and the nonurban vote is by no means neglected. As in all things, the situation is a relative one; but, relative to Congress, the Presidency is urban-oriented.

The Presidency and Urban Action

The President, of course, cannot unilaterally enact legislation; this depends heavily upon the cooperation of Congress. Nevertheless, in several ways the urban bias of the executive branch can make itself felt. One of these ways is by influencing, if not actually setting, the legislative agenda to be considered by Congress. Another way occurs during the implementation phase wherein it becomes possible through administrative procedures to shape a generalized statute into a measure which favors urban areas. In the first instance, that of influencing the considerations of Congress, it is generally conceded that the initiative for proposing legislation has now shifted substantially from Congress to the President. This is a result of a trend which has been in the making at least since the administrations of Theodore Roosevelt and Woodrow Wilson and which has subsequently received strong impetus from Presidents Franklin D. Roosevelt, Kennedy, and Johnson. Factors such as the remarkable growth of expertise in the executive branch, the President's political party leadership functions, and the mass media attention granted to the President's actions account for the shift.

The Chief Executive's concern for urban problems is reflected in the manner in which this legislative initiating function has been recently utilized. Most of the major federal endeavors for the relief of cities—programs such as the 1964 Economic Opportunity Act, the 1965 ESEA, the 1966 Model Cities Act, the 1967 Clean Air Act, and the 1968 Housing and Safe Streets Acts—originated with and were lobbied for by the President and his executive branch colleagues.

Certainly this is not to imply that congressmen never make proposals to benefit the cities; some congressmen, particularly Senators, do. It is difficult for individual congressmen, however, to muster sufficient support for their legislative proposals to overcome general congressional inertia and the rural bias of their peers. Some exciting programs for the relief of cities have been promoted by Senators, but they have never managed to reach fruition. The picture in the lower body, however, is more negative. It is very difficult even to identify a major, House-initiated urban proposal. The Senate does have several members who tend to speak for the cities (Ribicoff of Connecticut, Percy of Illinois, and, before his death, Robert Kennedy). Who performs such a function for the House: the Speaker, the Majority or Minority leader, powerful committee chairmen? The truth is that no one Representative nor any group of Representatives has emerged as an urban spokesman.

In addition to formulating and advocating legislative proposals, the executive branch manifests its concern for urban interests by shaping existing programs toward urban needs. This is possible because most pieces of legislation are enacted to meet problems couched in broad contexts and thus are open to being shaped in their implementation stages. A cabinet officer can decide to rearrange priorities within his domain. Such was somewhat the case when former Secretary of Defense, Robert McNamara, decided to accept 100,000 individuals who otherwise would not have met minimum draft requirements and supply them with compensatory preparation so as to make up for their educational deficiencies. The Secretary took his action within the discretion normally allotted a cabinet officer. Such was also the case when the former Secretary of the Department of Health, Education and Welfare, John W. Gardner, decided to establish a unit under his authority to coordinate HEW's urban activities. Former U.S. Commissioner of Education, Harold Howe, took similar action with a decision to concentrate the major portion of ESEA Title III funds over which USOE had authority in urban projects. These decisions did not require specific congressional authority. It is true, of course, that Congress could have acted to curtail these moves; thus, it could be argued that, because of its ultimate authority, Congress was responsible for the shaping of the programs for urban needs. However, the lack of negative congressional action is not strong evidence of concern for urban problems and is certainly very different from a positive executive branch decision. Thus our case remains that the Presidency is the major governmental unit exhibiting sympathy for urban needs.

Other Political Controversies

Up to this point our narrative has emphasized the detrimental effects of rural-urban tensions upon the quest for federal aid to city schools, but such is not the only problem involved. Efforts to gain federal assistance are also hampered by the highly controversial nature of school-aid legislation itself. Legislative proposals aimed at expanding federal aid to education, almost regardless of the kinds of schools for which such aid was intended, have historically encountered four categories of political controversies: race, religion, federal control, and financial distribution. These intense conflicts have played such a significant role in shaping school aid that each is worthy of at least a limited explanation(11). The following offers such an explanation; but the discussion will subsequently explain the manner in which the executive branch has taken the initiative over the last decade to compromise many of these issues, and thus further the cause of federal aid to urban schools.

Race

Historically, a bloc of congressmen (predominantly from Southern states) has voted against aid proposals which denied federal funds for racially segregated schools. Another bloc (predominantly from Northern areas with large Negro populations) has been able to prevent the passage of proposed legislation which would allow racially segregated schools to participate. This controversy has consistently provoked some of the most violent debates in the history of Congress, and on more than one occasion tempers have flared and name calling has occurred.

The typical pattern has been to submit a broad-scale school-aid bill which would not specifically exclude federal funds from racially segregated schools. A "civil rights" advocate, either in committee or on the floor, would then offer an amendment to prohibit federal funds to such school districts. During the 1950's, the amendment to prohibit became known as the "Powell Amendment" because of the frequency with which it was offered by the Democratic Representative from New York City's Harlem, Adam Clayton Powell. Once offered, the "Powell Amendment" typically drew support from two blocs: 1) Congressmen who for a variety of motives strongly supported civil rights measures, and 2) those who may or may not have felt strongly about civil rights, but who did disagree with the school-aid proposal and knew that a civil rights rider was a sure method for sealing such a bill's legislative doom. By voting in favor of the "Powell Amendment," this latter group (typically composed of fiscally conservative Northern Republicans) reaped the best of two political worlds; they appeared as favoring civil rights but ever-mindful of the alleged dangers of "creeping socialism" and "big" government.

From the moment the "Powell Amendment" was adopted a school-aid bill's eventual failure was assured. The prohibition of federal funds to segregated school systems motivated Southern Congressmen, who favored otherwise unfettered federal funds, to vote negatively; combined with the anti-federal aid bloc, their votes formed an unfavorable majority which prior to recent times proved to be an extraordinarily difficult barrier for broad-scale school-aid legislation to penetrate.

Religion

Many federal aid-to-education bills have failed because they either did or did not authorize funds for church-related schools. School-aid legislation is controversial for so many other reasons that the church-state partisans often swung the balance of power. If a proposed bill permitted federal funds to be used by church-related schools, opposition was mounted by "separationists." Conversely, if the bill lacked such permissive arrangements, legislators who were themselves Roman Catholic or who had large, influential parochial school constituencies tended to vote against it.

Federal Control

In the early days of school-aid proposals the federal control controversy was waged between advocates of an expanded federal role and those who contended that there existed no Constitutional bases for such action. It was the view of the latter faction that the language of the Tenth Amendment delegated education to the states and no authority for federal involvement existed. Over time, however, the liberal interpretation of the Constitution's General Welfare and Interstate Commerce clauses has created a firm foundation in precedent for federal support of social services such as education, and thus the nature of the federal control question is somewhat different today. A majority of both Republican and Democratic Congressmen now appear favorably disposed toward the concept of federal aid to education(12). The current controversy centers around the form such aid should take; more specifically, what level of government should determine the priorities for which federal money should be spent. Should priorities for federal funds continue to be established by Congress, or should such funds be allocated to states to be redistributed at their discretion to local school districts?

Generally, Republicans tend to favor the bloc grant school-aid approach whereby states determine objectives for federal funds. Conversely, Democrats, at least non-Southern Democrats, tend to favor the approach whereby federal funds are distributed in accord with specific congressional determined categories. Despite these general partisan tendencies, considerable controversy develops across party lines.

Financial Distribution

The distribution controversy contains at its core a conflict between educational desirability and political feasibility. It is generally conceded among educators that federal school finance formulas should in substantial measure be based upon the principle of "equalization"; that is, federal revenues generated in wealthy states should be distributed in a compensating fashion to less wealthy states. However, congressional spokesmen from poor states have seldom been favorably disposed to school-aid bills which returned proportionately less to their constituents than the latter had contributed in taxes to the federal treasury. Conversely, congressmen from wealthy states have seldom been favorably disposed to school-aid bills which did not allow their states proportionately more than their federal tax contribution. For several decades prior to 1965 no politically acceptable rationale could be found for an equalization formula, and many major school-aid proposals were defeated as a result.

New Tensions

Beginning with the 1958 enactment of the National Defense Education Act there has been an increasing amount of bipartisan support for school-aid bills. The questions thus facing proponents of such legislation are ones which are connected with the form federal aid should take, and there is growing controversy over the role that private interests should be allowed to play in federal programs. Not only the degree to which private nonproprietory schools should benefit from federal funds, but also the degree to which private proprietary interests should be involved is a question. Should it be legal, for instance, for profit-making firms to assist local school districts in writing proposals for federal aid in return for a consulting fee? Certain professional educational organizations contend that this should not be allowed and are actively pursuing the passage of restricting legislation. A number of private companies are lined up in opposition to such restrictions and can muster substantial rational justification and political influence in defense of their position.

Controversy of a similar sort of emerging over other topics. What proportion of federal education funds should go to higher education and what proportion to elementary and secondary schools? Similarly, what proportion to special education or vocational programs? Professional educators are themselves torn over the optimum means by which federal programs should be administered. Some contend that USOE should play the major role; others (and at the moment these appear to be in the majority) argue that the states should have the major role. And, whenever state control is proposed, religious groups and urban school spokesmen become somewhat "unglued" from their fellow federal-aid advocates because they fear their interests are not well served by the states which historically have been oriented toward rural and "Protestant" schools.

But, even among state administration proponents the question is fractionated. Some contend that state departments of education should run the federal programs; others feel that such agencies are inadequately staffed and too rigid organizationally to administer such programs effectively, and thus new state agencies should be established for the purpose. Then the question comes, however, as to who should control the new agency: the Governor, the state Legislature, the state board of education, etc.? These questions have few if any ultimate answers; there exist good reasons for taking action on both sides of most issues. These issues are mentioned here only to indicate that, even though some of the old political conflicts surrounding school aid have subsided or have been resolved, new tensions have risen in their place.

Compromising the Controversies

Over the last 80 or so years, heated political battles have surged back and forth over the above-described conflicts, and the life of literally dozens of school-aid proposals has been snuffed out in the conflagrations. Events of the last decade suggest that the conflicts are losing some of their intensity. Evidence for this point of view comes in the form of a number of pieces of significant legislation which have been enacted despite their potential to trigger all the traditional political controversies. In a substantial way the federal executive branch was responsible for initiating the political negotiations necessary to compromise the conflicts. This executive branch activity is illustrated nicely in the instance of the 1965 ESEA.

The 1965 ESEA

When it was enacted in 1965, the ESEA contained five substantive sections or "titles." Title I contains provisions for bolstering the education of children from low-income families. Title II provides federal assistance to schools (both public and nonpublic) for the purchase of textbooks and other instructional materials. Title III authorizes federal funds to be used in schools for developing and implementing new educational ideas and sources. Title IV amends and expands the previously enacted (1954) Cooperative Research Act, which authorized federal funds for research and development activities related to education. And Title V provides federal funds to strengthen state departments of education. (The

ESEA has subsequently been amended to include additional substantive sections which provide federal funds for special education, dropout prevention, and bilingual education programs.)

These provisions crossed a number of controversial lines. They enabled federal funds to be used for the benefit of children in nonpublic schools, and thus the church-state issue was present. Several of the programs authorized by the act were to be administered directly by U.S. Office of Education personnel, and thus those who feared federal "control" were placed on alert. The federal funds involved, in excess of $1.2 billion, were not to be allocated in equal amounts to all states, and those concerned over equal distribution of funds were therefore provided with a cause. Also, the previously enacted 1964 Civil Rights Act precluded the use of federal monies for racially segregated schools and, consequently, conditions were ripe to provoke Southern dissatisfaction. Furthermore, a substantial measure of the justification for the bill was based on the needs of urban schools: a rationale not likely to assuage the previously described antagonisms of rural congressmen.

Given this potential to trigger debilitating conflict, how was it that the ESEA was able to become law? The answer is by no means simple. A variety of prior actions such as the 1957 launching of the Soviet sputnik, which created a climate for educational reform, the Administration of John F. Kennedy and the reign of the liberal Pope John XXIII, which appeared to ameliorate public fears regarding the Roman Catholic Church, and the overwhelming 1964 election victory of Lyndon Johnson and the Democratic Party, all did much to facilitate passage of the ESEA. However, it is not likely that these fortuitous circumstances, even acting in consort as they did, would themselves have been sufficient to overcome the resistance to many of the ESEA's provisions. Rather, the view is persuasive that the actions of executive branch personnel in arriving at a series of ingenious compromises during the act's drafting stages and in coordinating the activities of key interest groups during the legislative process were the critical components accounting for passage. As was said previously, the manner in which such actions were taken is worthy of note because it illustrates the ability of the executive branch to influence the outcomes of Congress.

Attempts at identifying the origins of policy decisions typically involve an almost infinite regression and therefore are frequently fruitless. It is sufficient for our purposes to begin with a decision by Lyndon Johnson in mid-summer of 1964 to set in motion a White House task force to generate ideas for a landmark education bill. The task force was chaired by John W. Gardner, then president of the Carnegie Corporation and later to become Secretary of Health, Education and Welfare. At the same time the Gardner group was beginning its work on educational proposals, another cluster of idea men charged with much the same problem was gathered in the U.S. Office of Education. Eventually the ideas of the two groups were to be welded into one bill, but for purposes of making our point the actions of the USOE group are of greater interest.

A problem which the planning group knew would have to be met was that of financial distribution. The question was how to find a means and a rationale for distributing federal funds which would be both politically attractive and educationally sound. The solution had to meet a number of criteria: while satisfying genuine educational needs, it also had to contain some measure of fiscal equalization (so as to satisfy less wealthy states) and still guarantee every state (even wealthy ones) some minimum allotment. A principal problem was how to focus that minimum allotment for wealthy states in a fashion which would be productive of increased educational quality. The answer eventually resulted in the distribution formula embedded in Title I. The basis for that formula was the concept that federal funds should be focused to strengthen educational services for the so-called disadvantaged. This latter group was to be identified by the use of 1960 census figures indicating the number of children from families with annual incomes of $2,000 or less. Educationally speaking, this appeared practical because of the relationship which a number of researchers had demonstrated between low incomes and low levels of schooling(13). Moreover, the formula did contain an equalization component. Its outstanding feature, however, was that while providing the "bribe" funds to wealthy states necessary to gain their concurrence, the formula placed that "bribe" where it was educationally useful, on the noses of disadvantaged children.

A second major problem facing the USOE design group was the church-state issue. Two of the most influential interest groups in the area of education, the National Education Association (NEA) and the National Catholic Welfare Conference (which subsequently changed its name to U. S. Catholic Conference), had for years occupied opposite poles on the issue of whether or not federal funds should be used to benefit nonpublic schools and their students. A bill containing such features would be opposed by the NEA and, conversely, a bill devoid of such arrangements would not gain the necessary support of the Roman Catholic organization. In addition, other less influential interest groups were arrayed in satellite fashion around each of the major organizations and reflected their antithetical views. In order for a school-aid bill to pass, it was obvious that some sort of compromise was necessary because Catholic congressmen and those with large Catholic constituencies composed approximately one-fifth of the total membership of both Houses of Congress and held a balance of power.

No remarkably new strategy was utilized by executive branch personnel in their attempt to arrive at a politically popular and educationally feasible church-state compromise. Rather, the time-honored method of trial and error was employed. The then Commissioner of Education, Francis Keppel, along with several able assistants such as Samuel Halperin and Peter Muirhead, attended innumerable meetings with interest group spokesmen in an effort to arrive at educational programs and legislative provisions acceptable to all parties. A meeting with the NEA might result in a point which would have to be agreed to by the National Catholic Welfare Conference, which in turn might make changes which would need to be ratified by the National Council of Churches, which in turn, etc., etc. In time, however, the intellectual agility and emotional fortitude of Keppel and his colleagues paid off. By the time the ESEA was dropped in the legislative hopper, a coalition of church-state interest groups had been forged which, though somewhat shaky at times, managed to stay together throughout the crucial enactment stages. It was the first time such a coalition had been put together in behalf of a comprehensive school-aid bill, and the consequences were telling. The ESEA passed where all previous proposals of a like nature had been defeated. In substantial measure, the executive branch had made such success possible.

Other political controversies were subjected to much the same kind of tactics. Give and take transpired between executive branch personnel and civil rights groups, educational organizations such as the Council of Chief State School Officers, and various congressional factions. The end result of such executive branch initiative was a piece of legislation which had received a great deal of political polish long before it was ever subjected to the congressional tumbler. All that was needed for passage was the added Presidential push which Lyndon B. Johnson's landslide 1964 election made so easy.

By taking the initiative in framing legislative proposals and greasing the skids for their passage, the President and the executive branch can at least compensate for, and sometimes overcome, the rural bias of the legislative branch. However, the assumption of such initiative in large measure depends upon the President himself. The last two administrations, Kennedy and Johnson, have continued the tradition of the active Chief Executive and aggressively sought to initiate governmental policies. Eisenhower, however, did not perceive the President's role in the same fashion and a substantial portion of the policy-making initiative flowed back to Congress as a result. Eisenhower viewed the President's job as being primarily one of an executor of policy and thus relatively few proposals were sent to Capitol Hill from the White House. As to whether or not the executive branch continues in the Kennedy-Johnson tradition of policy initiation and concern for urban problems depends on the leadership style of Richard Nixon.

A Primer in Urban Educational Programs

The ESEA may be one of the most dramatic pieces of existing legislation of significance for urban education, but it is not the only one. The following section provides a "flavor" for the programs which have received congressional blessing and are in actual operation in urban areas.

The catalogue of federal assistance programs compiled by the Office of Economic Opportunity lists 459 federally sponsored activities dealing with domestic problems. In the specific instance of school aid the case is no more simple. During the five years of the Johnson Administration alone, Congress enacted 60 pieces of education legislation. This has resulted in 111 federal education programs costing approximately $13 billion annually. The matter is further complicated by the fact that these programs are administered by some 42 executive branch departments, agencies, and bureaus. The number of these programs and the variations in their operation make it difficult to assess those which are aimed specifically at urban concerns. In the following will be described a few programs which have obvious connections, in order to provide at least minimal understanding of what does already exist by way of federal programs for city schools.

USOE-Administered Programs

ESEA   Title I of the Elementary and Secondary Education Act is the primary federal program benefiting city schools. The Title I distribution formula is based primarily on: 1) the number of children from families with annual incomes of $2,000 or less, 2) the number of children whose parents receive AFDC payments(14), and 3) a multiplier of one-half the state or national (whichever is higher) mean annual per-pupil expenditure. The annual income component tends in some ways to discriminate against urban school districts. This is so because city living costs are higher than those of rural areas, and whereas $2,000 and above may enable one to live in a rural setting, it generally takes more than that to sustain the same living standard in a city. Many have argued that the ESEA Title I formula would be more equitable if the poverty definition were elevated to $3,000 or $4,000(15). The AFDC component, however, does tend to favor cities because it is here that such children are concentrated in larger numbers. Regardless of formula technicalities, Title I is still the primary federal program benefiting urban school districts.

The legislative provisions embodied in Title I allow for broad discretion on the part of local school district officials in deciding the best manner in which to spend the federal funds. The only major stipulations are that the money must somehow be focused on disadvantaged children and that it not be used for major construction. Given this decision-making freedom, school districts have created a vast array of new education programs designed to serve target groups of deprived students. Programs stressing reading improvement, counseling and guidance services, remedial mathematics instruction, extended school days, preschool activities, and inservice education of instructional personnel are common approaches to alleviating such problems.

It is difficult to assess the effects to date of Title I. The programs are only in their early years of operation, many have been seriously under-funded, and only in a few cities have sufficient resources been available to reach every disadvantaged child. These and other problems caused the Office of Education to suggest in its second annual report on Title I's operation that no glowing, overall successes could yet be claimed(16). This lack of immediate and dramatic results has led some critics to feel that compensatory education has been a failure. Such may indeed be the case, but it is our belief that the idea has not yet been given sufficient opportunity, and consequently does not warrant such a harsh evaluation. One of the difficulties may be that too many expected too much too soon. It probably is unrealistic to expect literally generations of poor social, medical, and educational conditions to be compensated for or eradicated in but a few short years. We can well understand the frustration of those who decry the lack of overwhelming positive results and who desire instant success, but we hope that sufficient patience can be mustered to allow the strategy more time to be implemented and improved.

ESEA Title III.   When originally enacted in 1965, this Supplementary Education Centers and Services title was not oriented specifically to urban educational problems. However, within the limits of its authority, the U.S. Office of Education has recently endeavored to focus Title III more closely on the needs of city schools. USOE has now developed a Central Cities Project which will direct 25 percent of USOE-controlled Title III funds to 24 cities. It appears too soon to assess the impact of this program, but the amount of money involved is not great and at best one can hope for the creation and development of new approaches. However, to implement these approaches on a vast scale will not be possible under present arrangements. If new ideas are conceived and perfected under Title III incentives, then other arrangements will probably be needed to achieve widespread dispersion and implementation.

Vocational Education   This is an area which has attracted sustained congressional interest for over half a century. Early efforts in this field were aimed at assisting the agricultural sector in obtaining sufficient numbers of skilled workers. Later legislative enactments concentrated upon the preparation of individuals for an economy which was reaching industrial maturity. Most of the programs were not geared to the needs of our present highly technical economy; thus, federally funded vocational schools have tended to benefit rural more than urban needs. Passage of the 1963 Vocational Education Act, however, slowly began to redress this inequity, and a recently enacted measure, the 1963 Vocational Education Act, appears to possess provisions which may redirect such programs even more. For example, several sections of the new legislation authorize the Commissioner of Education to give special consideration to depressed areas, and the "hard core" unemployed. These urban emphases plus the $3 billion authorized by the bill (for 1969–72) provide a glimmer of hope that vocational education may possibly reorient itself to the needs of urban youth. In that a large portion of the new program is to be administered by states, however, the grave risk remains that rural interests will warp the benefits of federal largess.

Higher Education   Though operating in a somewhat indirect fashion, there are a number of higher education programs which offer benefits to urban schools. Most of these are of a student-aid nature; that is, they provide financial assistance to students who otherwise might not be able to afford college. The newly enacted 1963 Higher Education Act (HEA) embodies several provisions of this general type: Economic Opportunity Grants, the Student Loan Insurance Program, and the Work-Study Program. In addition, this piece of legislation amended the 1953 National Defense

Act so as to allow up to 75 percent forgiveness on the college loans of those students who subsequently teach five or more years in schools where 50 percent or more of the children are from low-income families.

Another type of higher education program which encourages disadvantaged, but potentially very capable, students to continue their education into college is the Upward Bound project. This endeavor identifies exceptionally capable students who under typical circumstances would not pursue a post-high school education and provides them with tutoring and other special activities and incentives so as to encourage them to go on to college. This effort draws most, but not all, its enrollees from urban settings. Because of political controversies surrounding the Office of Economic Opportunity, Upward Bound has been a rather constant bone of contention among congressmen, and it appears that it may have lost some of its potential effectiveness in the process. The 1968 HEA transferred administration of the program from OEO to the Office of Education. One would hope that this older and more firmly established executive branch agency might provide Upward Bound with a better bureaucratic shelter and thus enable it to increase its effectiveness outside the glare of political controversy.

Other Office of Education Programs   The Office of Education administers several other programs which have the potential to benefit city schools. None of these is oriented exclusively toward urban areas, but Public Laws 815 and 874, the National Defense Education Act, the Education Professions Development Act, the Cooperative Research Act, and the 1964 Civil Rights Act all embody provisions which under certain circumstances make resources available to urban schools.

The Office of Economic Opportunity

The Office of Economic Opportunity, established to implement the 1964 Economic Opportunity Act, administers several programs which assist urban education. One of these programs,

The Job Corps, concentrates on youths unable to obtain satisfactory employment. It places them in residential training centers in an effort to prepare them with skills which will enable them to gain and hold a job. The Corps recruits among both boys and girls and city and farm youth. The training centers are located in rural areas (much like the Civilian Conservation Corps of the Great Depression) as well as in urban centers.

Perhaps the most famous of the OEO-administered programs is *Operation Headstart* which is now operated under USOE. This endeavor operates through a variety of local agencies, private schools, churches, community action groups, etc., to provide an intensive preschool experience to educationally and economically deprived children. In addition to emphasizing learning readiness skills, Headstart operations attend to the health and nutritional needs of children in the belief that the ability to absorb schooling is based on more than intellectual preparation alone. Headstart projects have appeared to have some rather remarkable results, but they are sometimes criticized because of the high levels of expenditures ($1,000 or more per pupil) apparently required to obtain those results. However, even if such expenses cannot be reduced by eventually identifying the most effective techniques, this appears to be a modest price considering the potential savings to society of subsequent expenses for welfare and institutionalization. Another fact to keep in mind, however, is that the intensified Headstart experiences appear to count for little if the student is then exposed to overcrowded, poorly equipped, and generally unsatisfactory primary school experience. In order to avoid this dilution and optimize the gains triggered by Headstart, the Office of Education implemented *Project Follow Through* in 1967. Here the effort is to provide Headstart youngsters with a sustained, high-level primary school environment.

The Office of Economic Opportunity also administers *Volunteers in Service to America (VISTA)*. This is a kind of domestic Peace Corps wherein volunteers work with the residents of depressed areas in order to upgrade their life. In some instances, big city school systems have capitalized upon the availability of VISTA volunteers to help teachers as paraprofessionals and to engage in community relations activities.

The Department of Labor

Several programs with educational significance for urban areas are administered by the Labor Department. One of the most promising of these is the Neighborhood Youth Corps. Emphasis is placed upon both economically and socially disadvantaged youngsters, and consequently the program tends to concentrate its efforts in urban areas. The purpose is to encourage youths from low-income families to continue their education. They can seek assistance at any of a number of locally situated Youth Opportunity Centers where they have access to services such as occupational guidance, testing, personal counseling, and job placement.

Other Labor Department programs relevant to urban education are the Special Impact Program, the National Apprenticeship Program, various Manpower Development and Training Act (MDTA) programs, and the Concentrated Employment Program (administered jointly with OEO).

Other Executive Branch Agencies

One of the difficulties with federal education programs is their fragmentation. As was described at the outset of this section, the variety and number of programs somewhat defies rationality. It is easy to understand how such fragmentation occurred. Legislation is seldom enacted in orderly fashion; programs are passed in fits and spurts and in bits and pieces. The Department of Health, Education and Welfare proposes and obtains one program this year, Labor the next year, and OEO the next. Such programs probably could not come about in any other fashion given our political system; nevertheless, such incrementalism makes for a certain degree of administrative chaos. Thus, while we have mentioned major programs in several executive branch agencies, we have by no means described all of them. Other departments such as Housing and Urban Development, Defense, and Transportation also administer programs with implications for urban schools. We will stop our descriptions here, however, and suggest that those interested in further information consult some compilation of federal-assistance programs such as the one published by OEO mentioned at the opening of this section.

Conclusion

In our tri-level governmental system—local, state, and national—consideration should always be given to the questions: 1) Is or is not a given function appropriately performed in the public sector? and 2) If so, to what degree and at what level? The arguments for public sector education are well known, and local and state governments have long been engaged in the provision of such services. Federal government involvement on any substantial scale, however, has come about only within the last decade and in some ways is still on a shaky footing. There yet exist a few individuals, particularly in the legislative branch, who question the legality and wisdom of federal government involvement in matters of social welfare generally, not to mention federal action in education and urban problems specifically.

I disagree strongly with the latter position. It is my contention that this nation faces no greater crisis than the social turmoil which currently inhabits our cities. The possibility of urban chaos constitutes as great a threat to our way of life as Fascist and Communist expansion, the proliferation of nuclear weapons, or the mounting dilemmas of air, water, and noise pollution. The American way of life is today an urban way of life. Some of the fuel for that life may flow from farms and mines, but the heart and nerves of America are in her cities. It is here that the economy is directed; it is here the most influential governments are centered; it is here that the writers and artists cluster. The cure for urban problems must be embodied ultimately in the actions of urban residents; I do not wish to contend that "Washington" can do it all. Nevertheless, the magnitude of the urban crisis is such that a large measure of the direction and coordination of our efforts and the resources for those efforts must come from the federal government. It is one of the few organizations with the perspective and potential power to accomplish the task. Because education has a major role to play in meeting the problems of urban areas, I believe the federal government should devote a substantial share of its efforts to improving urban educational systems. The degree to which it will be able to accomplish this objective depends in large measure upon two factors: 1) the speed with which recent social trends—urbanization—herein to be reflected more accurately in the makeup of

Congress, and 2) the view of the President of the federal government's role in meeting the urban crises. If the latter is resolved in favor of an active federal stance and if Congress moves further from its present rural bias, then the path is better paved for an extensive and well-coordinated federal attack on the problems of cities. Short of these two conditions, I am reluctant to predict the consequences.

Notes

1. Glendon Schubert, ed., *Reapportionment* (New York: Charles Scribner's Sons, 1965).

2. For an explanation of the factors which make the Senate more liberal than the House see Lewis Froman, *Congressmen and their Constituencies* (Chicago: Rand McNally & Co., 1963).

3. *Baker v. Carr*, 369 U.S. 186 (1962).

4. *Wesberry v. Sanders*, 387 U.S. 1 (1964).

5. *Branegan v. Grills et al.*, 390 U.S. 932 (1968).

6. The internal workings of Congress are described in many places. In this author's opinion, the following references offer the best general views of the situation: Clem Miller, *Member of the House: Letters of a Congressman*, ed. John Baker (New York: Charles Scribner's Sons, 1962); Charles Clapp, *The Congressman: His Work as He Sees It* (Garden City, N.Y.: Doubleday & Company, Inc., 1954); and Donald Mathews, *U.S. Senators and Their World* (Chapel Hill, N.C.: University of North Carolina Press, 1960).

7. For a detailed discussion see James W. Guthrie, "City Schools in a Federal Vise," *Education and Urban Society*, February 1970.

8. Nixon captured 43.36 percent of the vote in 1968 to Humphrey's 43.1 percent. The electoral votes were divided 301 to 191, with Wallace netting the remaining 46.

9. An interesting reversal occurs, however, when the Presidential election is so close as to place the decision in the House of Representatives. When this happens each state gets only one vote, to be cast in accord with the wishes of the majority of its congressional delegation, and the candidate who nets the most state votes is declared President. As can be readily seen, this procedure favors small, sparsely populated, rural states whose single votes are worth the same as the larger states.

10. Nelson W. Polsby and Aaron B. Wildavsky, *Presidential Elections: Strategies of American Electoral Politics* (New York: Charles Scribner's Sons, 1964), p. 19.

11. The best single source of information about the political controversies surrounding federal school aid proposals is Frank J. Munger and Richard F. Fenno, Jr., *National Politics and Federal Aid to Education* (Syracuse, N.Y.: Syracuse University Press, 1962).

12. For example, the House of Representatives passed the 1968 Vocational Education Act 390 to 0 and the 1968 Higher Education Act 389 to 15. The Senate vote was unanimous on both bills.

13. See, for instance, M. Thomas James, James A. Kelly, and Walter I.

Garms, *Determinants of Educational Expenditures in Large Cities of The United States* (Stanford, Calif: School of Education, Stanford University Press, 1966).

14. Aid for Families with Dependent Children, a federally subsidized welfare program.

15. In fact, the congressionally enacted 1967 ESEA amendments did raise the poverty standard to $3,000, but funding inadequacies have not enabled this new provision to take effect.

16. *Title I/Year II: The Second Annual Report of Title I of the Elementary and Secondary Education Act of 1965, School Year 1966–67* (Washington D.C.: U.S. Department of Health, Education and Welfare, U.S. Office of Education, 1968).

15

Urban Education
and the
School of Education

Robert J. Schaefer

Introduction

Historically, at least, any causal relationship between urban
location and a school of education's special commitment to problems of urban education could not be presumed. One was more
likely to find courses on city school administration at the University of Missouri in Columbia, Missouri, than at the University of
Chicago. Since the days of Frank Spaulding, Harvard has fixed its
gaze firmly towards Newton and Concord rather than towards
Boston or, down its nose, towards Cambridge. Washington University in St. Louis has traditionally attracted more students from St.
Louis County and the boot-heel of Missouri than from the city
itself. Life in the faculty apartments of Teachers College, Columbia University in the forties, if we are to trust contemporary
reports, was more like a small town in Iowa than any place in Iowa
itself.

Today, one finds a research and development center on urban
teaching the pastoral environs of the University of Wisconsin in
Madison. From Yellow Springs, Ohio, Antioch College establishes
graduate seminars on urban teaching in Putney, Vermont, and
sponsors a model subdistrict amidst the Washington, D.C., schools.
In the twin cities of Champagne and Urbana, the University of
Illinois pursues new approaches for teaching pre-school slum chil-

dren and interdisciplinary programs in the communication patterns of urban minorities. While many institutions located in metropolitan areas also demonstrate a current interest in urban education, the quick availability of live laboratories and even the presence of qualified faculty members guarantees no monopoly in the field.

At the moment, and presumably for some time to come, it seems advantageous to assert special enthusiasm and competence in urban education. State universities, even those which may be housed in relatively isolated rural settings, look toward the possible fiscal bias of legislators representing urban districts. Departments of education in liberal arts colleges are reminded that many of their students are recruited from the suburbs of great cities. Urban universities, themselves, make new and more positive assessments of their ecological circumstances. No one, to be sure, underestimates the difficulties of the city—its encroaching slums, its transportation problems and parking snarls, its racial hostilities, and its inflationary pressures—but there is fresh awareness of the intellectual excitement and the professional challenge which urban problems afford.

Given both the bandwagon pressures and a common recognition of the social importance of seeking to resolve urban educational problems, what are the appropriate strategies for schools of education? How should we deploy our resources; what programmatic changes are required; what organizational shifts are necessitated; in short, what stance should we assume? It would be presumptuous to imagine that any single perspective could fit the diverse circumstances which obtain in individual institutions, and downright fatuous to assume that any particular view could prevail in such a politically volatile area. Nonetheless, for whatever uses may be made of them, a few possible suggestions can be put forward.

Frank Admission of Our Ignorance About Urban Education

Of fundamental importance, if we are to encourage rationality in our stance towards urban education, is to admit the depth of our current ignorance about how to educate children from lower class homes. The plain fact, for which we have massive and overwhelming documentation, is that our state of knowledge and our technology are simply not adequate to the task. The public schools of the United States, individually and collectively, are failing to offset the educational handicaps with which lower class youngsters enter school. And, of course, the central problem of urban education is how to educate lower-class, and disproportionately Negro, children.

The Coleman Report

The degree of our ignorance in this area is clearly revealed in the literature. First, consider The United States Office of Education's 1966 report on *Equality of Educational Opportunity*—called the "Coleman Report" after its principal author, Professor James S. Coleman of Johns Hopkins University(1). The principal focus of the study was not what resources go into education—of course, education inputs were noted—but what product comes out.

The Report examined the results of education by measuring those areas of knowledge and achievement deemed most necessary for further progress in school, in higher education, and in the world at large—namely, verbal and reading skills and analytical and mathematical skills. What matters to the young adult, Coleman and his staff reasoned, was whether he was equipped at the end of school to compete with others, whatever his social origins. From the point of view of society, it assumes that what is important is not an ideological definition of equalized schools, but the assurance that children from all groups come into adult society so equipped as to guarantee their full participation in society. Since children do not come to school equally equipped to participate, the measure of whether the schools succeed or fail is whether or not they make a youngster's chances for academic success less dependent upon his social origins.

On this measure the public schools fail. It is true, of course, that minority children start school with severe educational handicaps; this gap is documented in detail by the Coleman Report, and quite obviously the deficiencies cannot be blamed on the schools. What can be blamed on the schools, however, is the fact that these youngsters face an even more serious educational deficiency at the end of their schooling. The gap between their achievement and that of white middle-class students is wider at the end of school than it was when they entered. More critically, in analyzing the various factors that bear upon children's academic achievement—for example, the quality of the school, the quality of their teachers, the nature of the student body, and the nature of the family from which they came—it is clear that the longer a minority child is in school, the less influence his school and his teachers have relative to the impact of family and student peer groups. By the time the minority youngster finishes school, therefore, his chances of academic success are even more dependent upon his social origins than when he entered.

Data from the Report demonstrate that schools are remarkably uniform in their effects, notwithstanding the apparent large diversity in their resources and the quality of their offerings. Thus, something between two-thirds and three-quarters of the differences that occur in students' achievement scores lies within the same school; only one-quarter to one third of the differences fall between schools, that is, reflect the effects of the schools themselves.

The school-to-school variation in achievement, small as it is, is due almost entirely to the social environment provided by the school—to the social, economic, and educational background of the students and teachers. When the backgrounds of the students and teachers are held constant, the differences in pupil achievement washes out almost entirely. Differences in class size, per pupil expenditures, homogeneous or heterogeneous grouping, number of books in the library show virtually no relationship to student achievement when the social environment of the school is held constant. In short, nothing we now do to improve education—at least, on anything like the scale we now do it—has any significant effect in freeing student achievement from the impact of the home and the social environment of the school.

Confirmation from Other Investigations

The major findings of the Coleman Report are not inconsistent with interpretations afforded by many other investigations. While careful evaluation studies of individual compensatory education projects have not been frequently undertaken, it is generally concluded that efforts thus far have proven unavailing. After reviewing the evaluations of various programs, none of which seemed to show any sustained academic improvement, the United States Commission on Civil Rights concluded that:

> . . . the compensatory programs reviewed here appear to suffer from the defect inherent in attempting to solve problems stemming in part from racial and social class isolation in schools which themselves are isolated by race and social class(2).

Similarly, the California State Department of Public Instruction's assessment of Title I projects conducted in 1044 school districts in the state revealed that only 2.3 percent resulted in statistically significant gains in student achievement(3). After examining the More Effective Schools project in New York City, the Center for Urban Education discovered that students, after two years, exhibited the classical pattern of increasing academic retardation(4). Even substantial reductions in the pupil-teacher ratios, without concurrent radical changes in pedagogical practice, failed to produce the hoped-for gains. As for the effects of ability grouping, the careful studies completed by Miriam Goldberg, Harry Passow, and Joseph Justman concluded that ability grouping per se has no important effect on the academic achievement of students(5).

Getting on with the Job of Knowing

To cite the literature attesting to our failure to know how to overcome the educational deficiencies associated with lower class and minority status is not at all to assert that we have no hope of knowing. It would be absurd to argue that under no circumstances could the effects of a student environment upon the development of academic competence be remedied in segregated situations. The lackluster results thus far are no basis for such a view. The question is not whether student performance could thus be improved, but rather how, with what programs, under what circumstances, at what level of investment, and with what major second-order effects? Our basic opportunity, once freed of the defensive posture of seeming to know, is to invest our full energies in getting on with the job of knowing.

The advantages of admitting our ignorance are many. In the first place, it focuses the attention of faculties of education upon the determination of appropriate priorities. Heavy investments of resources and personnel in research become obviously sensible. We are released from the pressure for honoring self-appointed experts and we have leverage for resisting pleas for ill-considered, immediate interventions. The challenge of considering more fundamental alterations of our traditional methods for keeping school becomes real. And, as the completeness of our failure in urban educational affairs becomes apparent to all, we can safely entertain proposals for the drastic revision of our programs for training practitioners. There is nothing so liberating than the shared knowledge that more, or improved versions, of the same hold no hope of sufficing.

Pressures to Maintain the Pose of Knowing

It will not be easy to assert our present ignorance nor to maintain the stance that fresh knowledge is urgently required. There are many, both individuals and groups, who hold that what schools of education and society at large lack is not knowledge but the will to act. Many believe, for example, that the core of the urban educational problem is lack of committing the resources to effect the necessary improvements. "Before we accept the slogan that money is not the answer," to cite Albert Shanker's oft-quoted remark as illustrative, "let's try the money answer just once"(6).

As Patricia Sexton's *Education and Income* well documents, there is certainly a relationship between social and economic status and the quality of education provided for children in the public schools(7). The data she presents demonstrate conclusively that curricula, educational standards, quality of teaching, educational facilities and materials, and academic achievement of the children are directly related to the socio-economic status of the majority of children attending a particular school. What is overlooked, however, is that while increased funds are patently necessary, money alone cannot buy the requisite services unless we have clear and intellectually defensible plans for how to spend it. The final evaluation of the More Effective Schools Project pointed out that drastic reductions in pupil-teacher ratios are only a necessary not a sufficient condition of effective compensatory education. "Observers noted that a majority of lessons they saw could have been taught to larger classes with no loss of effectiveness. . . . All levels of staff noted that the basic weakness of the program . . . centered about the functioning of teachers"(8). In other words, vastly increased expenditures could not in themselves generate the improved technology or the new instructional strategies which may have been required.

The Need for Dedication

There are other explanations of our urban crisis which threaten any effort to emphasize new knowledge. Critics seem to feel that it is primarily the small-mindedness and lack of dedication of the typical educational practitioner which is at fault. The urban school, so the argument runs, draws a disproportionate share of indifferent teachers, counselors, and principals who not only have little concern for their pupils but accept the common stereotype that most of them are incapable of learning. As a result of this low estimate of potential, the self-fulfilling prophecy of the ineducability of lower-class students is perpetuated. As Mel Ravitz has described it, "The children are not encouraged to learn very much; the teacher expends little energy on anything but maintaining order and bemoaning his lot; as a consequence, the children fulfill the low expectation, which in turn reinforces the original assumption"(9).

Fictional and autobiographical writers on teaching in city schools tend to support such "benighted individual" explanations of our urban educational problems. Most of the educators in Bel Kaufman's *Up the Down Staircase* are made to appear obvious idiots, but despite the inanities of the system and the low character of her "professional" associates, the heroine manages to perform creditably, nay, even nobly, as a teacher. Patently, what is needed in the New York City schools is not fresh knowledge about how to reach lower-class children, but how to attract more sensitive and humane teachers and the destruction of a particularly foolish bureaucracy. Similarly, what comes through in Jonathan Kozol's *Death at an Early Age,* John Holt's *Why Children Fail,* Herbert Kohl's *36 Children* and James Herndon's *The Way It Spozed To Be* is not a plea for systematic inquiry into the pedagogical problems of ghetto schools, but the consistent theme that what is wrong is the dearth of persons of the requisite humanity and faith. While no one can deny the schools' need for patience and sensitivity, possession of those traits, if one is to judge by the fact that none of the writers cited teaches any longer, does not necessarily lead to long-term dedication nor make the urban school a viable place in which to work.

The clear implication of such writing is that we should rely on the so-called "Peace Corps spirit" of existing or potential teachers to attract highly motivated individuals to ghetto schools. It assumes that missionary idealism will overcome racial and social-class prejudice, and what are admittedly poor working conditions, and thus reverse the present maldistribution of competent teachers. "With respect to missionary idealism," as David Cohen has observed, "there are no precedents for the hope that it will be widespread. It exists in limited quantities, and although one must applaud and encourage dedication which is not patronizing, it simply is not an everyday quality. Wise policy cannot be made on the assumption that most people will be heroic"(10).

It is probably true that in recent years a greater number of young persons imbued with the Peace Corps spirit, especially those whose induction into the armed services appeared imminent, have accepted positions in ghetto schools. But as Peter Buttonweiser of the Philadelphia Advancement School has attested, the turnover rate is incredibly high. In New York City, also, young enthusiasts attracted to experimental districts in Bedford Stuyvesant and in the I.S. 201 complex have rarely lingered long enough to accumulate tenure. In general, as data from the Coleman Report indicated, the better teachers are least likely to prefer teaching in predominantly Negro, or blue-collar schools. High-ability Negro teachers in ghetto schools are—of all groups—the teachers most likely to be dissatisfied with their present teaching position. Clearly, missionary zeal alone, without the requisite knowledge and technology to make it effective, is insufficient.

Mood of the Black Community

One further difficulty in maintaining the position that to meet its responsibilities in urban affairs the school of education should primarily engage in research and in the development of new technology is the present mood of the Black community. There is a pervasive conviction that schools are massive white barriers to Negro education and freedom. What seems needed is hardly new knowledge, but breaking the white monopoly on educational resources and providing the kind of educational plant and teaching staff affluent schools in Scarsdale or Winnetka have traditionally enjoyed. Francis Ianni has characterized this mood thusly:

> Our neighbors in Harlem have laid the responsibility for what they consider a socially and intellectually irrelevant, almost criminally negligent school system equally at the foot of the schools and the schools of education that prepare people to operate these schools. They see the experimentation and demonstration programs which were the touchstones of the search for quality as somehow precious and alien to their own problems. Sophistication of research seems futile to them when seen against the backdrop of incredibly ill-kept, ill-supplied, and over-crowded ghetto schools and teachers who don't seem to be able to make any difference in the lives of their children. For them, the school has become a conservative, almost reactionary institution in a revolutionary society. To most of the people of the ghetto who think about such things, it is the community which must lead and the schools which must follow.

> This same attitude colors the relationship between the school of education and the people of the ghetto. Paternalism, no matter how positive and sincere, has no place in today's urban education programs. In a very real sense, the people of the ghetto are demanding the right to make their own mistakes and not to have them made for them by others. Time and again educators are met with the maddening and seemingly irrational twin accusations of never having been interested in helping the people of the ghetto and now trying to impose middle-class white solutions on black peoples' educational problems. . . . We are told that experimentation and demonstration, the principal methods of our

craft, are unwelcome and unneeded in the ghetto, and that we are unwilling to look at major educational problems. What is perhaps most disturbing to the liberal educational reformer is that he is now being told that he is no longer needed and that the ghetto will find its own solutions to its own problems(11).

Given such feelings and assuming they will be expressed with increasing frequency and vehemence, it is easy to anticipate the pressure upon schools of education to deliver developed talent and resources rather than to analyze problems. The Black community can hardly be expected to respond patiently to any stance which threatens, with seeming heartlessness, to postpone ameliorative action. Careful inquiry and experimentation, no matter what their promised potential for effecting lasting educational improvements, is bound to appear to be another put-off. But to cite the problem is not to suggest capitulation of its dilemma. While it is clear that in the present circumstances, research that is not cooperatively planned and executed, or technologies that the community as well as the university do not jointly support, are politically untenable, it is certainly possible that the requisite collaboration can be developed. Rather, it seems likely that an openness and honesty about how little we know and how much we might jointly discover could serve to build mutual trust.

Emphasis Upon Disciplined Field Study

One of the factors which has contributed to community skepticism about the importance of inquiry in improving urban education is simply the fact that there has been so little of it. For the most part we in schools of education have been content to engage in didactic discussion of urban problems from the security and isolation of university classrooms. Comparatively rarely have faculty members been visibly involved in field investigations. When we have joined in community discussion, it has often been only to offer generalized and global advice about such matters as non-graded classes or the importance of being earnest. When we have ventured into the live arena, it has frequently been with a noticeable thud; i.e., New York University's efforts to manage, in model fashion, a Brooklyn school or Harvard's attempts to advise Roxbury parents about modern school facilities. The obvious fact is that most professors of education, and equally most specialists in educational administration, have been content to prescribe generalized remedies for the particular pathologies of metropolitan districts without going through the travail of diagnosing the true nature of the urban world.

There have been exceptions, of course. The University of Chicago has long sponsored careful empirical investigation of educational problems associated with race and class. Daniel Griffiths' et al., study of personnel practices and Frank Lutz's analyses of contract negotiations in New York City have not been of the armchair variety(12). The Community Resource Centers established by Teachers College have been located geographically and conceptually in actual Harlem neighborhoods. New programs for developing educational leadership, too, have not been campusbound, but have required a variety of internship experiences and situational analyses.

The current mood of university students, their restless insistence upon combining study and action has, fortunately, spilled over to professional schools of education and contributes to our capacity for first-hand examination of the phenomena of urban education. There is a general disenchantment with wholly verbal analysis of social and professional problems and an ebullient faith in the possibilities of learning through immersion in the full complexities of the real world. At best, this rejection of the merely academic need not be anti-intellectual nor even a-theoretical; abstractions can indeed be illuminated through concrete instances and viable theory cannot afford a permanent separation from live data. Field study and experience can certainly be wholly legitimate forms of the current insistence upon educational relevance.

But our present enthusiasm for taking education out of the classroom is not without its neurotic tendencies. As I observed in another context:

> To some students and faculty members involvement in social action situations is itself fully educative and requires no concurrent effort to organize such experience intellectually and to relate it to what disciplinary studies can potentially or have already

revealed. While we may all decry the overly cognitive emphases of traditional education, there seems little sanity in dismissing analysis and conceptualization as irrelevant vestiges of an evil past. Certainly understanding and the capacity for effective action can be enhanced by field experience, but only if students are helped to impose meaning upon what they observe and feel. If advocacy of intellectual structure becomes merely one among many competing political positions in the educational world, there can be no university. We might just as well send students into the streets and after suitable exposure to experimental learning encourage them to mimeograph their own degrees(13).

While there is danger in rampant student activism, the need for greater involvement in the urban scene, both in research and in participation, exceeds the risk. There can be no hope of understanding, let alone remediation, of severe problems if institutions capable of it do not commit manpower and resources to an on-location study of urban education. One fundamental element of a recommended response to urban educational problems, therefore, is a vastly increased emphasis upon disciplined field study.

Preparation for Fluid Occupational Roles

As we recognize the problem of educating lower-class youngsters and what to do about it—and field study, I believe, is bound to deepen our awareness—we are forced to question the viability of the structures and organizational patterns which currently prevail. It may well be that attempting to prepare "better" teachers and administrators for urban schools as they currently exist can only perpetuate chaos and futility. To the degree we are successful in adjusting new personnel to the present environment, we may be disqualifying them for roles which have a greater chance of effectiveness. If our students are prepared primarily to cope with present difficulties, they may be dissuaded from seeking basic changes in their environment. Given our massive failure to date, it seems imperative to train, not for static occupational positions, but, more fluidly, for roles not yet fully conceived.

Consider, for example, the problem of recruiting and maintaining teachers for urban schools. As indicated earlier, reliance upon missionary idealism has not paid off, and present inequities in the distribution of teacher quality can probably be reversed only if the status of urban schools is raised by dramatically improving working conditions. At a minimum, we need to recognize that the problem of teacher maldistribution will not be solved by the voluntary action of individuals. In general, teachers prefer to teach academically oriented students and, by definition, this preference assigns low priority to urban schools and to the possible satisfactions in teaching Negro and other lower-class children. Teaching in deprived-area schools is conceived as precisely equivalent to teaching in suburbia—similar pupil-teacher ratios; essentially synonomous, if watered down, curricula; an identical system of grades, tests, gold stars for rewards, and punishments; comparable teacher autonomy, and an equivalent expectation that beneficial results will somehow occur. Teachers in urban schools have to bear a heavy burden of guilt for being unable to resolve difficulties which, according to the implicit expectations of school appointments, require no special analysis or talent. Is it so surprising that most who are there want to get out?

Since the hazards of urban teaching have become so apparent, it seems unconscionable for schools of education to prepare new practicioners for mere coping-behavior. The emphasis instead should be upon equipping prospective educators with the attitudes and insights essential to modifying their work environment. One tactic might be, as I have argued extensively in *The School as a Center of Inquiry,* to prepare teachers who can conceive of their classrooms not simply as places of instruction for the young, but as laboratories for adult study of pedagogical problems. Robert Dreeben has made much the same point in his "The Nature of Teaching: Schools and the Work of Teachers." He states:

To take a page from the medical book: physicians have had an on-going tradition of *clinical* research. Doctors, *in the course of their practice,* have often written up their experiences in the treatment and management of particular diseases: 50 cases of kidney stones, 100 cases of bronchial asthma, and the like. These studies are not necessarily experimental, they do not employ random samples, they do not necessarily contain the most desirable set of varying examples; but they do reflect systematic work, intensive knowledge, and direct relevance to practice. Equally important, the research is carried out by practicioners and it is published so that others engaged in the treatment of similar illnesses can benefit by the experience of men with intimate knowledge about the disease. The knowledge, in other words, ceases to be private; no claim is made that it is definitive.

There is no reason that research of this kind cannot be undertaken in schools by teachers. It is necessary that they know the rudiments of doing the research—the skills can be taught in the normal course of their training—and that time be made available for them to do it. Is there any reason why teachers, alone or in concert, cannot investigate, for example, strategies for dealing with able learners in classes where academically unmotivated pupils predominate? Techniques for providing structure for students who particularly mistrust adult authority or experimental approaches to teaching reading suggested by individual language usage patterns? Methods for establishing control in classrooms where many pupils hate school? At least three benefits can result from such efforts: 1) *useful* material can be gathered and disseminated among teachers confronting similar problems; 2) a medium of communication can be established within an occupational group whose members work largely in isolation; and 3) the content of this research can feed directly into the theoretical and empirical problems studied by academicians in the social and psychological sciences(14).

If nothing else, an interest in such an anthropological mode of investigation may free the teacher from the guilt associated with not being fully equal to his urban assignment. The possibility of developing inquiring scholar-teachers, however, is intended as an illustrative response to the problem of creating satisfactory working conditions. The point is simply that means must be deliberately developed which have some chance of attracting and retaining able teachers for deprived-area schools. Another approach might simply be to ensure that all prospective educators have full opportunity for the systematic and objective, rather than tender-minded and sentimental, exploration of the problems and difficulties of urban education. A variety of new occupational roles and alternative modes of instruction—developed with as much imagination and intelligence as schools of education can command or borrow —must be made constantly visible to the student. Our responsibility is not preparation for an ineffective, if structured, present but for a hopefully more efficacious if indefinite future.

Educational Leaders Needed

A similar point of view might very well guide our efforts to produce educational administrators for urban settings. Surely, the economic, political and social pressures which now, and in the future will increasingly, beset city schools, dictate new approaches to producing educational leaders. There is obvious need for persons who conceive of education broadly, and who recognize the significance of educative influences which go beyond mere schooling. We require persons who are prepared by disposition and training to cooperate with many public and private institutions in the education of the populace. Our need is less for fully certificated administrators who have learned to survive within the system and more for persons capable of building the political power necessary to change the system. We need to concentrate our resources upon more thoughtful programs for nurturing educational leadership and to select candidates, not upon the basis of their acceptability within some tightly knit bureaucracy, but because of their potential for intellectual and professional development.

In attempting to envisage new patterns of educational leadership it is, of course, impossible to describe all of the substantive elements which may be necessary in preparing persons for roles which are not yet fully defined. Certain features are clear, however. We must encourage an individual intellectual style appropriate to the continuing study of social and educational policy issues. Training must incorporate experiences in a variety of educative setting, not only in schools, but in foundations and in state, local, and national governmental agencies which bear upon the development of urban youth. Above all, the conventional wisdom must always be open to criticism and the disposition for pursuing new structures and new relationships carefully nurtured. The as yet unyielding difficulties of urban education require not fixed knowledge but the trained capacity to recognize and to exploit promising leads.

Building a Long-Term Commitment to Urban Research

Training the kind of sensitive and flexibly minded practitioner urban conditions desperately require can probably best be accomplished in institutions committed to research and to the development of new technology. The need is not to indoctrinate the prospective urban educator with particular nostrums, but to surround him with the intellectual commitment and questioning spirit which inquiry generates. Nor can research programs be conceived simply in decision-oriented terms, as short-range and direct investigation of immediate urban problems. As the Committee on Educational Research of the National Academy of Education has pointed out, significant improvements in educational practice have also derived from research motivated simply by the curiosity of the inquirer rather than by its perceived applicability to problems of practice(15).

Education, like other efforts to change and to influence people, rests on bodies of knowledge provided by the humanities and the social sciences, disciplines that are relatively undeveloped theoretically and not well suited, at present, to provide clear guidelines for occupational practice. Although we need not dismiss technological developments that "work" for reasons we don't understand—there are many medical treatments of precisely that character—in the long run, we can expect to find a general correspondence between advances in teaching and those in the behavioral sciences. Since advances in the social sciences or the humanities cannot be delivered upon demand, we may have to wait a long time for some important technological developments in teaching. We cannot, therefore, limit ourselves to classroom experiments or to investigations of the politics of diffusing ideas and practices, but must also promote scientific research that has no obvious, short-term relevance to the crisis of urban education.

Schools of education which expect to be seriously concerned

about urban education, therefore, must plan for the long rather than the short haul. And if we are to generate much sustained pulling power, we will need to engage the resources of the university as a whole in tandem effort. In recommending that schools of education seek to attract university scholars to problems of urban education, let it be clear at the outset that arts and sciences faculties are not teeming with experienced and knowledgeable urban experts. It must be admitted that except for periodic flurries and intensive work by a few individual scholars, the university has been relatively unresponsive to the cluster of interlocking problems centering around poverty, slums, and the Negro. John Gardner's sermon about the university's sins of omission has been certainly justified:

> One would like to think, that the universities have been the primary source of intellectual stimulation and enlightenment in those issues. One would like to think that university research on these matters had laid the bases for significant action. One would like to think that university people had played a key role in formulating the public policy alternatives, and in suggesting the factual or value considerations involved in each alternative. Unfortunately, this is far from the truth. . . . One cannot say that the universities are a significant intellectual base for the main attack. In fact, a good many university people whose fields should give them a legitimate interest in these matters barely understand what the relevant problems are. Many are debating policy alternatives left behind five years ago. Few are planning the kind of research that would sharpen policy alternatives(16).

A Harmony of Study

One advantage of the school of education over the university as a whole in this area of responsibility is simply that it has had a head start. More importantly, the basic mission of a professional faculty encourages a harmony of study and action and a commitment to thoughtful efforts to improve practice. It may be, as Gardner observed, that "intentional change in human institutions is associated with activities and roles which the academic man holds in very low esteem: administration, management, politics, leadership"(17). To the school of education, however, these very activities and roles comprise its central concern. We regularly seek to enhance our work through field engagement. It is only sensible to attempt to increase the effectiveness of our efforts by engaging university colleagues to help us in developing the necessary substratum of basic theoretical knowledge.

It is apparent, therefore, that now, and increasingly in the future, it will be mutually advantageous to collaborate in studying and serving the urban community. Attempting to utilize and develop whatever substantive forms and content the university as a whole and the school of education may develop, is an important aspect of any serious professional commitment to urban education.

Developing and sustaining meaningful research also requires that the school of education strengthen and smooth its relations with urban school systems. There cannot continue to be an attitude of hostility, suspicion, or contempt between college personnel and public school officials. There can be little inquiry if each piece of research has to clear every office-holder in the system; there can be few trials of experimental materials or instructional treatments if schoolmen lack confidence and respect for those who have designed the interventions. A fruitful set of relationships cannot simply be proclaimed, of course, and the requisite mutual support and understanding will have to be carefully cultivated. Research in school settings carried out by teachers may be necessary to build the common values and perspectives required. Robert Dreeben has commented as follows:

> A form of research indigenous to schools has direct relevance to those in the universities working on general problems that subsume the specific school-related ones. Accordingly, a natural linkage based on common interest can be established, not by telling teachers and academicians to like each other and to pay attention to what the other is doing—an approach doomed to failure—but by each becoming involved in different aspects of the same line of inquiry. Under these circumstances, the generalized scientific knowledge of the academic can inform the subsequent work of the teacher doing "clinical" research in the schools; and, of course, the flow of knowledge also travels the other way. In effect, they have something to say to each other just as the physician doing clinical research, say, on endocrine disease, has something to say to the biochemist, and vice versa, even though each is engaged in a separate research enterprise. In this way, I can envisage a break in the traditional barrier be-

tween schools and universities and the establishment of alliances between previously hostile parties. It is difficult, moreover, to imagine the development of teaching technology without direct contact between the two institutions and their members, and contact is not likely to be made without a universe of common discourse and actual pieces of research relevant to each. The basis of such discourse can be established by the creation of knowledge in schools deemed valuable by both(18).

Whatever the mechanism for the rapprochement, however, more cordial and more efficient working relations are essential. The two institutions, in turn, both need to develop more viable relations with the Black communities they supposedly serve. There can be no research if parents feel it requires the use of their children as experimental "subjects." There can be few changes in pedagogical practice unless community members are enabled to understand and to appreciate their potential utility. As I have indicated earlier, we must face up to the fact that in the urban ghetto paternalistic attitudes and the self-appointed status of the expert will no longer be tolerated. The Black community recognizes the role of education in achieving group goals, but it wants no gifts from a "master" and insists that it be consulted in developing any educational innovation. A continuing commitment to research, therefore, carries with it comparable willingness to seek workable, if always precarious, forms of collaboration.

Conclusion

This, then, is a partial set of suggestions for schools of education who would contribute to the resolution of urban educational problems. By realizing our present problems, by resisting pressures to pretend wisdom we do not yet possess, by venturing fearlessly into the real world of urban schools, by training for occupational positions not yet clearly defined, and by emphasizing inquiry at the expense of missionary zeal, we may hope to make a small difference. Even if the difficulties proved resistant to whatever energies and talents we could muster, we would, at least, by a constant insistence upon rationality, have protected schools of education from the familiar hazards of tender-mindedness. In the field of education generally, our commitment to research is as yet so tenuous, our grappling seriously with the reciprocal relations of theory and practice as yet so tentative, our faith in the "authority" of the processes of inquiry as yet so fragile, and our resistance to the appeal of political positions as yet so incomplete, that a sentimental response to urban education might erode many of the gains of recent years. Despite our vulnerability, I am confident our actual response to the dilemmas of the urban scene will strengthen our capacity for reasoned action.

Notes

1. James S. Coleman et al., *Equality of Educational Opportunity* (Washington, D.C.: U.S. Government Printing Office, 1966).

2. U.S. Commission on Civil Rights, *Racial Isolation in the Public Schools* (Washington, D.C.: U.S. Government Printing Office, 1967), I, 139.

3. California State Department of Public Instruction, *The First Year of Title I, ESEA* (Washington, D.C.: U.S. Department of Health, Education and Welfare, 1966).

4. D. J. Fox, *Expansion of the More Effective Schools Program* (New York, Center for Urban Education, 1967), p. 63.

5. Miriam L. Goldberg, A. Harry Passow, and Joseph Justman, *The Effects of Ability Grouping* (New York: Teachers College Press, Teachers College, Columbia University, 1966).

6. Albert Shanker, "What's Wrong With Compensatory Education," *Saturday Review,* January 11, 1969, p. 56.

7. Patricia Sexton, *Education and Income* (New York: The Viking Press, Inc., 1961).

8. Fox, op. cit., p. 122.

9. Mel Ravitz, "The Role of the School in the Urban Setting," *Education in Depressed Areas,* ed., A. Harry Passow (New York: Bureau of Publication, Teachers College, Columbia University, 1963), pp. 19f.

10. David K. Cohen, "Policy for the Public Schools: Compensation and Integration," *Harvard Educational Review* (Winter 1968), p. 125.

11. Francis A. J. Ianni, "Conservative Schools in a Revolutionary Society," *Perspectives On Education,* Teachers College, Columbia University (Winter 1968), pp. 20f.

12. Daniel E. Griffiths et al., *Teacher Mobility in New York City* (New York: Center for Field Research and Services, New York University, 1963); Frank W. Lutz and Joseph J. Azzarelli, eds., *Struggle for Power in Education* (New York: Center for Applied Research in Education, Inc., 1966).

13. Robert J. Schaefer, "An Editorial," *Perspectives On Education,* Teachers College, Columbia University (Fall 1969).

14. Robert Dreeben, *The Nature of Teaching: Schools and the Work of Teachers* (Chicago: Scott, Foresman & Co., In Press).

15. Lee J. Cronbach and Patrick Suppes, eds., *Research for Tomorrow's Schools: Disciplined Inquiry for Education,* Report of the Committee on

Educational Research of the National Academy of Education (London: The Macmillan Company, 1969).

16. John W. Gardner, "Universities as Designers of the Future," *Educational Record* (Fall 1967), p. 318.

17. Ibid., p. 319.

18. Dreeben, op. cit.

Conclusion

There was a time in the not too distant past that the public school systems of our great urban centers were examples of the finest education available to large masses of pupils. Today this picture is changed. Few, if any, central-city schools can claim the distinction of providing high-quality education for all or even most of their pupils. Nearly every urban school system in the country is plagued by issues with which it is not prepared to cope. Large groups of the urban poor are charging that the school systems have passed them by and that their children are disadvantaged as a result of the educational organization built to serve the city populations of 30 to 60 years ago.

Nearly every urban school system has been threatened by or has already felt the impact of teacher strikes. In the fall of 1968 the New York City school system, serving more than a million school children, ground to a halt—and the system failed to operate as an educational system for the first quarter of the school year. Neither its administrative officers, its central board, the Mayor of New York City, nor the Commissioner of Education of New York State could provide the necessary impetus required to set the organization in motion again. As one recognizes that a public school system is an echelon of government, and as it is clear that the established offices and processes of government could not compel the orderly processes of that government to function, one is forced to the conclusion that a social revolution had overthrown that government and that anarchy prevailed.

In a statement on October 30, 1968, Governor Nelson Rockefeller of New York State indicated that he might be forced to convene the state legislature and intervene in the crisis. He commented, "Really, this move would mean that the Mayor, the Board of Education, the Regents, and the Commissioner of Education had failed." Yet it is unfair to place the responsibility for all this on these men and the groups they represent. What had failed was the processes and structure legislated for governing public education in New York City. The oarsmen were not resting on their oars. In fact, it is likely that they were more capable oarsmen than had ever manned the ship before. They were rowing well and hard in a craft designed to meet the challenges for navigating a ship during a time when sails and oars were adequate equipment for steering and propelling large complex educational organizations during the early 1900's. They now found themselves in the deep part of the ocean of the late 1960's and in the middle of the storms and hurricanes of the social revolution of our times. Their equipment simply was and is inadequate.

Suburban school districts have inherited the title of the world's champion in the seas of public education. This is probably not because their personnel are oarsmen of greater stature, nor are their vessels of improved quality. Rather they are riding the relative calm on the edge of the storm that is presently engulfing the urban school districts. But the storm is spreading. Some of the small craft are already floundering. Others are beginning to see signs of the impending storm. Unfortunately, still others float serenely in the belief that they will continue to be exempt from the storm. This is not likely to prove true. The problems of urban and metropolitan public education will soon engulf both center-city and suburban districts. Unless rapid and drastic changes are made in the basic structures provided for public education in the United States, it is entirely possible that metropolitan public education in the core cities and satellite suburban areas alike will find their outmoded vessels completely overwhelmed by the crushing social problems of the 1970's.

Several of our authors have mentioned the power of teacher groups. It appears clear that teacher demands and power will continue to play a major role in fiscal, curricular, personnel, political, and structural decisions of urban education. This fact places a major responsibility on administrators to develop appropriate mechanisms to handle these demands. Most urban administrators keenly feel this press. But to teachers this new responsibility is sometimes less keenly felt. It is easy for an individual teacher psychologically to escape the responsibility for union action. Unaccustomed to power, teachers may find themselves in situations that can be dangerous. Their education has not prepared them for the responsibilities of membership in strong militant organizations that affect every aspect of public education. What is the teacher's responsibility for the election and supervision of the organization's leadership? What is his responsibility to the elected leadership? What is the organization's responsibility for teacher welfare as balanced with the responsibility for the education of children in urban centers?

In addition, it is clear that the present internal structure of urban school districts must change if the demands of the new urban society are to be met and urban education is to regain a position of excellence. The strong, centralized, often authoritarian structures developed to serve in a different decade will no longer suffice. Decentralized structures that provide a large measure of local autonomy and community participation must be developed. Nor can such decentralization stop at the local school district level. Individual schools must be given the freedom and resources to devise creative programs to meet the unique needs of their specific clientele. Formulas for the allocation of fiscal resources must accompany the decentralized decision-making power if it is to be more than a hollow promise. Some of the other problems must be solved on an even larger metropolitan basis. The problems of Newark, Great Neck, and New York City cannot be treated as if they were independent. Some form of a federated system, crossing county and state lines when necessary, must be put in use—yet without weakening the decentralized participation and decisions of local community groups.

Such changes in educational structure must be accompanied by changes in the roles of school administrators. As changes are contemplated, the political nature of education becomes apparent. As they are realized, the political role of the superintendent must become overt rather than covert. Principals, realizing that they are not trained to be an expert teacher in every area, will turn their attention to administration and their leadership ability to the development of an educational organizational climate where education can take place. Leadership no longer will be directed toward teaching the teacher to teach. Instead it will be directed toward providing the atmosphere in which he can teach. As building administrator, the principal's organizational and administrative expertise, such as his ability to develop a master schedule, will be his forte.

Federal concerns, operationalized in programs such as the Office of Economic Opportunity and the Elementary and Secondary Education Act titles, will continue to impinge on urban educational systems. Federal policy will play an increasing role in the formulation of local urban educational policy. Urban city government will of necessity begin to treat educational systems as partners, and the educational systems will be unable to resist that pressure. The specter of graft and favoritism often raised in defense of the unrealistic slogan "keep politics out of education" will give way to the realization that to keep politics out of education has only served to keep educational decisions apart from the people and has allowed the politicians to escape the responsibility for failing to provide adequate support for public education. Government by the Philosopher Kings is usually advocated by the ruling kings who are too often not very philosophic. It has no place in the American democracy. Caught up in the new merger of city and educational governance, the urban school superintendent may find himself director of the department of education of the urban city, rather than head of his own special governmental unit.

Parallel to such a movement, the federal and state governments will have to recognize and assume their responsibilities to urban centers. The outmoded notion that urban centers can and should support rural areas of the state and nation must be effectively attacked and defeated. New tax structures must be devised to finance the requirements of the modern urban centers and their educational systems. The federal system, although slow to move, will likely come to this realization sooner than the more rurally oriented state governments. Such a situation cannot be tolerated for long. Continued frustration of federal intent by state governments can only precipitate radical federal action. The nation cannot survive without socially healthy urban centers. One solution, as old as Charlemagne's Holy Roman Empire, is the federalization of the major urban centers.

Major universities, including some of the more rurally oriented land grant institutions, must reexamine their commitments. Their efforts can no longer overlook the plight of the urban centers. Theory and research must leave the ivory tower, be operationalized and disseminated. In doing this task, the difference between the social missionary and the social researcher-practitioner must not be clouded. While the missionary wipes the brow of the ill, making them feel better while they die, the researcher-practitioner studies the dying so as to discover the cause of death and uses the information to heal future generations. Time is running out for the researcher-practitioner. It already has run out for the social missionary. Additionally, corn, cotton and cows can no longer be the *major* concern of the land grant institutions. We must recognize that we no longer live in a rural, agrarian society. Our society is urban and universities must adjust to that fact. Universities must rededicate themselves to the teacher training programs using the science of human behavior. Teachers must be taught to be *effective* in combating the learning problems of the inner city rather than the methods of "keeping school" in a middle-class community.

Students in urban schools will increasingly become recognized as individuals and human beings capable of participating in decisions and having the inherent right to do so. A philosophic, humanistic basis for decision-making in our political and mechanistic society must be at the foundation of all of our efforts if those efforts are not to be in vain. The education of all educational practitioners, including administrators, must include the humanizing effects of a strong philosophic core.

Selected Bibliography

Allen, Rodney F. and Charles H. Adair (eds.). *Violence and Riots in Urban America.* Worthington, Ohio: Charles A. Jones Publishing Co., 1969.

Allport, Gordon. "The Psychology of Participation." *Personality and Social Encounter.* Boston: Beacon Press, 1960.

Argyris, Chris. *Interpersonal Competence and Organizational Effectiveness.* Homewood, Ill.: Dorsey Press, 1962.

Barnett, Homer. *Innovation: The Basis of Cultural Change.* New York: McGraw-Hill Book Co., 1953.

Bromage, Arthur W. (ed.). *Manager Plan Abandonments.* Chicago: National Municipal League. Pamphlet.

Burkhead, Jesse. *Input and Output in Large City High Schools.* Syracuse, N.Y.: Syracuse University Press, 1967.

Callahan, Raymond E. *Education and the Cult of Efficiency.* Chicago: University of Chicago Press, 1962.

Carlton, Patrick W. and Harold I. Goodwin. *The Collective Dilemma: Negotiations in Education.* Worthington, Ohio: Charles A. Jones Publishing Co., 1969.

Clapp, Charles. *The Congressman: His Work As He Sees It.* Garden City, N.Y.: Doubleday and Co., Inc., 1954.

Coleman, James S., *et al. Equality of Educational Opportunity.* Washington, D.C.: U.S. Government Printing Office, 1966.

Cronin, J. M. *Big City School Boards.* New York: The Free Press, 1970.

———. "The Board of Education in the Great Cities, 1890–1964." Unpublished Ph.D. dissertation, Stanford University, 1965.

———. "A Typology of School Board Members." Unpublished manuscript, Harvard University, 1966.

Cunningham, Luvern L. and Raphael O. Nystrand. *New Forms of Citizen Participation in Urban School Affairs.* Washington, D.C.: The Urban Coalition, 1969.

Donovan, John C. *Politics of Poverty.* New York: Pegasus, 1967.

Gallaher, Art, Jr. "Change Processes in the Public Schools." Eugene, Ore.: University of Oregon, Advanced Study of Educational Administration, 1965.

Giardino, Alfred A., Francis Keppel, Antonia Pantoja, Mitchell Svindoff, Bennetta B. Washington. *Reconnection for Learning: A Community School System for New York City* (The Bundy Report). McGeorge Bundy (chairman). New York: Mayor's Advisory Panel on Decentralization of the New York City Schools, 1967.

Graff, Orin B., *et al. Philosophic Theory and Practice in Educational Administration*. Belmont, Calif.: Wadsworth Publishing Co., Inc., 1966.

Hartley, Harry J. *Educational Planning-Programming-Budgeting: A Systems Approach*. Englewood Cliffs, N.J.: Prentice-Hall, Inc., 1968.

————. "Twelve Hurdles to Clear Before You Take on Systems Analysis." *American School Board Journal* Vol. 156, No. 1 (July, 1968).

————. "PPBS: The Emergence of a Systemic Concept for Public Governance." *General Systems* XIII (1968).

Heidegger, Martin. *Being and Time*. London: SCM Press, 1962.

————. *An Introduction to Metaphysics*. Garden City, N.Y.: Anchor Books, 1961.

Heller, Robert W. "The Coleman Report Revisited." *Urban Education* Vol. 3, No. 4 (Winter, 1968).

————. "Needed: A Rationale for the Middle School." *New York State Education* LVI, No. 4 (January, 1969).

Iannaccone, Laurence. *Politics in Education*. New York: The Center for Applied Research in Education, Inc., 1967.

James, M. Thomas, James A. Kelly, and W. I. Garms. *Determinants of Educational Expenditures in Large Cities of the United States*. Stanford, Calif.: Stanford University School of Education, 1966.

Jankowitz, Morris. "Alternative Models of Change for Inner-City Schools." *The Quality of Inequality: Urban and Suburban Public Schools*. Edited by Charles O. Daly. Chicago: University of Chicago Center for Policy Study, 1968.

Kierkegaard, Soren. *Concluding Unscientific Postscript*. Translated by David F. Swanson. Princeton, N.J.: Princeton University Press, 1964. (Completed after his death and provided with introduction and notes by Walter Lowrie. Printed for the American Scandinavian Foundation.)

Lewin, Kurt. "Group Decisions and Social Change." *Readings in Social Psychology*. Edited by T. Newcomb and E. Hartley. New York: Holt, Rinehart, and Winston, Inc., 1947.

Lutz, Frank W., Lou Kleinman, and Seymour Evans. *Grievances and Their Resolution*. New York: Interstate Printers and Publishers, 1967. For background on the subject of "Bureaucratization and Role Modification, see pp. 79–84.

———— and Joseph Azzarelli (eds.). *Struggle for Power in Education*. New York: The Center for Applied Research in Education, 1966.

Mathews, Donald. *U.S. Senators and Their World*. Chapel Hill, N.C.: University of North Carolina Press, 1960.

McGregor, Douglas. *The Human Side of Enterprise*. New York: McGraw-Hill Book Co., 1960.

Miller, Clem. *Member of the House: Letters of a Congressman.* Edited by John Baker. New York: Charles Scribner's Sons, 1962.

Mourant, John A. "Thomistic Existentialism." *Essays in Philosophy.* Edited by J. M. Anderson. University Park, Pa.: Penn State University Press, 1962.

Munger, Frank J. and Richard F. Fenno, Jr. *National Politics and Federal Aid to Education.* Syracuse, N.Y.: Syracuse University Press, 1962.

Nietzsche, Friedrick Wilhelm. *Thus Spoke Zarathustra.* Baltimore: Penguin Books, 1966.

Ohm, Robert E. and William G. Monahan. *Educational Administration—Philosophy in Action.* Norman, Okla.: University Council for Educational Administration, University of Oklahoma, 1965.

Perry, Charles and Wesley Wildman. *The Impact of Negotiations in Public Education: The Evidence from the Schools.* Worthington, Ohio: Charles A. Jones Publishing Co., 1970.

Peterson, Paul E. "City Politics and Community Action." Unpublished Ph.D. dissertation, Department of Political Science, University of Chicago, 1967.

Roaden, Arliss L. (ed.). *Problems of School Men in Depressed Urban Centers.* Columbus, Ohio: College of Education, Ohio State University, 1969.

Sartre, Jean-Paul. *Being and Nothingness.* New York: Citadel Press, 1965.

Sherwood, Robert Petersen. "Cost Implications of Specific State Legislative Requirements: An Application of Program Budgeting to Selected California Unified School Districts." Unpublished Ed.D. dissertation, University of California, Berkeley, 1965.

Stanford Research Institute PPBS Staff. *Planning-Programming-Budgeting System in the New York City School System . . . An Introduction.* (OPPB Bul. No. 1, 1967–68 series) Office of Business and Administration, Board of Education of the City of New York, June, 1967.

U.S. Commission of Civil Rights. *Process of Change—The Story of School Desegregation in Syracuse, New York.* Washington, D.C.: Clearinghouse Publication No. 12 (June, 1968).

U.S. Commission on Civil Rights. *Racial Isolation in the Public Schools.* Vol. 1. Washington, D.C.: U.S. Government Printing Office.

Index

DATE DUE
REMINDER

Please do not remove
this date due slip.